Bradman and the
BODYLINE

Previous books by the same author:

Simply Human Beings

The Australian Sugar Industry

The Blackbirders

A History Of Indian Cricket

Bradman and the BODYLINE

E.W. Docker

ANGUS & ROBERTSON PUBLISHERS

ACKNOWLEDGMENTS

For their assistance in the making of this book, I should like to thank firstly Sir Donald Bradman, as well as the late E. W. Adams of Rockdale, J. Ahern of the staff of the S.C.G. Trust, G. O. Allen, M. J. C. Allom, L. E. G. Ames, Alan Barnes, Secretary of the Australian Board of Control, O. W. Bill, Michael Bruer, Mrs. Frank Cush, P. G. H. Fender, Mrs. June Gordon of Glensloy, Stephen Green and the staff of Lord's Library, C. V. Grimmett, R. A. Hamence, W. A. Hunt of Balmain, E. W. Kann, H. Larwood, Geoff Leahy of Cootamundra, P. K. Lee, the library staff of Australia House, London and the Mitchell Library, Sydney, H. W. Parks, C. E. Pellew, Ray Polkinghorne, John Priestley, Terence Prittie, the late J. Ryder, Mrs. Lilian Sproule of Campbelltown, N.S.W., W. W. Thomson of Brisbane, Harold Toose of Moss Vale, Mr. and Mrs. Brian Turner of Adelaide, B. H. Valentine, M. G. Waite, T. W. Wall and R. E. S. Wyatt.

For the photographs I wish to thank Central Press, Lord's, the Press Association, the Radio Times Hulton Picture Library, and finally for their typing Phillipa Bird, Ngaire Blackstock and Mrs. Everest.

ANGUS & ROBERTSON PUBLISHERS
London • Sydney • Melbourne

First published by Angus & Robertson (UK) Ltd, 1978
This paperback edition 1983

ISBN 0 207 14805 8

Printed in Australia by Hedges & Bell

In memory of my father

Contents

CHAPTER ONE

Discovery of a Star

On 18 August 1926 the Australians lost the final and deciding Test match at Kennington Oval and three weeks later at the annual general meeting of the New South Wales Cricket Association the principal topic of conversation was still the loss of those precious Ashes. Holding the Ashes, winning at cricket, was no less a matter of personal pride to Englishmen than it was to Australians, except that for the latter much more than personal pride was involved. Theirs was a "young" country, they believed, its potential still unrealised, and its young people, more active, more virile, more self-reliant than the population of the "Old Country", were the ones to realise this potential. The argument was used quite unselfconsciously as though Australians, products of a rugged environment, possessors in excelsis of all the essentially outdoor skills that had enabled them to conquer this environment, were bound to prevail in any contest where the young manhood of the country was concerned.

And yet they had been defeated! But the 1926 side, it was pointed out, had contained too many "old" men. For instance Bardsley had first represented Australia in 1909. Collins was 37. Nobody dared to mention the name of Charlie Macartney who was older than Collins, nor suggest that he was past it, but the mood of the meeting generally was to single out the older players as the ones who had let their country down. "Just as well we have lost the Ashes", commented the Sydney *Referee* (29 September, 1926), "or the deifying of veterans would have got worse".

Primarily though, it was the bowling of the 1926 side that came in for condemnation, and the Association after great discussion decided to institute a search for young bowlers. Country and junior matches were to be watched. Parks were to be visited and on various Mondays throughout the season, youths from all over the State (theoretically) were to be invited to the Sydney Cricket Ground No. 2 to practise under the eye of such famous old cricketers as C. T. B. Turner, Dr H. V. Hordern and the veteran Tom Garrett. They would be divided into four classes, fast, left-hand, medium and slow; but the net was to be cast widely. Batsmen too might be included and thus on October 5 the secretary of the N.S.W.C.A. wrote to a young Bowral cricketer, as follows.

"Dear Sir,

The State selectors have had under consideration your record in cricket in the past season, and in view of such record, they particularly desire to see you in action.

For this purpose, I would like you to attend practice at the Sydney cricket ground on Monday next. Practice commences at 4 p.m. and continues throughout the afternoon. My association is prepared to pay your return fare from Bowral, and should you deem it necessary to remain in Sydney overnight you will be reimbursed to the extent of your accommodation.

I sincerely trust that you will give this matter the consideration its importance warrants, and hope that you will realize that this is an opportunity that should not be missed. . . ."

The name of Don Bradman had been known, if rather vaguely, to the N.S.W. selectors, for some time. "But let me say first and foremost," said one of the selectors years later, when that name was rather better known, "that the selection committee of 1926–27 didn't discover Don Bradman. He was a player of infinite skill before we ever saw him." Grade sides from Sydney sometimes visited the Southern Highlands and brought back word of the young prodigy. But the innings which first brought him to the city's attention was one of 234, for Bowral versus Wingello. Now Wingello was but a hamlet, the size of an English country village perhaps, whereas Bowral was a small town; yet it possessed a cricket team formidable out of all proportion to its scanty population, as well as a bowler, Bill O'Reilly, who was already known in Sydney where he was studying to be a school-teacher. Unfortunately this tall, husky young man was now rarely available for Wingello, but this occasion was important enough for him to be intercepted at Bowral railway station on his way home for the week-end and fitted out in borrowed togs for the match.

Wingello won the toss and sent Bowral in, as one normally did in these local competition matches spread over two Saturday afternoons, and young Bradman made 234 not out in something under four hours, a score completely unheard of before in that class of cricket. He was but seventeen, small for his age and quite slim, and though briefly uneasy against O'Reilly's fast-turning leg-spinners on a matting-over-concrete wicket, was rarely in trouble thereafter and finished the afternoon in a blaze of fours and sixes. The following Saturday at Wingello the twenty-year-old, six-foot and more O'Reilly, thoroughly nettled by the youngster's *sang froid*, by his air of unshakable self-confidence, particularly by his lack of inches, gave the ball just that extra amount of vicious tweak and bowled him first ball.

Bowral went on that season to qualify for the final of the Berrima District competition, where it was to oppose the neighbouring township of Moss Vale. Bowral and Moss Vale, twin stars in the little firmament of the Southern Highlands, tended to behave like any two entities too closely attached to one another. There was mutual antipathy between them, grievances and matters of dispute reaching back many years, and when Bowral won the toss and batted it was in the grim determination that no quarter would be given to Moss Vale on this occasion. Finals were played out to a finish, upon however many Saturday afternoons were necessary to reach a decision, and at the end of the first Saturday Bradman was 88 not out. At the end of the second afternoon he was 279 not out; George Whatman, his uncle and Bowral's captain, being 121 not out; and although Bowral was now 1 – 479, Whatman still didn't think of declaring. Bradman was eventually out on the third afternoon for 300, but Bowral's innings didn't come to an end until some time on the fourth Saturday when the ninth wicket fell at 672. Whatman hadn't declared however. His brother, Dick Whatman, had a broken toe and couldn't bat, so the team was all out. It was now 5 June, well into the football season, and Moss Vale weakened by football demands could manage only 123 and 200 in reply and was beaten outright.

The Moss Vale players would never forget this match. How could they? The fame of it reached Sydney where a cartoon depicted a young country batsman starting out at the beginning of his long innings, growing steadily older as the saga unfolded, Saturday upon Saturday, until finally, an ancient with a beard reaching down to his waist, he is seen at the Gate of Heaven asking the way to the cricket ground. Although he had never played an innings of this calibre against them before, the Moss Valers none the less were already accustomed to Don Bradman. They could remember him, a boy of twelve in white knickerbockers, coming out to bat No. 11 for Bowral after somebody had failed to turn up and Bowral's young scorer was called on to put on the pads. He made 37 not out on that occasion and then opened for Bowral in the second innings, displaying all those qualities of patience and unflagging concentration that were to be revealed in an even more remarkable light in his innings of 300 five years later.

He was not a great one for conversation on or off the field, but they all liked him, accepting his youthful mastery as something that just had to be endured. Occasionally Stan Tickner, their fast-medium right-hander, might slip in a few short ones, which Bradman would pull to the boundary in the greatest glee, but generally they were proud of the fact that their district had produced such an outstanding young player, one who was obviously a little bit different from the rest of them, who would continue from hundred to hundred, never taking a definable risk, never playing a stroke that might seem to give the bowler a chance. Englishmen believed that colonials usually won at cricket because the whole population was cricket-mad. It would be more correct to say that the great mass of Australians were as indifferent to the game as the majority of Englishmen, but that individual Australians tended to play it more keenly and competitively, even at the humblest level.

So the famous Bowral–Moss Vale final ended on 12 June 1926, the very day England and Australia were due to begin the first Test match at Nottingham, and four months later in October Bradman set off for Sydney in the company of his father to answer his country's call for young talent, primarily bowling talent. He batted in the nets. The N.S.W. selectors and various ex-internationals stood solemnly around and watched, and though nothing very much was said he must have impressed, since a Sydney grade side, Cumberland, asked him to play with it and soon afterwards another telegram from the N.S.W.C.A. invited him to a trial match at the S.C.G. No. 1, Possibles v. Probables. Perhaps a little too expectant at this stage, unaware of the number of other young hopefuls in the selectors' eye, Bradman felt that he could be well in the running for the N.S.W. side shortly to visit Queensland.

With the exception of one or two, it was likely to be a completely new team. Of the 1926 tourists, Oldfield and Taylor had remained in England; Bardsley and Gregory were still on their way home; Collins was in Melbourne; Macartney rumoured to have retired. It was Armstrong's old 1920–21 side, in the throes of disintegration, in the process of being rejected by the rest of the cricket community. Collins, Ryder and Hill had chosen the 1926 tourists, and now all three, along with Warwick Armstrong, had failed to win re-election on their respective State selection committees. The case of Sidney Smith, manager of both 1921 and 1926 sides was even worse. As a Gordon committeeman and delegate to the N.S.W.C.A., he was dropped from the committee while the team was still in England. Smith was another member of the "Old Guard", too much in with the players, it was alleged. As manager he collected the receipts of the matches in England. As manager his would be the chief voice in deciding how much the players were to receive by way of a bonus above their normal expenses allowance.

Rumours, impossible to prove, impossible to refute, abounded. They didn't directly concern young Bradman at this stage, except that dissatisfaction with the performance of the 1926 side was helping to keep alive the issues originally aroused by the omission of Alan Kippax. What did one have to do to be chosen? Now nearing thirty, Kippax had played once for Australia, in the final Test in Sydney in 1924–25 after the series had been decided, though he possessed a Sheffield Shield batting average of over 90, unequalled, unapproached by any other N.S.W. batsman alive or dead, a record second only to that of the Victorian champion, W. H. Ponsford. He was also a brilliant fieldsman at a time when the standard of Australian Test fielding was notably declining. It was all the more extraordinary, said Kippax's admirers, since Herbie Collins, Australia's Test captain for many years was also Kippax's Waverley club captain in Sydney grade cricket.

Jealousy was mainly the trouble; jealousy, ever on the bubble, ever on the stir, agitating the hearts and minds of the most unexpected people. Conceivably Collins was jealous. Some of the old hands at the S.C.G. certainly were. Since the day of Victor Trumper's death, they had lived in hopes of another Trumper turning up, and when a possible candidate did come along, self-confessedly modelled on their idol, wearing his sleeves rolled half-way down the forearm à la Trumper, they had been first elated and then furiously jealous – because he was scoring so many more runs than Trumper. The over-prepared wickets of the modern game were the only reason for these mammoth scores, was the ceaseless complaint. One couldn't compare Ponsford and Kippax, they said, with the giants of the past, Bannerman, Murdoch, Hill, Trumper, etcetera. Their runs had been produced on natural wickets where the bowler had a chance. "We cannot tell whether our bats are stars or not", said Warwick Armstrong, "until they are tested by good bowlers, and we don't have even decent second-class bowlers."

So if Kippax laboured under a sense of grievance, he had some justification. Anyway, Collins being currently at odds with the N:S.W. selectors, Kippax was the logical choice to lead the N.S.W. side for the opening match of the season in Brisbane. This at last was his chance to break from the past. He had a side composed largely of complete newcomers to first-class cricket, all eager and full of enthusiasm, beside whom the twenty-nine-year old Kippax looked an absolute veteran. Bradman however was not amongst them. He had batted safely and soundly in the trial for 37 not out, yet without daring to make too many strokes while still uncertain of the pace and bounce of turf wickets, and very much more impressive on this occasion was a certain Archie Jackson, one year younger than Bradman, though with one year's more experience of Sydney wickets. Jackson went north instead, but Bradman's effort in the trial was not completely wasted. The selectors were still very much interested in him and a few words from them in the right quarter ensured his being chosen in a Southern District side to take part in the Country Week tournament beginning on 22 November.

In fact his omission from the Shield side was probably a blessing in disguise. In the country he had developed a pull-shot to counter the ball pitched short of a length and rising uncomfortably high for a little fellow facing grown men. He would go back and across with the right foot and pull the ball between mid-on and square-leg. It was a shot which required exceptional eye-sight, but it was a perfectly safe shot for Bradman on matting wickets where a uniform bounce could be relied upon and the ball tended to rise to just over stump height. On the less predictable turf however much greater care and judgement was necessary in executing the shot and this was why a week of cricket on Sydney turf wickets, playing day after day against cricketers from both city and country, was just what he needed.

Country Week then was a marvellous opportunity for practice on turf, though it presented certain hazards as well. The idea was to pit the country cricketers against one another (or this year against Sydney Grade cricketers as well) and hope that sooner or later another Charlie Macartney, another C. T. B. Turner would emerge. However it never seemed to work out like that. In practice the country players rarely did themselves justice in the city, inclining to believe that the city-dwellers were laughing at them behind their backs, sniggering at their clothes, their manners, their general lack of familiarity with city ways. In 1926 the gap was considerable. A story grew up about Don Bradman in 1926 and steadily improved in the telling from year to year. In his first big match in Sydney, it was alleged, he stepped jauntily out of the pavilion, bat over shoulder, wearing a pair of black trousers held up by braces. The game was instantly stopped. An umpire sent him back to the dressing-room from which he eventually re-emerged properly clad in white flannels enabling the game to be resumed. He went on to make a hundred.

It was pure invention, based on the tiny fact that country cricketers of those days sometimes wore braces. However people who had never seen Bradman in their lives, except perhaps distantly on the cricket field, would swear that they remembered him batting in the Sydney nets dressed in black trousers and braces. In sober fact Bradman was an inconspicuous figure in Country Week, quietly correct in his dress, correct in his behaviour, saying very little while eyes and ears missed nothing. Cautiously at first, but with mounting confidence, he made a few runs, took a few wickets and was very fast and sharp in the field. Cumberland remarkably enough had decided it couldn't afford Bradman if it meant paying his travelling expenses to and from Bowral each week. But now, before the end of the week he received another invitation to play in Sydney, this time from St. George and this time he accepted, starting that coming Saturday.

How much he had improved in one week was illustrated by his first innings in Sydney grade cricket. Batting No. 6 for St. George v. Petersham at Petersham Oval he looked like a lamb thrown to the wolves. As he took guard and looked round, the field moved in, T. J. E. (Tommy) Andrews, the international, going right up to silly-point, the position he had once fielded to Gregory and McDonald and made famous. Petersham were a tough bunch. They didn't exchange a cheery word or two, as they mostly did in the country. They just stared at you. Whether or not he was disconcerted, Bradman played forward to one before he had scored and pushed it straight into the hands of Andrews – who dropped it. The tension eased. Soon he was middling the ball with the greatest aplomb, evidently not at all impressed by the fact that Sam Everett, Petersham's opening bowler had just returned from England with the touring side. How would he go if suddenly confronted with Maurice Tate, somebody had asked him years before in Bowral. "I don't know," Bradman had smiled back, "but I wouldn't allow myself to be put off by his reputation". He was eventually out for 110 made in 128 minutes and Everett was so disgusted with his form that he told the Petersham committee after the match that he didn't want to bowl any more in grade cricket.

Where or how does one acquire such marvellous self-confidence? Obviously there can be no cut-and-dried answer, but it certainly does help to be brought up in a secure home, safely isolated from the harsh realities of life during one's most impressionable years. The father, George Bradman was the backbone of the family, a tall, strong, God-fearing man who had been born a farmer on the south-west slopes and plains of New South Wales and subsequently moved from the wide, open spaces of Cootamundra to the more restrictive environment of Bowral for the sake of his wife's health and the mountain air of that region. Actually both families, Whatman on his mother's side, Bradman on the other, hailed originally from Bowral or thereabouts and Donald George, youngest by four years in a family of five children, grew up among a crowd of elder sisters, uncles and aunts who undoubtedly tended to make much of him, to make him feel that he had a meaningful part to play in a meaningful world.

In later life he would sometimes be pictured as a lonely youth who shunned the company of his fellow youngsters, but the fact was that he simply didn't have the time to be gregarious, to hang around in gangs and so on. He was foremost in almost every school activity, cricket, football, athletics. . . . In the week-ends there was his uncle's tennis court, his father and elder brother to go shooting with, and his music. Every member of the Bradman family played a musical instrument, Don played the piano and violin, and all were involved in musical evenings, entertainments and local functions of all kinds, since Bradman senior was a great organiser and pillar of the local community, whose happiness was to see everybody else organised and happy. The only time the youngest Bradman had to himself, when he wilfully cut himself off from the society of others, was when he came home from school in the afternoon, slung his satchel in a corner of the porch, and thud, thud, thud, all the family could hear was the sound of a ball being relentlessly driven up against the side of the tank-stand. His mother might easily have been demented by the sound and chased him out of the backyard. His sisters might have complained that they couldn't concentrate on their music lessons with such a racket (it was only a small house), but being the kind of people they were, fond, forbearing, unusually indulgent towards the little chap, they said nothing and by the time he was old enough to play cricket with the men he had already acquired the reflexes that were to make him unique.

In the circumstances he could hardly have failed to be confident.

Bradman has written of this early part of his career that he was "almost a total stranger to that species of nervousness common to most people whenever involved in an unusual happening". Don't presume from this however that he suffered none of the batsman's usual palpitations while waiting to go in to bat. He didn't mean that he had no nerves; only that he had no fear of failing. The concept of the wicket as a castle to be defended never occurred to him. He had never met the bowler who could get a ball past his bat; he never suspected that such a person could even exist. The only feelings he could remember when he went out to bat were feelings of "great joy", like one embarking upon a glorious adventure.

Not that he was always successful. After his striking debut against Petersham he achieved nothing further of note in grade cricket season. Chosen for N.S.W.'s second eleven against Victoria he played two innings of 43 and 8, but it was always very comforting in this period of trial and experiment to know that he had good friends close at hand. Dick Jones, his first St. George captain, kept an eye on him while he was in Sydney. So did another State selector of that year, A. G. (Johnny) Moyes. It was a nuisance travelling from Bowral to Sydney every week-end, but Percy Westbrook of the Bowral real estate firm of Davis and Westbrook, his first employer, did not grudge him the Saturdays off. Further in the background his father and Alf Stephens, his father's great friend and one-time Mayor of Bowral, made sure that he didn't lack for anything.

Perhaps it was a bit disappointing, having to put off until the following season all hopes of realising his highest ambitions, but really the future looked bright for batsmen. Just before the second eleven match in Sydney, Victoria's first eleven made 1107, a world record, against Alan Kippax's sadly inexperienced N.S.W. side in Melbourne. "Cripes, I'm unlucky," Ponsford is said to have exclaimed as he looked back to see his bails dislodged with his own tally, 352. In 1922 he had made 429 against Tasmania, five more than MacLaren's record score against Somerset in 1895, and then been chagrined to find that although the Australian Board of Control recognised the fixture as a first-class match, MacLaren and the English governing authorities apparently did not. He had been hoping to put the issue beyond all doubt in this match against N.S.W. Woodfull, Hendry, Ryder and Kippax were other heavy scorers during the season but the batsman being most talked about was the newcomer, Archie Jackson. A sequence of extraordinary second innings performances against the various States had earned him the sobriquet of "second-innings Jackson".

Bradman of course could hardly contain himself waiting for the 1927–28 season to begin, waiting for the opportunity to follow in Jackson's footsteps, yet when the season did finally arrive, wetly and overdue, he just couldn't do himself justice. He played one innings of

130 not out against Paddington and Jack Gregory at Hampden Oval, but a succession of rain-affected wickets were no help to him and his average after five innings was only 37·50. He was not chosen for City in the annual match against Country; he was not even in the State practice squad of 29. Finally on 6 December twelve players were chosen for the southern tour to Adelaide and Melbourne and his last chance seemed to have gone.

However on the previous Saturday against Marrickville at Hurstville Oval he had scored a brisk 40 not out and felt in his very best form. It was an omen, a sign that his fortunes were about to change. On the Wednesday Gregory dropped out of the N.S.W. side and was replaced by Bradman's St. George clubmate, Albert Scanes. On Thursday Hammy Love, wicket-keeper-batsman also withdrew and miracle of miracles Bradman was chosen. He must have been very fortunate that Dick Jones was one of the selectors. Though obviously only the twelfth member of the touring party, not at all assured of winning a place in the eleven, he gave no thought to that in the excitement of getting away.

For the moment things just continued to run his way. It was terribly hot in Broken Hill where they played against a local side on a concrete wicket with concrete approaches to the wicket; still terribly hot when the team reached Adelaide. But Bradman didn't care, for by this time Archie Jackson had developed a boil on his knee and the twelfth man was automatically in the side. It proved to be a marvellous game of cricket against South Australia, a personal triumph for Bradman and a tremendously hard-fought contest in which fortunes were constantly fluctuating and South Australia just got home in the end by one wicket. Seven thousand spectators were there to watch the finish on the fourth morning; 7000 who rose to their feet as one man and urged the ball on as a delivery from MacNamee narrowly missed the wicket, beat the 'keeper and just managed to reach the fence for the winning runs.

But the memory which the winners would cherish most was of young Don Bradman coming in to bat at No. 7. He looked so vulnerable and boyish looking; they planned to get him down at the end facing Grimmett before he had a chance to overcome his newcomer's nerves and settle down. (What irony!) Scanes, his batting partner, seemed equally intent on shielding him from Grimmett for as long as possible, and the manoeuvrings continued for an over or two until Bradman was finally brought face-to-face with the arch enemy, and promptly responded by racing yards down the pitch and striking him for two fours.

Clarrie Grimmett was an extraordinary little gnome of a man. In his own view he was the greatest bowler in the world, an opinion which he managed to convey to people without in any way making it sound like showing off. And very likely he was in 1927. For more years than Bradman had practised hitting a ball against a tank-stand, Grimmett had practised spinning one. For instance he could pitch a tennis ball onto a spot on his carpet some yards away and because of the spin on it make it simply bounce up and down on that spot until it came to rest. He had taken some dreadful hammerings in Australian cricket, particularly from Ponsford, but he had never stopped persevering and experimenting on wickets where sometimes not even a tennis ball could have been made to turn without the utmost difficulty. The accepted way of playing him was by using the feet, but he gave the ball very little air on these occasions and getting out to him was not easy, as Bradman discovered after the exuberance of those two opening boundaries. He did succeed in mastering him that day however, going on to make 118 in his first Shield innings, and doing even better, many thought, in his second innings when he made 33 on a pitch where the ball was beginning to turn quite a lot.

He was now in the N.S.W. side to stay but he had an awful lot to learn. While Bradman was making his maiden first-class century in Adelaide, Ponsford was engaged in setting up a new world record, 437 versus Queensland in Melbourne. (There was no doubt about the genuineness of this achievement. From England MacLaren was the first to cable his congratulations.) For the moment the burly Victorian seemed invincible. Abandoning all hope of getting him out, the bowler turned to means of purely containing him and even in that he had scant success. For the medium-pace of Cecil Thompson, Queensland's skipper, Leo O'Connor placed almost his whole field on the on, and had Thompson bowl well down the leg-side. Ponsford overcame these tactics very simply – stepping away to leg before the ball was delivered and driving to the off. Next week, for N.S.W., Arthur Mailey concentrated outside the champion's off-stump, only to see anything the least bit short despatched instantly to the leg boundary with a blow like the kick of a mule. Andrews tried round-the-wicket leg-theory; Kippax bowled without a soul on the leg-side, but Ponsford went on to another double-century, 202 in 286 minutes, before Bradman caught him off MacNamee. He was undoubtedly the greatest player of slow and medium-paced spin of his day, his art lying mainly in his foot-work, in his ability to use the full width and depth of the crease in order to make the ball into any length that suited him.

Bradman would have dearly loved to imitate these methods, but for the moment he was too puzzled by the flight and variations of pace of the veteran off-spinner, Don Blackie, to be able to think how Ponsford might have coped. He only narrowly avoided being stumped off Blackie in N.S.W.'s first innings and Tommy Andrews, his partner, was so perturbed by his habit of leaping out of his crease almost the moment he reached the wicket that he walked down the other end to speak to him about it. Bradman stayed home instead. But it made no difference. He went cheaply for 31 in the first innings. Blackie bowled him for 5 in the second.

It is very difficult, the relationship between teacher and pupil, particularly when the pupil is the more gifted one. Another habit which many didn't like was his manner of drawing away to leg in order to square-cut the faster bowlers. The lynx-eyed old men in the pavilion certainly grumbled about that. It might be alright for a Charlie Macartney, but in one so young? They shook their heads. To make it worse, Bradman would sometimes only grin when these "faults" were pointed out and the oldsters would go away and say, "You can't tell him. He knows it all already". Which side was right? He made only 0 and 13 in his first Shield appearance on the Sydney Cricket Ground against Queensland. Then 2 and 73 in 74 minutes against South Australia. Bradman believed that he was along the right lines; that the only way to learn is to make the mistake and find out how to do it correctly the next time. His enemies retaliated that he "relied entirely on his eye-sight." When that deserted him, they said, his "bad habits" would find him out and he would quietly fade from the scene, the fate of so many promising young N.S.W. batsmen in recent years, particularly of those "who wouldn't learn."

In fact he hadn't the smallest desire to offend people or rebuff them. He grinned a lot because he was enjoying life so much, "relishing" it, as he would say. He was always ready to accept advice, provided it was good advice. For instance he was still a poor judge of a run and happy to admit it. More than once he would start haring down the track when every S.C.G. regular knew there was no single in it; or else, having safely made the first run, hesitate and refuse the second when there was an easy two to be had. Lack of experience of playing on first-class grounds was partly the trouble; that, together with too much experience of bumpy little country grounds where the ball is apt to bound erratically from pebble to pebble and running between the wickets tends to be a matter of impulse. On one occasion that season he was dashing down the wicket on the wrong side when he smacked full-tilt into his partner. Before long, during a country tour with other members of the N.S.W. side, Tommy Andrews would take the opportunity of instructing him in the finer points of calling and running between the wickets.

Meanwhile the major event of 1927–28, for Bradman the most important match of his career to date, was N.S.W. versus Victoria beginning on Anniversary Day. Victoria had already won the Sheffield Shield, but the 30,386 who turned up on the opening day didn't care particularly about the Shield. They had come to see Bill Ponsford, the world record-holder, in action. He had made a century in each of his previous 11 first-class matches in Australia, his last four scores being 437, 202, 38, 331. It *was* exciting to be an Australian in 1928. A member of the most exclusive and privileged little sporting community in the entire world, one believed. Tens of thousands went to the races every Saturday, not because they were compulsive gamblers, simply because it was such an utterly Australian and patriotic thing to do. If cricket had some exciting personality of the moment to offer, they would go to the cricket instead.

Flags fluttered noisily from mast-heads all round the ground; the band was playing, the French and Australian Davis Cup players were all looking on as Jackson and Gregory walked out to open the innings for N.S.W. Across the ground from the players' pavilion the new giant score-board was waiting to record every detail of this great encounter. In fact the first day's cricket was not specially memorable. For much of the time the Victorian attack was in the hands of a'Beckett and Blackie; the one, fastish-medium, bowling consistently just short of a length; the other, concentrating on leg-theory to a circle of three men just behind the wicket.

The second day was very much better. Oldfield and Charlie Nicholls added two more centuries to N.S.W.'s overnight 7 – 349 and then came the pièce de résistance, Ponsford versus Gregory. The fast bowler's appetite for the fray had become somewhat jaded of late, it was felt. But the coming of Ponsford had evidently stimulated it afresh. He had been training hard for several weeks and was still a fearsome sight as he lolloped up to the wicket with great strides, a huge leap, arms flailing, and the ball was liable to rear sharply off this S.C.G. wicket, perhaps chest-high. It would be an epic duel between/the two, the Press had hinted. A cartoon had depicted Gregory armed with cannon-balls. "Fee-fi-fo-fum. I smell the blood of an Englishmun". Nicholls was perhaps not quite as fast; but, a bigger and burlier man even than Jack Gregory, he was able to keep up the pressure from the other end, and Ponsford, having never looked comfortable against the short ones, very soon played all over a ball pitched well up to him and was bowled Gregory, 6. In the second innings he was to be caught by Gregory off Nicholls for 2.

How are the mighty fallen! Their thrones o'erturned and scattered in the dust! Ponsford the scourge of the batting world, the destroyer, whose blade was a broad-sword reputedly the widest in the land! Now Ponsford, the uncertain, the all-too-human, offering the bat tentatively. The greater the batsman's reputation, the harder the bowler will be trying to dent it. And there is not just the bowler to contend with, but these vast crowds with their craving for excitement, the demands which they make on one, the price they are sure to exact if they are disappointed, all part and parcel of the nervous strain that is cricket at the highest level. Not long before the end of the N.S.W. innings, Ponsford running hard for a catch in the outfield had the misfortune to put it down – which caused many of the Hillites to stand up and cheer uproariously. If Bradmen had learnt much from watching Ponsford's long innings in Melbourne, there was even more to be learnt from the example of these two much briefer visits to the crease in Sydney.

He was not going to be put off by speculations like these however – not at his age. In the first innings he had been stumped off Blackie for 7. In the second, he came in with the score 4 – 86 and Blackie on a hat-trick. There was a fair breeze blowing across the ground and the tall off-spinner coming in on his long, diagonal approach was making the ball float beautifully in the air before breaking sharply away to leg where a strong on-side cordon was waiting. Bradman averted the hat-trick alright, then found himself pinned down for over after over, against Blackie at one end, Ironmonger at the other. A lot of people hadn't realised he had the patience. But the nerves are never stronger than they are at 19 or 20. When Blackie came off at the end of 26 consecutive overs, N.S.W. through Bradman and Oldfield had survived a difficult period with great credit. The team was now absolutely safe from defeat and Bradman blazed happily away, reaching 134 not out before Kippax declared. That was his last first-class innings of the season and there was no longer the slightest doubt, whatever the reservations in certain minds, that Australia had acquired a new Test match batsman.

And a new outfielder as well. After Ponsford had departed in Victoria's first innings and Gregory had been taken off, Woodfull and Hendry went on, looking wonderfully safe against the spinners. Woodfull was imperturbable. Speed didn't frighten; nor spin confuse him. But he did have one moment of alarm. As he jogged back for a leisurely second run, a throw-in from the fence suddenly shattered his stumps. He was almost run out. He looked up in amazement. Hendry looked. Bradman stood by the distant fence, hands on hips, unmistakably grinning.

He had a terrific, bullet-like throw, having spent so many hours of his boyhood pinging a golf-ball against a certain rail in a paddock-fence. The ball had to hit the rail in just the right place at just the right angle, otherwise he had a long walk to fetch it. Being a perfectionist, he went on until he could hit the spot almost at will. Similarly, with this same golf-ball, he was accustomed to throw it up against the wall with his left hand, using a two-handed grip on an old cricket-stump to keep the ball on the go, studying the rebounds with minute attention until his eye was so good, his reactions so sharp, that he rarely made a mistake. So it was with his music. If he heard a piece he particularly liked, he played it over and over till he had it off pat.

So Bradman had been discovered; with Jackson, another exciting young batting prospect to throw in against the Englishmen when they arrived in 1928–29. However no exciting new bowlers were to be observed anywhere; no obvious captain to lead Australia following the rumoured retirement of Herbie Collins. Australian cricket, like it or not, was going through a period of decline. The fact was more apparent now than it had been even in 1926 and there was just no immediate remedy to hand. The crowds were greater than ever before; the revenues were larger, but they only seemed to bring worse head-aches. The State associations which had originally created the Australian Board of Control now believed that the Board was attempting to take over from them altogether – to confine them, each to its own local back-water, where its influence on the main course of the game would be minimal. When the 1926 side returned for instance, the N.S.W.C.A. looked forward to the profits being split in the traditional way, the lion's share going to the three major cricketing States which provided all the players and did all the work. The Board saw matters differently. The money ought to be divided equally among all the States, Queensland, Western Australia and Tasmania included, declared Aubrey Oxlade, the Board treasurer; it should be spread throughout the continent for the good of the game generally instead of going into piles of bricks and mortar for the greater glory of Sydney and Melbourne.

The Oxlade party carried the day at a Board meeting held in Sydney on 7 January 1927, the same season which saw Queensland admitted to the Sheffield Shield for the first time. Though this was nothing to the shock in Sydney the following year when it was learned that Brisbane was to be awarded a Test match, the first of the series against the M.C.C. in 1928–29. Sydney being the centre which now lost one of its Tests in order to make way for Brisbane, the N.S.W.C.A. took the opportunity to point out to the Board that over a period of 20 years and more N.S.W. had spent £3000 nurturing the game in Queensland, while Victoria and South Australia had provided not a penny. If such a state of affairs was allowed to persist, the N.S.W.C.A. threatened to secede from the Board.

While the administrators aired their grievances and didn't hesitate to take their quarrels to the Press, the players themselves were discontented, mainly because the associations were taking more and more in gate-money each year and not increasing the players' allowances in anything like the same proportion. After Queensland came into the Shield, N.S.W. players were obliged to spend an average of 52 days a season away from their homes and their jobs, the 20 shillings per diem allowance covering immediate expenses, but hardly making up for the chances of preferment lost in their normal employments.

The associations, and in its turn the Board, had come into being to serve the interests of the players. They didn't need any Board for instance to organise the itinerary for a tour of England and make all the necessary travelling arrangements. They could do that well enough themselves. But when it came to such delicate matters as dividing th profits and apportioning the various responsibilities attached thereto, there obviously had to be some over-riding authority; some body which they could turn to to arbitrate in their disputes. But how quickly the servants became the masters. The players soon found that all that they had done was to create a hierarchy of officials, or non-players, whose interests were often enough diametrically opposed to their own. Inevitably, clashes of personality occurred. There was the spectacle of a captain of Australia, Warwick Armstrong, being dropped from the Victorian eleven at the behest of a Victorian official, E. E. Bean, while a Test series against England was actually in progress.

The Associations were bad enough. The Board of Control, as it grew in strength and gradually emerged as the real power behind the scenes, the focus of the most intense politicking, was infinitely worse. About one thing the players were certain: that the game had fared far better, a more general satisfaction had obtained all round, when they themselves had the running of affairs. For example the Board now appointed a committee to choose the umpires for Sheffield Shield matches, a task formerly entrusted to the Shield captains who, one presumes, were better placed to make the choice than a panel of non-players. The result of course was that the overall standard of umpiring was on the down grade. "For God's sake, stop shouting, willya?" the Victorian wicket-keeper told the bowler after his appeal for lbw had been turned down by the Queensland umpire for the umpteenth time, "Doncha know they don't play lbw up here?"

The Queenslanders made the same sort of complaint when they travelled south, but the ill-feeling wasn't confined to these two States or to differences of opinion about the umpiring. The Anniversary Day fixture between N.S.W. and Victoria wasn't a great advertisement for the game either. There were various on-the-field incidents, culminating in sections of the crowd hooting the Victorians at one point. Nobody could accuse Woodfull of being a bad sport, but he showed what he thought of Kippax's delay in declaring N.S.W.'s second innings by putting Ponsford on to bowl. The match ended with Kippax bowling high lobs to no outfield and Woodfull and Rigg making no attempt to run easy singles. What the game seemed to lack for the moment was an outstanding personality; a figure of undeniable authority who would take charge of them all and stand up for them, even against the Board if necessary. Another Warwick Armstrong perhaps?

CHAPTER TWO

First Tests

In September 1928, the first Test being little more than two months away, Don Bradman left Bowral to become permanently resident in Sydney. He was devoted to his family. He didn't particularly like the idea of leaving his little home town with its happy memories, but there seemed no other way, if he wished to make certain of his place in the Australian eleven. It was a big step to take however, much bigger in 1928 than it might seem today. To visit Sydney from time to time was safe enough. Actually to live there was another thing. There were youths in Bowral in Bradman's day who would no more have thought of setting foot in the big city, snares and temptations bristling on every side, than they would have ventured into the lion's den. However Alf Stephens and other friends of the family had contacts in Sydney, and after much anxious debate, Davis and Westbrook finally made it possible, appointing him secretary of their newly-opened Sydney office. Bradman went to stay with the G. H. Pearce family of Concord West, where he would remain until it was necessary for St. George qualification purposes to reside strictly within St. George territory.

It was to be a testing time all right. He started off in grade cricket in great form, but his first big match of the season, the Test trial in Melbourne in mid-October, was a sad disappointment. The selections had been disappointing to begin with. Only one of the originally selected "Australia" side was under 30. The Rest were even older. Kelleway, Ironmonger, O'Connor, Thompson, Jack Scott! A newspaper photograph of the time depicts a group of well-seasoned Sheffield Shield warriors, a lined-and-leathery collection beside whom Bradman and Jackson in the Rest side look mere youths, positively cherubic.

The two sides in fact strongly reflected the personalities of the men who had chosen them. There was firstly dour Warren Bardsley, who, having failed to win a place on the N.S.W. selection committee, so noted for its encouragement of its youth and progressive outlook, had then stood for the Australian selection panel and been successful. Bardsley at least had a distinguished background in international cricket. Of the remainder only C. E. Dolling (South Australia) could lay claim to any real first-class experience. E. E. (Ernie) Bean, stalwart of the Victorian Cricket Association, had played twice for Victoria; Jack Hutcheon, occasionally for Queensland in the days before Queensland was recognised as possessing first-class status. But they were all experienced Board men, well versed in the business of trading A for B, your 'keeper in exchange for my man as captain, and so on. What made it worse this year was that they were four instead of three following the addition of a Queensland representative, and that the fourth was Jack Hutcheon, the strong-man of Queensland cricket. Hutcheon would not be content with a relatively passive rôle, commensurate with Queensland's modest standing in Australian cricket. He was a force to be reckoned with in any gathering.

It was on the cards then that the selectors would play safe, plump for experience rather than youth, though none of their selections was as surprising as that of Jack Scott. The fast bowler was nearing 40. Eighteen years had elapsed since he had first played for N.S.W. against South Australia and been carted all over the Sydney Cricket Ground by Clem Hill. True, the country no longer possessed any really penetrative opening bowler; true, the old war-horse was as fit and enthusiastic as any of the younger men coming along. But surely, he had been at his best years ago and not good enough to get into an Australian eleven then.

Anyway, he was a great trier and an adaptable bowler, ever ready to experiment. For instance, off-side shots against the faster bowlers having become unfashionable, Scott would sometimes shorten his length and direct his attack at or outside the leg-stump instead. However leg-theory, as it was called, used habitually to be scorned in Australia in those days; it was regarded as a purely negative tactic, an admission that the bowler had thrown in the sponge as far as taking wickets was concerned and was merely trying to keep the runs down. Herbie Collins, N.S.W.'s skipper and sole selector for some years, absolutely forbade anything resembling a leg-side field-setting for a fast bowler, with the result that Scott was in and out of the N.S.W. side for a number of seasons, never having the opportunity of trying out his new method, at least not at Sheffield Shield level.

In fact leg-theory was a more sophisticated, more rational means of attack than most Australians supposed. Very simply it was the bowler's answer to batsmen who no longer trusted their off-side shots; who rarely attempted to drive through the covers for example, lest the ball swung in and took their leg-stump. They tended now to play back instead of forward; had developed a variety of on-side strokes that made up to some extent for the loss of the cut and the drive. To counter this growing trend, Root of Worcestershire, to take one example, had perfected a medium-fast delivery which pitched roughly in line with the middle and leg stumps and swung sharply away to leg. Where a leg-trap was in position. The ball couldn't be ignored because every now and again he would straighten one up and the batsman would be found with his pads in front. That was positive leg-theory; successful in keeping the runs down, successful also in taking a vast number of wickets.

But Scott of course was really fast, and the theory behind this new-fangled Australian style of fast attack had quite a different origin. He was a fiery and belligerent character whose unusual slinging action enabled him to get considerable lift from the pitch. He just loved to disconcert the batsman with his shorter ones; to see him eventually lose his head and perhaps get himself out. Evidently it was not the length that worried the batsman as much as the line. He was made to feel that *he* was the target instead of the stumps. Thus, as the focus of the fast bowler's attack gradually shifted to leg, so did his field gravitate in that direction also. One or two men close to the bat were there for the catch cocked up in self-defence. Leg-slips replaced the conventional off-side slips; there was another man or two deep for the hook-shot. The hook-shot was the answer to the whole business, but not many batsmen hooked, Scott found, or at least not consistently and well.

Almost nothing was seen of Scott's leg-theory however, until the season of 1924–25 when Collins was occupied almost exclusively by the matches against the visiting Englishmen. Playing for N.S.W. versus South Australia in Adelaide in January 1925, Scott was intrigued to find L. T. Gun, little more than an occasional Shield bowler, bowling fast-medium leg-theory with six men behind the wicket on the leg-side. Gun was hardly fast enough to cause great concern, but at least somebody had been brave enough to try out a new idea, and two weeks later in Sydney, when N.S.W. took the field under a stop-gap skipper, Andy Ratcliffe, a poor crowd was treated to a sensational opening burst by Jack Scott. With an arc of fieldsmen stretching from the 'keeper round to square-leg, Scott began firing down bouncers, launching himself at the crease with such furious energy that his first over contained five no-balls, all for "dragging." But it was an effective first over just the same. Clearly rattled by the unexpectedness of it, Edgar Mayne, the Victorian skipper, swung wildly at successive deliveries, hooked one to the fence, snicked two more boundaries and was "bowled" by a no-ball. Finally the last and thirteenth ball of the over bowled him out.

This was the only notable achievement of the new theory however. Liddicut and Willis murdered the short stuff in the latter part of the innings and a few weeks later arrangements were made for Scott to settle in Adelaide where he would have at least the sympathy and full moral support of his new skipper, Vic Richardson. However, he rarely achieved very much for South Australia. What induced Richardson to bring him over to Melbourne for the Test trial and suddenly to switch his field over to the leg-side after only two overs, can only be surmised. Did he hope to unsettle Ponsford, as Gregory had reputedly unsettled him in Sydney? Or, alternatively, to give him practice against this mode of attack in the event of the Englishmen adopting the same tactics?

The battles of Test cricket, as Bradman would soon have to learn, must be waged to the hilt, using every means, strategical and psychological, at one's disposal. Test cricket is not total war. There are rules, but one needs to be cold-blooded in one's approach. It is folly not to play the game as hard as the rules permit and in this case there was nothing in the laws of cricket to cover the kind of bowling that a batsman might be disposed to regard as dangerous or intimidatory.

Scott however was simply not accurate enough to be really dangerous. He was not Test class, never had been, and Ponsford played him or evaded him with some ease. Another who failed signally to impress was young Bradman. Grimmett had him caught behind for 14 in his first innings. Oxenham bowled him for 5 in the second. It was his first tilt with the wily Queenslander and he had never looked likely to get to grips with his well-flighted leg-breaks.

His double failure was a severe blow to his hopes of making the Test side. Yet how often when the little man was down, when one bowler or another was reputed to have gained the mastery of him, would he come out the next time and completely annihilate his enemy. It was as though the ability to bring out his very best was controlled by some unconscious mechanism inside him; which wouldn't go off until a situation of the direst emergency arrived to trigger it into action. The following week for N.S.W. against Queensland at the Brisbane Exhibition Ground, he wiped the unfortunate Oxenham virtually off the map. One particular delivery in the slow bowler's bag of tricks was a top-spinner disguised as a leg-break. It had earned him countless lbws against batsmen accustomed to playing back, but of course it could always be countered by quick movers like Bradman, not afraid to use their feet. After looking a certainty for the first Test on his own home ground, Oxenham lost all confidence and eventually failed to win selection. He was actually in the original Test match twelve, whereupon he begged Hutcheon to leave him out of the forthcoming Queensland game against the M.C.C., lest the Englishmen, like Bradman, sort out his wiles before the Test match. Hutcheon was adamant however, so he played and duly bowled himself out of the Test. "Oh God," Arthur Mailey is alleged to have remarked on reading in the morning newspaper that he had the measure of Don Bradman. "That's the end of me."

It was possible, in this game against Queensland, to see how far Bradman's batting had advanced in the two seasons since leaving behind him the matting wickets of Bowral and the Southern Highlands. He didn't have a great range of shots at this stage, but he had clearly spent the intervening time eliminating some of the inelegancies he had brought with him from the bush, using every match to perfect the strokes he did possess. One day for instance, playing for St. George against Gordon at Chatswood Oval, he told skipper Ted Adams that he intended to practise his leg-glance. In fact he hit the ball exclusively to leg during this particular innings, polishing up not only the glance, but the hook, the forcing shot off the toes and finally the gem of the whole collection, the pull wide of mid-on from the shortish ball pitched on or outside the off-stump.

There are more ways of making a stroke than are set out in the illustrated text-books, he had discovered. The ball may be played early or late. A late cut may be hit with the middle of the bat, or the inside edge, or the outside edge, according to the disposition of the field and the direction in which it is desired the ball shall travel. If the outfield is very slow it may pay to keep the ball off the ground, as Bradman demonstrated one memorable afternoon at Coogee Oval. He obtained his runs off the Randwick bowlers this day, almost entirely by the aid of lofted strokes that safely cleared the infield and landed mostly just inside the fence. In later years there was the famous occasion at Chatswood when he hit a six over the head of point. "You could never do that again," remarked Bertie Oldfield from behind the stumps. "Couldn't I?" said Bradman and repeated the shot off the next convenient half-volley. By this time he had acquired the ability to play two or more shots off the same delivery, making it just impossible for the bowler to set a field for him. Move a man from one spot and he was sure to hit the next ball through that very spot. He had a photographic memory for this sort of thing. A quick glance or two around the field and as he settled down over his bat, he seemed to know the exact location of every man.

He was not yet as proficient as this in 1928, but he had an absolutely precocious talent and it was all very discouraging for the Queenslanders. They had not only Oxenham, but Hornibrook, the left-hander, who must have been desperately unlucky not to have gone to England in 1926; a new fast bowler in "Pud" Thurlow, and Dr. Otto Nothling, recently returned from N.S.W. With this steady and well-varied attack, they had been all set to show the world they were entitled to their first-class status, entitled to their first Test match, when Bradman arrived and blighted their hopes. In N.S.W.'s first innings he made 131 out of 248; in the second, after his side had trailed by 76 and needed 399 second-innings runs to win, he was 133 not out when N.S.W. reached its mark with six wickets to spare.

Queensland had no answer to him for the moment. The State would just have to search for fresh bowlers, but in the meantime a new challenge had appeared. The M.C.C. side that reached Sydney in November may not have been the greatest England had ever sent out, but it must have been close to it. It was rare to find a touring party so well-balanced: between youth and experience, between speed and spin, with as much depth in the batting as there was in the bowling. On the opening day of the match against N.S.W. the M.C.C. batted first and made 3 – 372, the highlight being an innings of 140 by the amateur, Douglas Jardine. The ease with which he handled Gregory, intended spearhead of the Australian attack, was really quite alarming. His height helped him, as well as his cast-iron composure. But mainly it was his immaculate Winchester and Oxford technique, "coming forward with his left foot to the ball, his head right over it, the body balanced well forward with the weight over the left leg, the right arm close to the body and his immobile face looking down at the ball over his left forearm and turned wrist." On the second day, before a crowd of 43,117, Hammond and Hendren took over, scoring almost at will after lunch, confirming the pessimists in their worst fears about the state of Australia's bowling resources. At one stage Kippax had to resort to Bradman with his occasional leg-breaks.

Wally Hammond would never forget his memory of this first meeting. The latest bowler was "a slim, shortish boy with a grim, nervous face whom I have never seen before . . . he looked about nineteen and not very formidable." He asked Hendren who he was. "Oh, he's a lad from the back-blocks called Bradmen. Bats a bit, they say. But he looks too frightened to do much today." Hendren may have underestimated his opponent however. After cracking the new bowler for a four and two sixers, he failed to get hold of one properly and was caught in the outfield. Hammond made the same mistake. Bradmen had just been taken off, having conceded 55 runs in 5 overs, when Leyland called for a quick single to deep mid-off. Mid-off moved in like lightning however, gathering and returning the ball in a flash, and Hammond at the 'keeper's end was just a trifle too slow. 5 – 622; last batsman, 225, run out Bradman. Chapman didn't declare until seven wickets were down for 734 and N.S.W. was left with half an hour or so in which to bat.

Australians love an underdog. No nation on earth rejoices more in the spectacle of David slaying Goliath, of the little man taking on the established authorities, cocking his snook at Goliath and getting away with it. Bradman was already a firm favourite with the Sydney crowd, following his deeds of the previous season, but never had it shown so much emotion as when he came out to bat, fair-haired and capless in the fading light, after three N.S.W. wickets had gone for a mere 38. It was a situation made to order for him of course – just when the Englishmen joking and jubilant, under their very effervescent, public-schoolboyish captain, Percy Chapman, seemed to have gained the upper hand.

The week before they had shattered Victoria through the sheer pace of their fast bowler, Harold Larwood. Larwood had since suffered a strained shoulder, but this week Tate seemed likely to be the wrecker. The redoubtable Maurice Tate! On his favourite Australian ground where he had taken such a huge swag of wickets in 1924–25! How would he fare if suddenly faced with Tate, Bradman had been asked one far-off day in Bowral. "Oh, I wouldn't worry," he had replied, and now here he was facing the great man in the flesh, facing him with the bowler's tail up and grinning his familiar broad grin, and playing him just as calmly and confidently as he had promised. Kippax was a great encouragement at the other end and together they survived the evening and carried their partnership to 90 the next morning.

Nevertheless, the M.C.C. attack overall was a class or two higher than anything he had previously encountered. Not only Tate, but Freeman also was a problem still to solve. He didn't as yet dare to use his feet against those cunningly-contrived leg-breaks. Rather he found himself being forced back and back onto his stumps, until, finally, perhaps inevitably, a bigger leg-break than usual spun past his bat, on to his foot and thence onto the wicket. He had scored 87 and N.S.W. was now 5 – 196. The side was all out 349, had to follow on 385 runs behind, but at least it gave Bradman another chance. Not many bowlers would ever get the better of Don Bradman a second time and so it happened to Freeman. In the second innings he succumbed to those nimble feet, was driven repeatedly through the off-field, and thus with Bradman making one century and Kippax another, the match was easily saved. Larwood hadn't been able to bowl much in N.S.W.'s first innings, but he came on in the second innings, bowling to one slip and a cluster of three short-legs, evidently in an effort to cut down the run-rate of this dangerous pair. He proved to be the only one able to keep them quiet on a wicket that was now very easy-paced and ideal for batting. Perhaps it was these kind of conditions that had originally driven Jack Scott to leg-theory.

The rôle of Jack Scott in Richardson's strategy was by this time more apparent. On the second day of the M.C.C. versus South Australia game, as soon as it became clear that the Englishmen, no more than some Australian batsmen, were likely to be tempted by anything outside the off-stump, Richardson gave the fast bowler seven men on the leg-side, a field very similar to the one he had set for him in the Test trial in Melbourne. The only difference this time was that he went over the wicket instead of round. Hammond, nearing his century, was obviously the danger man and he certainly didn't seem to like Scott's change of direction, flicking rather dangerously at several head-high deliveries, until Chapman came along to hook the fast bowler out of the firing line for the time being. After Hammond was out and Scott had been eventually brought back, Larwood laid into him with no less vigour, and one might have thought that all chance of Scott's winning a place in the first Test side had definitely disappeared – until he was chosen for an Australian Eleven to meet the M.C.C. in Sydney immediately following the N.S.W. game.

This was the fixture granted to Sydney in compensation for the lost Test match, but the Eleven chosen by the N.S.W.C.A. on this occasion were hardly as representative of Australia as the public might reasonably have expected. There was not a single Victorian in the side, (the Victorians claiming that the £1 per day expenses allowed them were totally inadequate); only one Queenslander, Dr. Nothling, but no fewer than seven from N.S.W., plus three from South Australia – Vic Richardson (skipper), Gordon Harris (opening bat) and Scott.

Whether Scott was intended to be Australia's answer to Larwood or the other way about, it didn't matter, because the match and indeed the entire series was decided not by any new-fangled theory, but rather by the old-fashioned virtues of pace, guile and accuracy in which the M.C.C. attack proved far superior to their rivals'. It was Sydney's first taste of the real Larwood and it made the members sit up. He was curiously similar to Jack Scott in build, short in stature for a fast bowler, but with the same powerful arms and shoulders, the same ability to make the ball lift sharply off the wicket. But there the similarities ended. Scott was primarily a slinger with little control over length and direction; Larwood on the other hand possessed an action like velvet, an approach to the wicket "like a rubber ball bouncing over a cobbled path" as it was once described. If all the snicks and mishits of the Australian Eleven had gone to hand, he would have had better figures than 3 – 80 and 2 – 81, but it was already apparent that he was too good for Richardson, too good for a number of Australia's front-line batsmen. Only Bradman and Jackson in this match played him with confidence, and they were having their work cut out coping with Tate and the slow left-hander, White.

The crowd took to Jack White. A benevolent-looking figure with whitish hair, he started off his short run on the right side of the wicket, crossed behind the umpire and delivered round the stumps very wide out. They liked anything unusual like that. "Try the other arm," they yelled, when he was hit for four. Or, at the end of a particularly tight maiden over, "Garn, you couldn't get him out with a corkscrew. Come on Corkscrew, give somebody else a go." It was this M.C.C. side's second only appearance at the S.C.G. and already the Hill had established its own special kind of relationship with various of the players. "How the hell did you get into the team, Hendren?" somebody called when the little man once misfielded near the boundary. "Didn't you know? We were picked for our looks," Hendren grinned broadly back at them. "Look at old Leyland over there." Soon after it was Maurice Leyland who put down a difficult one in the outfield. "Ya big mug. Why don't you use your mouth next time?" "If I had a mouth as big as yours, I would," Leyland snapped back.

If only Jardine too could have made some response like that, at least waved back in recognition of their good-humoured raillery, he would have been forgiven everything. But he emerged from the pavilion on the final day of the N.S.W. match wearing a large Panama hat, a silk handkerchief at his throat, sleeves buttoned down to his wrists. He usually wore his multi-coloured Harlequins' cap to which they had already taken exception. Was he deliberately trying to annoy them further? Who did he think he was? The great white hunter? "What's the hat for? To get a catch?" But Jardine treated all their taunts with icy contempt and would just have to suffer their laughter and resentment for the rest of the tour.

Meanwhile Bradman, pinned down by Tate and the uncanny accuracy of Jack White, was playing almost the slowest innings of his first-class career. He was 58 not out when the Australian Eleven was dismissed for 231, and so having now scored 277 for only once out against the tourists, his choice for the first Test in Brisbane was a foregone conclusion. In his autobiography he recalled how the selectors' deliberations had gone on until such a late hour that he decided not to wait up for the wireless announcement of the team, but to get a good night's sleep instead. However he had not properly dropped off when he heard the names being read out from the wireless in the next room, his own being the first on the list in alphabetical order. "I cannot say I was unduly elated. I was not conscious of excitement, but of course was pleased that I had accomplished a task which I had definitely set out to do. To me it acted as a sleeping-draught – in fact I slept so soundly I was late for work next morning."

Perhaps the Victorians were lucky they hadn't played in Sydney after all. None of the Australians, with the exception of Bradman and Jackson, did their reputations any good, M.C.C. going on to win the game by 8 wickets and confirm their present clear-cut superiority. Woodfull, Ponsford, Ryder, Hendry, and Ironmonger were the five Victorians to win places in the Test twelve; Kippax, Oldfield, Gregory, Kelleway and Bradman (N.S.W.), Grimmett (S.A.) and Oxenham (Q'ld.) making up the rest of the team.

It was most unfortunate about Vic Richardson. A great favourite w th the public and almost everybody's choice to captain the Australian side, it was thought that he would have been the Board's choice also, except that in September 1927 it had passed a new ruling upon the procedure to be adopted in choosing a captain. It was now laid down that the selection committee having chosen twelve players and passed the names on to the Board for its approval, it would then be the task of another committee to select the captain and vice-captain from the names submitted. After his showing against Larwood in Sydney, there was just no way the selectors could envisage him in his usual position, opening the innings for Australia. To an older generation of cricketers it was inconceivable that the captain of the Australian team should have no hand in choosing his side, but anyway this was the way things were done in 1928 and the committee's choice eventually alighted on Jack Ryder. Rumour alleged that Woodfull may have been its first preference, but he was suffering from a bad attack of 'flu at the time and his fitness was in some doubt.

So Bradman's first Test match didn't begin under the best possible auspices. Though it wasn't entirely the Board's fault. For weeks beforehand, at least four candidates for selection had been contributing their opinions to various newspapers, not hesitating to pass judgment upon the form of other likely candidates, freely indulging in speculation about the possible make-up of the side. In the Melbourne *Herald* for instance Ponsford included himself of course, but couldn't find a place for Bradman. Kelleway wouldn't have had him either. But Bradman didn't care. As one of only two newcomers in the Australian team and by far the youngest, he was less involved in their shenanigans than any of them, yet he couldn't help noticing the very marked absence of team-spirit that prevailed when the side finally assembled in Brisbane; the smouldering ill-will between certain players that actually led to blows in one case.

However the articles that were to have the most damaging consequences for Australia in the long run were those by Ponsford in the *Herald.* He still retained bitter memories of the Australian tour of 1926, it appeared. At Folkestone, near the end of the tour, Larwood had bowled deliberately short at the Australian batsmen, he believed, with the obvious intention of intimidating them. He had made no secret of his dislike for the fast bowler since then; who was also, it happened, a great contributor to the Press in his own country, as well as a great reader of the stories published about him in other people's newspapers. "He gives the impression," he wrote about Ponsford in the *Sunday Chronicle* (3 June 1928) "that his ultimate ambition is to score 1000." He made it sound as though the batsman was actuated by malice; as though his underlying object was to deprive every honest, hard-working bowler of his livelihood. He foresaw drastic consequences for several Australian batsmen when the M.C.C. arrived in Australia in October.

Ponsford wasn't going to be bluffed by any of this sort of gammon however. "Judging from what I saw when in England," he hit back in the *Herald* (26 September), "I have very definite doubts about certain of the new bowlers succeeding in Australia." They were not fast enough, he hinted. Larwood was livid when the team actually arrived and he had a chance to catch up with the newspapers. But Ponsford stuck to his guns and backed up in print by his colleague, "Stork" Hendry, he reiterated his opinion that Larwood could be knocked out of contention by a determined assault. Not even the fast bowler's great performance against Victoria could make him change his mind. "McDonald," he said after this match, "is the greatest fast bowler in England," and while conceding that Larwood also had claims to be considered speedy, "yet he is not as fast as Scott."

It was all most unfortunate, because after England had made 521 in its first innings in Brisbane, Australia was all out 122, Larwood's figures being 6 – 32. The pitch was green and very fast, no scythe having been used to finish off the work of the mower, but where Gregory was merely awkward during his opening spell, Larwood was devastating from start to finish. Woodfull was out to a wonderful gully catch by Chapman in Larwood's first over; Ponsford was yorked by the second ball of his third over and Australia was 2 – 7. In the second innings he was caught behind off Larwood for 6, after which he graciously conceded (*Herald* 8 December) that "although Larwood was not as fast as may be thought, he and Tate are undoubtedly the world's greatest bowlers. He has great control and is always attacking the batsman. Many fast bowlers might profit from Larwood's example."

Bradman didn't have much of a match either. He came in at No. 7, when five wickets had fallen for 71 in Australia's first innings, batted very nicely for 18 in 33 minutes including four boundaries, and was then lbw to Tate's slower ball curving in and keeping low. (He still hadn't altogether mastered Tate.) Gregory couldn't bat, having broken down with an old knee injury, and that was practically the end of the Australian innings, of the worst display of batting by an Australian side that anybody could remember. Soon afterwards, with a lead of 399, Chapman decided his team would bat again.

England's second innings proved to be an even worse ordeal for the Australians. Kelleway was also incapacitated, following an attack of "ptomaine poisoning", so Ryder and Hendry shared the new ball. In great heat, interrupted by the occasional shower which only made the humidity worse, England went on to 342 before Chapman at last declared, leaving just enough time for Larwood to get rid of Ponsford before bad light stopped play for the day. The following morning it was all over in next to no time. Heavy overnight rain succeeded by hot sun had converted the wicket into a glue-pot and Australia was dismissed for 66, losing by the colossal margin of 675 runs.

Bradman took it very much to heart. "To me and my countrymen this Test in Brisbane will ever remain a painful memory. It was some grounding for a lad of 20 to play on a side defeated by the greatest number of runs in Test history." He had made only 18 and 1 and missed a catch, offset to some extent by his brilliant running-out of Hobbs in England's first innings. But it wasn't only the consciousness of personal failure that haunted him, if that bothered him at all. He just couldn't understand why England had batted on and on in its second innings, making no attempt to force the pace against such a weak and dispirited attack. It simply didn't accord with his youthful notions of how Englishmen played the game. Jardine for instance, who had batted so attractively in Sydney, went to the wicket with his side 516 runs in front, seven wickets in hand, and stayed over three hours for 65 not out. Was he deliberately trying to rub Australian noses in the dirt? Possibly at the time he didn't realise how far English cricket had become committed to defensive tactics, ever since the days of Warwick Armstrong's Australians; had been conditioned by the series of 1924–25 in particular into believing that Australian pitches would last for ever.

Still it was disillusioning. Nor would he ever forget Maurice Tate calling jocularly to White as he made his way back to the pavilion for the second time in the match, "You've pinched my rabbit, Jack." Tate hadn't meant to hurt his feelings. He was given to indiscreet, unconsidered remarks, but this one he would have to pay for. Bradman had a long memory for certain things; was apt to take perhaps too personal a view. Be that as it may, his experience in Brisbane would do much to shape his attitude to Test cricket in the future.

CHAPTER THREE

The Making of a Champion

Australian cricket was at its lowest ebb since the ill-fated tour of 1912. Gregory and Kelleway, great names to conjure with once, were gone; Ponsford had been reduced to nonentity by Larwood. The final blow was self-inflicted. In the twelve for the second Test in Sydney, Bradman was advised by his captain fifteen minutes before the match began that he was to be twelfth man. It was logical in a way. At Brisbane he had gone in last in the batting order of those chosen solely for their batting and failed along with the rest. So it was perhaps logical, and at the same time incredible, considering amongst other things that he had scored the most runs by any batsman, English or Australian, in first-class cricket that season; the most by any Australian against the English bowling thus far on the tour. He had made more runs and saved more runs. After his work in the out-field, his marvellous running out of Jack Hobbs in particular, never again would a member of this M.C.C. party risk one for his throw.

Anyway Bradman was dropped and the all-rounder, Otto Nothling, batted in his place at No. 7. It is impossible to account for such a gross miscarriage of justice, unless it be Nature's way of correcting the balance, of going to such lengths in order to demonstrate the blindness of those who seem determined to lead us to destruction. Nothling was a perfectly competent Shield cricketer, simply not of Test class. Anybody could see that. Nevertheless he acquitted himself, in his only Test match appearance for Australia, with all the spirit and assurance to be expected of an international Rugby Union full-back. *He* certainly didn't let his country down. Australia would have lost the second Test, with or without Nothling; with or without Bradman.

Nor did it make a great deal of difference to Bradman himself in the long run, bitterly disappointed though he was at the time. Ponsford having been hit on the hand by Larwood and forced to retire from the match soon after lunch on the first day, the twelfth man was obliged to field throughout the entire English innings and thus had the opportunity of watching Walter Hammond at close quarters.

One didn't need to be a connoisseur to enjoy Hammond at his best; the manner in which the strokes simply flowed from his bat, no effort seemingly required. The crowd could sense his greatness. Bradman in the covers could appreciate the technical command, the art which made it look so easy. These great English batsmen didn't have a tremendous array of strokes. To the ball that an Australian might be tempted to cut, Hammond mostly stepped across his wickets, pads guarding the stumps and ignored it, beautifully. But the straight drive along the ground or over the bowler's head, the forcing shot off the back foot past mid-off, he played to perfection. Bradman himself had not too many attacking shots at this period. But he had a different temperament from Hammond. His development would be along different lines altogether.

Hammond's 251, following his 225 against N.S.W., confirmed the impression already created that here was another great English cricketer to place alongside Hobbs and Sutcliffe, Hendren and Woolley. It was not a bright outlook for Australia. England's total of 636, after Australia had been all out 253 on a perfectly good wicket, was the highest for any Test in any country. Another record against Australia had been set up and in its frustration, in its disappointment with the failure of its own heroes, the huge crowd vented its wrath, first upon one, then upon another, English or Australian, with remarkable impartiality. On the first day Duckworth was the focus of its resentment. Duckworth, the aggressive little wicket-keeper! With his too raucous, too frequent appealing! The next day, though, it was more Larwood. In Brisbane he had pitched the ball up and swung it around in the heavy atmosphere to great effect. In Sydney he found it paid more to keep the ball short, to make it fly. Richardson had been restored to the Australian side to open in place of Ponsford, but neither he nor Woodfull was any match for the fast bowler at the start of the Australian first innings. Larwood had them both hopping from foot to foot, fending off one ball, just getting the bat out of the way of another. Woodfull, the more skilful, didn't get a touch. Richardson, after numerous snicks, was bowled Larwood, 27.

The spectacle of one's fellow-countrymen so plainly outclassed must naturally be disappointing, but crowds are not particularly steadfast in their allegiances, or not in Sydney at any rate. They are always ready to cheer their opponents if they should prove the more worthy. No, it wasn't Larwood's success that irked the Hill. The fast bowler wasn't barracked to any extent until the second morning of the match when he made his bumpers fly at the head of the amiable Ironmonger, 41 years of age, and in batting terms completely inoffensive. That, they felt, was most definitely unfair, a sort of gut-reaction stimulated by the sight of Larwood standing hands on hip, the very embodiment of physical menace, glaring down the pitch after his last delivery had narrowly missed decapitating the batsman. "He is not particular where the ball pitches," Alf Noble was to write of Larwood after the tour was ended, "uses his head, has his field well-placed for intentional long-hops, and doesn't mind who gets hit."

Fortunately, though, in Australia's second innings Larwood was not nearly as deadly. The wicket was now quite gentle in pace after three days of hard play and hot sun, and if the fast bowler's field tended to shift progressively across to leg as the innings proceeded, it was clearly nothing more than a defensive tactic designed to reduce the flow of runs. In the event Woodfull scored 111, Hendry 112, Ryder 79, and although the Australians were easily beaten by eight wickets this encouraging performance by the three Victorians, together with the reinstatement of Bradman and the inclusion of the promising young Victorian all-rounder, a'Beckett, ensured another wonderful gate for the third Test in Melbourne.

In fact the crowd on the first day was a world record for a cricket match, over 60,000, not including all those packed on the roofs of nearby buildings, nor perched in trees outside the ground where at least they might get a glimpse of the score-board. Australia again won the toss, Harold Larwood took the ball, and for a boy of 20 playing only his second Test match, the scene, the occasion, the spectacle of Larwood very deliberately measuring out his run, would remain indelibly etched on his memory. "I have never at any time seen faster bowling than that of Harold Larwood on this day. The ball seemed literally to fly through the air and come off the pitch at terrific speed." He would never forget either Jack Ryder going for a hook, snicking it and seeing the ball fly over the wicket-keeper's head and on over the fence for six. Or rhe sight of another attempted Ryder hook, when the ball "hit Duckworth on the forehead, bounced off it and landed on the sight-screen."

The fast bowler certainly had the best of it at the outset. Woodfull went to Tate, but Larwood had Richardson caught behind, Hendry caught hooking and though Ryder and Kippax were still there at lunch they had been kept desperately defending. But how often the fortunes of a game of cricket are upset by lunch; by those subtle changes of pitch and atmosphere that cause the delicate balance in favour of bat or ball to tilt from one to other. Only the week before on this same ground Kippax had scored 260 not out for N.S.W. against Victoria, so no one was better acquainted with the changing moods, all the little quirks and vagaries of this Melbourne wicket. After lunch he decided to hook. In Larwood's first over he hit him for three fours, two from hook-shots. Twenty-three came from the fast bowler's first two overs after lunch and he was soon taken off to be used thereafter in even shorter spells, as little as two overs at a time.

Larwood wasn't the only sufferer. Jardine deep on the fence at long-leg had to do most of the running and retrieving, to the usual jeers and cat-calls from the outer. He had held two catches in the morning, yet couldn't help reflecting, had he been captain, that he would never have surrendered the initiative in this way; at least a more scientific arrangement of the field would have saved some of the runs now being given away.

The Australians now seemed on the way to evening their score with Larwood and when Bradman came in late in the day and began to hook and glance in turn, he was quickly forced to pitch them up instead. Bradman however was more worried by White. Clearly he was still apprehensive about moving out to meet the ball. Time after time he would drive determinedly from the crease but fail to budge Chapman at silly-point. He stayed in the end to make a solid 79; Australia reached a very respectable 397, and then England by the same cautious, painstaking means made 417 in reply. There now appeared very little between the two sides. Chance as much as anything else would determine the final result.

Bradman was again fourth-wicket-down in the second innings, coming in with the score 143 and White in the middle of another long stint. Up and over went White, ever on the spot. Back and back went Bradman, picking up a single here and there, moving from 9 not out at lunch to 60 not out at tea. All at once a faster ball beat and almost bowled him. Bradman was instantly transformed. No longer did he seem forced back all the time. Rather he suggested a tiger, crouched, waiting to pounce. Two or three times an over he sprang, lashing the ball with almost incredible ferocity, causing Chapman to retreat to deep mid-off where repeatedly he was made to wring his hands after stopping the ball. Bradman's first 50 had taken him 143 minutes; his second occupied only 83. The vast assembly of the first two days had shrunk to less than half its former size, yet the ovation when he reached his first Test century was described as "the greatest ever heard on any Australian cricket ground." So prolonged was it in fact, that many of the Englishmen who had joined in enthusiastically at the beginning wearied of it and lay down on the grass waiting for the noise to subside.

Bradman changed his bat, handed his cap to the square-leg umpire, and was indulging in some very pretty late-cuts when a hoarse scream from Duckworth rent the stadium and he was given out caught-behind off Geary. The crowd seemed dazed as he turned towards the pavilion and began to walk out. Then he turned back and a huge sigh of relief went up. He was not out after all, then? But no. It was only to retrieve his cap from the umpire.

It was not the Australian batting this time which lost the third Test. It was the English batting which won it. On a really bad pitch, in conditions more familiar in England than in Australia, Hobbs and Sutcliffe began England's second innings, their side needing 332 to win the match and thus the series. Owing to the prevailing practice of covering the wicket in Sheffield Shield cricket, the country no longer possessed anybody who really knew how to exploit a wet wicket, but even so the Englishmen's courage and technique were beyond all praise, the stuff of which the English love to weave legends. Almost it recalled the historic occasion at The Oval in 1902 when Rhodes was last man in, England needing just 15 runs to win, and Hirst walked down the wicket and is supposed to have said, "We'll get 'em in singles, Wilfred."

In this case Hobbs, pretending to require a new bat at one point, took the opportunity to get a message to Chapman in the England dressing-room, "If a wicket falls this evening, send in Jardine." Clearly he trusted Jardine best in these very trying circumstances. Hammond and the others would thus be saved for later. And so it proved. When Hobbs was out, Jardine came in and held out with Sutcliffe until the wicket eased the next day and England's task became relatively simple. The Englishmen's craft and resource, their patience in adversity, contained many a lesson for Bradman, but none better than the way in which they had gone forward to smother the ball, getting right over it and taking the knocks if it unexpectedly popped; or, alternatively, had gone back ready to withdraw the bat at the very last instant if they judged it didn't need to be played. If he was to make runs in England, he foresaw, he would have to learn more about wet wickets.

For the fourth Test in Adelaide the selectors brought in the nineteen-year-old, Archie Jackson. Despite his curiously fluctuating form, they had long had him in mind as a possibility and now, after the failure of Australia to recover the Ashes, the failure of Ponsford and Richardson as opening batsmen, they took the plunge and entrusted the responsibility of opening the Australian innings with Woodfull to this youth. After all the harsh things said about the selectors that season, their love-affair with the over-40s and so on, it is pleasant to record that their enterprise was handsomely rewarded on this occasion.

Jackson was quite different in style from most of the others. He didn't crunch the ball like Ryder, or lash it like Bradman. He didn't give the same impression of solidity as Woodfull and Ponsford gave. Yet when he executed a glance, or a late-cut, or forced the ball off his toes to square-leg, or leant well forward to cover-drive, going down almost on one knee, it made one gasp. Trumper had the same effect on people. At the end of the day their average is not outstanding. Yet their great innings stand out in the memory, long after the match and all else is forgotten, like some immortal painting glimpsed but once whose beauty haunts the beholder for ever after.

Jackson's first innings for Australia, after England had laboured to 334, was one of these innings. The first three Australian wickets had fallen for only 19 when Ryder joined Jackson. The tough, lean Australian skipper was a hard-hitter when the occasion demanded and very slowly and carefully at first, but with increasing acceleration later on, they carried the score to 145 when Ryder was lbw White for 63. To their partnership of 129, each had contributed in equal measure. Bradman was next in and fresh from an innings of 340 not out versus Victoria in Sydney, he was the picture of confidence, outscoring

Jackson at first. The latter continued quietly, serenely on however, and soon it was he who began to dominate the partnership. Larwood came back and tried leg-theory, with six men on the leg. Was it a lure, to tempt one or both of these two youngsters into an ill-judged glance or hook? Larwood himself wrote years later, "I bowled rising balls on the leg stump . . . a desperation move to dislodge batsmen on top in tough conditions. Both seemed to play it well enough."

Immediately after lunch Jackson square-drove Larwood to reach his 100 and although Bradman was soon caught by Larwood in the slips off Tate, Jackson now proceeded to take complete charge of the attack. Here was the difference between the Australian approach and the English approach. When the Australians got on top, they attacked. When their opponents gained the advantage, they generally plodded on doggedly as ever, faithful to the methods that had brought them out of many a sticky situation from Waterloo onwards. Even under such a dashing leader as Percy Chapman.

Jackson eventually made 164, which looked likely enough at one stage to ensure victory; though tragically, in the end, it did not. Australia was 6 – 308 in its second innings, needing 349 to win and Bradman 58 not out, when Oldfield called his partner for a quick single off the last ball of an over. It was one of those small misunderstandings that just seem to occur from time to time. Bradman, who would now have lost the strike, was not expecting the call, was slow in starting and just failed to beat Hobbs' return and Duckworth's scrambled efforts to break the stumps. White quickly cleaned up the tail and Australia was beaten by 12 runs.

Four defeats in a row, one might imagine, must have been a shattering experience for a people supposedly cricket-crazy, long accustomed to success, at least on Australian wickets. But not at all. Nothing like it. All over the country the Adelaide Test was hailed as a great triumph. It was as though a miracle had occurred, the scales had fallen from the nation's eyes and Australia suddenly saw this shining young man, Jackson, as the saviour of his country, the herald of a wonderful new era in Australian batsmanship. Could it be that this great continent had given birth to another Trumper? He was reputed to have modelled himself on Kippax who had modelled himself on Trumper.

Since Bradman's brilliant innings against Queensland a very youthful N.S.W. side had been responsible for a series of exceptional performances in Sheffield Shield cricket, yet without attracting very much attention in a season dominated by the Test matches until this sudden flowering of Archie Jackson in Adelaide. Interstate matches were one thing, it seemed, Test matches against the Englishmen another. For instance, of Bradman's 340 not out against Victoria, the *Sydney Morning Herald* merely had this to say: that it had been achieved against a very weak Victorian eleven; that he ought in fact to have been run out five times. But now, one looked again at these young players. Besides Bradman and Jackson, there was McCabe, Fingleton, Alex Marks, Charlie Andrews, all batsmen, Alan Fairfax, an all-rounder from the same St. George club as Bradman; Harold Davidson, a young wicket-keeper ready to step into the shoes of Bertie Oldfield.

Before the last Test in Melbourne, N.S.W. met South Australia in the final Shield match of the season at the S.C.G., an engrossing contest in which the advantage ebbed and flowed and much remarkable cricket was produced. Between them the two young 'keepers, Walker making his debut for South Australia, Davidson for N.S.W., took part in 17 dismissals in the four innings, eight stumpings and nine catches. But the most exciting period of all was when Jackson and Fairfax opened the N.S.W.'s second innings to the bowling of Scott and Wall. Four seasons ago the thirty-five-year-old Scott transferring from N.S.W. had managed to displace the youthful Wall from the South Australian side, and now Wall was back and bowling to a conventional slip-field while Scott's field was described in the "S.M.H." as "ultra-modern leg-theory."

Fairfax and Jackson had a glorious time with it. With the abandon of youth, they steered the ball down between the leg-slips, hooked it over their heads, stepped back and square-cut, lifted towering shots to the many vacant places in front of the wicket. They ran to 60 in no time until, intoxicated by success, they struck out in the same impetuous fashion at Grimmett and were both instantly stumped as a result. Bradman, now first-wicket down for N.S.W., was more circumspect. At first. He wasn't taking any liberties against Wall who had dismissed him for 5 and 2 in Adelaide. He always had regard for Grimmett. But when Scott returned for his second spell he began hooking and glancing with the same quiet intensity, the same precision and deadliness of aim as once he had fired a golf-ball at a paddock-rail fence. It must have seemed to the bowler, as it would seem to many an unhappy toiler after him, that he would pick a spot on the distant boundary and hammer it until a man was placed there; when he would turn his attention to another target. His first 50 took 90 minutes; the second 37; the third, next morning, 59, and he was finally out for 175 after three and a half hours. N.S.W. won the match by 60 runs.

Seven days later in Melbourne Bradman went in, fourth wicket down for Australia, after only 722 runs had been scored in sixteen and a half hours of the most gruelling Test cricket imaginable. Leyland had ground out a century; Woodfull another, and all the time the heat had grown worse and worse, the barracking more sustained and monotonous than ever. "Most unfriendly things, Test matches," said Chapman after he got back to England. "I would rather play club cricket any day." Bradman however raced to 50 in 71 minutes, slowing down before he reached his century in 172 minutes, but contributing easily the most exciting batting of the series, or at least since Patsy Hendren's 169 against an uninspired Australian attack in Brisbane. Larwood quickly reverted to leg-theory when Bradman first came in, but where Woodfull, Jackson, Ryder and Kippax could do little with him, he was no trouble to Bradman. He only tried the short ball once or twice. After that he pitched them up and Bradman several times off-drove him, hitting him harder than he had ever been hit before.

That was the end of fast leg-theory as it had been practised in Australia up to that time by Scott, Larwood and others. Scott never played first-class cricket for South Australia again; Larwood, 1 – 168 in this final Test, took the ship home a few days later, grumbling about the heat in Australia, the flies, the crowds, the hard grounds. . . . "Don were cruel", he would say in after years, "there's nobody like him na-ow".

Meanwhile Bradman's 123, in particular a record partnership of 183 for the Australian fifth-wicket between the two young colts, Bradman and Fairfax, was arousing 20,000 odd spectators to paroxysms of excitement; to "cheering in great waves of sound, round after round, amid hats being waved in the air with parasols and handkerchiefs." Australia finally got home by five wickets on the eighth day, Ryder (57) and Bradman (37) tearing off the field to escape a multitude of well-wishers, and a long, long season had at last come to an end. One certainly needed to be young for that sort of thing. No wonder so many Australian cricketers retired in their early thirties.

It was very strange, but after the tumult and the shouting had died down a little, there was a disposition in more informed cricket circles to see not Bradman, but Jackson and Hammond as the two batsmen of the future. Their strokes, it was felt, suggested the truly cultured approach to the game so that all playing or merely looking-on would feel some-how raised to a higher plane. Bradman evidently didn't achieve this effect. Maurice Tate, for instance, told him plainly before the M.C.C. left Melbourne, "Don, learn to play a straighter bat before you come to England, or you will never get any runs." Duckworth thought much the same thing. "There were flaws in his off-side game," he believed, "calculated to be fatal on English pitches." (*Sydney Morning Herald* 30/5/29)

Finally and conclusively, Percy Fender, most eminent of English county captains, acknowledged authority on all matters connected with the technique of the game, had this damning report to make. "Bradman was one of the most curious mixtures of good and bad batting I have ever seen . . . one minute one would think him a grand player, and the next he would look like a schoolboy. If practice, experience and hard work enable him to eradicate the faults and still retain the rest of his ability, he may well become a very great player, and if he does this, he will always be in the category of the brilliant, if unsound ones. Promise there is in Bradman in plenty, though watching him does not inspire one with any confidence that he desires to take the only course which will lead him to a fulfilment of that promise. He makes a mistake, then makes it again and again; he does not correct it, or look as if he were trying to do so." (*Turn of the Wheel*, p. 329)

Writing about Jackson, on the other hand, Fender was lyrical. "Here we saw a nineteen-year-old lad producing strokes of all descriptions and a perfection of execution which I have never seen in any lad of a similar age in this country." Bradman of course was not as orthodox in all his strokes as Jackson. We know that. But at the end of the Australian first-class season, 1928–29, he had made 1690 runs, 1143 more than Jackson, 137 more than Hammond, a record in fact which still stands today. Again, his average, 93·88, compared with Hammond's 91·35 and Jackson's just over 60.

He was not altogether orthodox in other directions as well. He didn't drink for example; didn't particularly discuss the game with the other players; didn't really indulge in any of those forms of camaraderie which help to ease the strain of Test cricket; to soften the rivalries and sharp exchanges which inevitably occur on the field of play. However he did have opinions which he wished to share with others. He didn't always agree with his captain about tactics for instance; nor with the selectors concerning all their selections; nor, sometimes, with the critics and commentators in what they had to say and write about the game. He didn't hesitate to declare openly at one stage that some of the N.S.W. selectors were too busy playing grade cricket themselves on Saturday afternoons to have any chance of watching promising young players in action somewhere else. He was probably right, but it was a moot point. Alf Noble had continued playing grade cricket when he was a N.S.W. sole selector.

In the circumstances he may have been better advised to keep his mouth shut. But that was his trouble; he was outspoken, even with the knowledge that some of his colleagues didn't like it, that some of the visiting Englishmen didn't like it. He was too cocky, was their general opinion, too perky for his own good. Going back on the boat they often discussed the merits and demerits of their late opponents. They liked Jackson and believed and were inclined to hope that he would do well in England. But they were not so sure about Bradman. They felt he rather deserved to fail. And yet in Sydney grade cricket, there was scarcely a more popular player. It was quite common in Sydney for Test stars and even Shield cricketers to adopt a somewhat off-hand attitude towards their clubs. But not Bradman. Even when he became the owner of an Australian blazer, he continued to turn up for St. George occasions in the proper club cap and blazer. From early boyhood he had had instilled into him a horror of "skiting", of appearing to seek personal publicity. His name would soon be on everybody's lips whenever cricket was mentioned. People who knew nothing about the game would travel hundreds of miles just to see him bat, and yet his demeanour among his club-mates on Saturday afternoons was of one who preferred to efface himself.

For instance in his batting. Occasionally, in order that his side should win the match, he might hit a double century. But dozens of times he deliberately threw his wicket away after reaching 100, and always he forgot about his own batting for the sake of shielding a partner or giving him the strike so that he could get his century first. He still didn't drink after a match or go out of his way to make friends with his St. George colleagues. It was constantly said that the idolising of one particular player by the public was bad for the game, but his team-mates didn't seem to mind. To them he was only, affectionately, "Braddles", and "Braddles" he will always remain in their memories, though of course they cannot forget the crowds, the excitement, the lustre that his presence added to the game in those golden years. At St. George's Hurstville Oval attendances rose from roughly 1000 (at 6d a head) in the year of his arrival to the region of 10,000 when he left the district in 1933. And not only St. George, but all the Sydney grade clubs gained the benefit. There was no doubt about whom the crowd had come to see whenever Bradman was playing. One day at Manly Oval he and Eddie Kann were engaged in a dashing partnership before a crowd which Manly club officials gleefully estimated to be at least 3500, easily a ground record. All too soon Bradman was out, but Kann continued in great form, wholly absorbed in his innings, not realising for some little time that the crowd had grown deathly quiet. He gazed round the ground and slowly it dawned upon him that almost everybody had gone home. It was uncanny, sometimes unnerving for the batsman who had to go in next, and would sometimes be obliged to struggle towards the pavilion-gate through a mass of spectators already on their way out of the ground.

Shield cricket however was slightly different. When he made his first Interstate tour with the N.S.W. team certain of the older players, Kippax and Oldfield were two, decided he needed taking down a peg or two. He was subjected to various pranks which, as he afterwards admitted to Wally Hammond, affected him more than he was willing to admit at the time. He possibly didn't understand then, that playing cricket with ten others on Saturday afternoons is different from going on tour with them, having to live in their company for weeks at a time. That imposes certain obligations to conform with majority practice, a sense of which Bradman appeared to lack. Alan Kippax would probably have liked to take a fatherly interest in the lad; to instruct him in a few little points. But Bradman was too self-sufficient for that. He had successfully made the transition from Bowral to Sydney. He would manage on his own, thank you. Such faults, minor though they may be, are hard to endure in a young man of small stature, of apparently humble background, who yet possesses a talent, a temperament, a determination manifestly greater than one's own. It was worse than unendurable. It was grossly unfair.

So he began to grow away from his contemporaries. Some of these were inclined to sneering remarks behind his back, an unhappy state of affairs which events only served to accentuate. The bally-hoo that followed Australia's Test victory at Melbourne was typical. He was the "Bowral boy", the fair-haired young darling of the Press, to the point where there seemed to be almost nobody else in the team. Everywhere he went people lionised him. In January 1929, Davis and Westbrook having closed its Sydney office, he accepted a position with Mick Simmons Ltd, the big sports store, a job which enabled him to travel widely on business, to own a car, and once to fly in an aeroplane. He took up golf, which few first-class cricketers in those days had time for and played tennis socially with Jack Crawford. In this period also he moved permanently from Concord to stay with the Cush family in Rockdale.

It was now necessary for him to live in the St. George district and Dick Jones, N.S.W. and Australian selector and a great friend of the Cushes, arranged it for him. Frank Cush was a member of the Australian Board of Control and young Bradman was soon one of the family, going for an early morning dip with other members of the household, playing ping-pong with them in the back-room, throwing peanuts into the air at the dinner-table and catching them expertly in his mouth – to amuse the Cush children. In the evenings, if he had no work to do, he might listen to Mrs. Cush playing the piano. Or play the piano himself. "But I only play," he wrote modestly in his autobiography, "when I cannot listen to somebody else."

Rarely had the Cushes struck a young man so meticulous about the house; so considerate of those around him. The telephone would go all through dinner, said Mrs. Cush, but their young lodger never cursed nor complained. Just politely left the table and dealt with it. He never wasted words, didn't talk much sport, but would prefer perhaps to listen to a talk on the radio about the state of the economy. All the time he was drifting further out of the society of his fellow-cricketers, into the company of those more likely to be helpful to him in a business way, though cricket and the coming tour of England forever dominated his thoughts.

No international side, with the exception of an M.C.C. party on its way to New Zealand, was due in Australia in 1929–30 and so the main interest of the season was in the composition of the touring side to be chosen at the end of January. There were no certainties, Bradmen felt. He didn't even feel too certain about himself. Suppose the selectors were influenced by what some of the English critics had written about him? His tall scores in Australia would count for nothing then. For others, batting was primarily a matter of "style", which Bradman, they said, with his partiality for the cross-bat, just didn't have. Leyland had been similarly accused before being chosen for Australia in 1928. His methods smacked too much of the "village green", it was sometimes alleged, and not even the 137 he scored in his Test match debut in Melbourne would make them admit that he might now be a better bat than Frank Woolley.

Bradman was therefore very pleased, in his first match of the season against Queensland in Brisbane, to find himself batting on a difficult, rain-affected wicket, with the ball turning sharply the whole time. He managed to stay in for three and a half hours in scoring 66 and N.S.W. won the match narrowly by 23 runs. He had learnt quite a lot about wet wickets since watching Hobbs and Sutcliffe on that "sticky dog" in Melbourne.

It was now conceded, even by Bradman's severest critics, that his batting "might have lost some of its earlier crudities"; that his running between the wickets for instance was now very much better. Certainly these were improvements noted in his favour during the summer of 1929–30, but they would go very little distance in removing the major stumbling-block in so many minds. It is just not possible in one or two seasons to shift minds that have been made up in advance; to overcome prejudice that is ingrained. Jackson's batting, people said, took them back to the old days, to Trumper and MacLaren, R. E. Foster and A. O. Jones. All style. Could Bradman cover-drive like that? Or late-cut, with such delicacy? As one used to see.

On 6 December at the S.C.G. a Test Trial match commenced, Ryder's Eleven v. Woodfull's Eleven, to sort out players for England. Jackson and Ponsford opened the innings for Ryder's team and their first-wicket partnership of 278 proved to be the foundation of a huge score, 663, which just seemed to grow steadily more mountainous, more remote, when Woodfull's men went in and found themselves at bay against Grimmett and Oxenham. With the great prize of a tour of England in the offing, Grimmett, so it was said, had spent the whole winter practising in his back garden with all sorts of new spins, and he was now a greater puzzle than ever. "Some of the balls he sent down to me," Bradman would write of Grimmett's bowling that season, "were the most difficult I have ever been called upon to play." However he managed to get the hang of them after a while, of Oxenham as well, and by the close of play on Saturday evening he was 54 not out after batting for just over an hour.

He went on to 124 on the Monday morning, but the rest of the batting then collapsed against the two spinners and Woodfull's side had to go in again 354 runs behind. This time Woodfull took Bradman in with him and it turned out to be inspired decision because by stumps

Bradman was 205 not out, having now scored 275 in one day in two separate innings. The athleticism of this performance, the number of hard-run twos and threes obtained between morning and early evening, was almost beyond computation. "For God's sake, slow down, Don," his partners used to beg him. But Bradman was inflexible. Every run was all-important. It had been necessary for him in the first innings to farm the bowling at one stage, which he achieved in some cases not by running singles, but by running threes. In the end he made 225, Kippax made 170 and seemingly inevitable defeat was turned, very nearly, into a famous victory. Their opponents, left 188 to win, struck a rain-damaged pitch and scrambled home by only one wicket. The *Sydney Morning Herald* man was very impressed with Bradman's performance, no doubt about it, but felt obliged to point out that after passing 150 he had "discarded artistic methods and substituted unadulterated slogging."

There were still a number not absolutely convinced about Bradman. Others who may not have even wanted him to succeed. Indeed it was to be an up-and-down sort of season for him in some ways and it so happened that in his next innings at the S.C.G., for N.S.W. versus Queensland on 3 January, he made only three after being sent in to open the innings in place of Jackson, unavailable through illness. He frequently seemed to fail when asked to open. But the luckless Queenslanders were not going to get off as easily as that. N.S.W. was all out 235; Queensland made 227 and soon after lunch on Saturday afternoon, Bradman was in again, first-wicket down this time. He was quickly into his stride: 50 in 51 minutes, 100 in 104, 200 in 185. At stumps he was not out 205.

Though the fielding hadn't noticeably slackened at any stage, Bradman felt himself to be in such wonderful fettle that it seemed no trouble making twos out of shots hit straight to a fieldsman on the fence. He certainly needed to in order to keep up that pace. A deep-set field made boundaries none too easy to come by, although it must have been very hard on poor Kippax, his partner. In that previous match in Sydney they had put on 218 together; this time it was 272. "How's it going, Kip" Vic Richardson asked his old cobber when the South Australian team reached Sydney that month, and Kippax grinned and muttered something about "being sick of acting as a running partner for the Boy Wonder."

It was understood at stumps that Kippax would bat on for a substantial period on Monday, thus giving him a marvellous chance, it seemed to Bradman, of surpassing Ponsford's world-record 437. When the Cush family returned home that Saturday evening, they found him stretched out on a divan in the hall-way. "You're tired, Don?" Mrs. Cush asked. "No, not at all. But I'll need a bit of a rest if I'm going for the record," Don smiled back. He did want that record, but he would have to hurry if he was to get there before Kippax declared. His 300 came in 288 minutes; 400 in 377; 29 minutes later he was almost there. Thurlow pitched one a fraction short on the leg-stump; Bradman seemed to be already in position for the shot and hooked it straight to the fence. The Queenslanders raced in from all directions to wring his hand and O'Connor called for three cheers. Whatever the state of the game, it was a tremendous physical effort which any sportsman could appreciate. All round the ground the cheering resounded. After a while it died down a little on the Grandstand side, only for it to be heard more plainly on the Hill. It was splendid, thrilling for the 7,000-odd spectators, as though a feast had been provided specially in their honour. Kippax finally declared at tea, with Bradman 452 not out, whereupon several members of the crowd jumped the fence and raced towards him, vying with one another for the privilege of chairing him off. He was put down when they reached the gate and he ran lightly up the steps and into the dressing-room, as though he had just popped out onto the field a few minutes before.

It would be alleged of course that his only interest in this match was in breaking the record and piling up runs for himself. And it is perfectly true that on this occasion and on certain other occasions he set out deliberately to break records. After all he was only twenty-one and already he had gathered about him a small army of detractors, like that man on the *Sydney Morning Herald* who now said about his 452 not out that it was "an innings which could not be compared for speed and artistry with Macartney's famous effort of 345 in less than four hours at Notts. Macartney's flashing strokes could not be contained. Bradman throughout held himself well in control." What should he do to please?

Others were ever ready to crow with delight if he failed, so it wasn't surprising that he sometimes sought to hit back, to wipe off a few smiles. Though human motives are seldom so simple. He loved batting and, if his batting gave other people pleasure as well, he enjoyed it all the more. A week or two after the State game against Queensland he represented Gladesville Mental Hospital in a match against the *Sydney Morning Herald.* He hit up 228 not out in two hours. The ball landed on the roofs of adjoining buildings, knocked chips off the tops of the surrounding trees, flew among the cars and the trams in the street outside. The patients frequently had to join in a search for the lost ball, but it was a day they would remember all their lives. Bradman had insisted upon playing, even though he had also been invited to lunch at Parliament House that day.

These were some of the great moments of this great Bradman summer. Though there were other moments as well, moments when it seemed as though some malignant fate had planted a gremlin in his cricket-bag and was forever trying to trip him up in revenge for such phenomenal success. Against South Australia for instance Bradman came in with the score 1 – 27 and endeavoured to open his account, in his usual way, with a single off the first ball. He made to go, bounced a yard or two out of his crease, then turned back hastily as Grimmett in the covers gathered the ball in a flash and let fly: The return hit Bradman on the left temple and he fell like a log.

After about half a minute he struggled to his feet, stood awhile slowly pulling his gloves on and off, and finally tried to face up again. But it was useless. He had to go off and remained in the pavilion until after lunch, looking dazed and shaky and complaining of feeling sick. N.S.W. in his absence didn't fare too well. So at 5 – 163 he went in again to join McCabe, this time successfully completing his single off the first ball. He was missed when 3 and again when 10, but held on for 89 minutes, by which time two of N.S.W.'s exciting young prospects, McCabe and Allsopp, had entirely mastered the bowling, Grimmett included.

His stamina was amazing; his courage no less. He came back to the Cushes one afternoon, obviously under the weather, asking to be excused from dinner; he had had a tooth out. Several hours later a very faint voice was heard calling for a doctor. He had had in fact four teeth out and the wounds had gone on oozing blood until the bowl beside his bed was full to the brim. A doctor came and managed to staunch the bleeding, and Bradman turned out the next day for St. George and nobody ever realised from his batting that he was not his usual self. On another occasion at the S.C.G. a spectator happened to remark to one of his team-mates that the little man appeared in fine form that day. "Oh, yes, not bad," he was told, "considering he's got a splitting head-ache."

Meanwhile however the race for places in the 1930 touring side was approaching an exciting climax. On 30 January, immediately following the N.S.W. versus Victoria game in Sydney, a Board of Control meeting had been arranged when the selectors, having made their final choice, would hand in their list and the Board would review their selections and announce the names. For three days though the start was held up by a persistent misty drizzle, and the players had little to do but speculate on the likely team. There was a strong rumour, for instance, that Jack Ryder would miss out. Ryder was himself one of the selectors, yet the deeds of Bradman and Jackson had created such a strong public reaction in favour of youth, that the other selectors, Jones and Dolling would not dare oppose the tide, it was claimed. In 1926 experience and previous knowledge of English conditions had been the decisive factors determining the side. Now in 1930, where all else was equal and the choice lay between an older and a younger player, youth would gain the preference. Thus Fairfax and a'Beckett, McCabe and the wicket-keeper, Charlie Walker, were all strongly in the running; others such as Ryder, Richardson, Oxenham and Ironmonger were more doubtful cases. Not even Grimmett nor Ponsford were absolute certainties.

Everybody claimed to have positive inside knowledge, but then the match was under way, N.S.W. being sent in to bat on a drying wicket. Andrews, Kippax and Jackson all went cheaply, but Bradman was still there, in complete command on a bowler's wicket, and by the time he was out for 77 in 103 minutes, the pitch was much easier and the later batsmen thrived. What a terrible power resided in that dazzling blade! It had once before destroyed Oxenham, and now, if Ironmonger was on the selectors' list as a slow left-hander likely to succeed in England, he would surely have to be crossed off again. Blackie similarly. In the end the rumours proved to be remarkably well-informed. Woodfull was elected captain; Richardson, vice-captain, and the full side, 15 in all were: Bradman, Fairfax, Jackson, Kippax, McCabe, Oldfield, all N.S.W.; Hornibrook and Hurwood (Queensland); Grimmett, Wall and Walker (South Australia); a'Beckett and Ponsford (Victoria).

Only one slow bowler had been selected. It was shocking bad luck for the Queensland-born Ironmonger and Oxenham, particularly for the latter who for so many years had been the bulwark and main support of Queensland cricket, and now that Queensland had achieved near-parity with the other states, at least with South Australia, found himself unexpectedly supplanted by the little-known Hurwood. The latter's principal recommendation, it seemed, was that in the course of Bradman's marvellous 452 he was the only bowler to have managed to keep him relatively quiet.

The deliberations of the Board of Control were secret of course. But even behind the locked doors and brick walls of the N.S.W.C.A. rooms, Pressmen could hear the familar tones of Jack Hutcheon raised in angry expostulation. He was fighting for the inclusion of a sixteenth player presumably, (the question of how many should go, 15 or 16, still hadn't been resolved), though whether it was in the interests of Oxenham or Ironmonger or whoever, the reporters couldn't be sure.

By this time Bradman had departed for Bowral to be with his own family for a few days; so that at 3.15 on the afternoon of the 30th, the moment of the team's announcement, the moment the rest of Australia had been waiting for, he was actually incommunicado, in the bush somewhere shooting rabbits with his brother, Vic. He was not so cool however when they got back and found that he had been picked. "It seemed too good to be true; it took me some time to realise that I was really going Home, to begin an adventure upon which every Australian, whatever his station, sets his heart." Shortly after his return to Sydney the Cushes found him in their back-garden, surrounded by suit-cases and pots of paint, inscribing his name very neatly in green and gold letters on every item of luggage. The great adventure was about to begin.

CHAPTER FOUR

Conquest of England

Colombo, Aden, the Suez Canal, Cairo and the Pyramids! The long voyage to England used to be an unending succession of delights for Australians. With the Union Jack flying everywhere, or almost everywhere. Not all Australians are impressed by the rest of the world, but a group of young men on their first trip abroad want to see everything. From their ship they cabled the Board of Control seeking permission to disembark at Naples and continue overland; which the Board granted, provided they arrived in England not a day later than the boat. So then Pompeii, Rome, Milan, Switzerland and the first sight of snow for many of them, some rollicking times in Paris, and finally London, the hub of it all. Some of the more seasoned travellers, like Vic Richardson, were inclined to make light of most things. Others, like Bradman, were just overwhelmed – by the sights, the hospitality, the important people one met, a world so much wider than they had ever imagined. There was not much time to take it all in at first though. After a brief visit to Lord's, to Wembley for the Cup final, and so on, it was down to business. The first match of the tour was at Worcester, beginning on 30 April.

The newcomers in the Australian side tended to be amused and a little bit puzzled by the "Englishness" of their reception at Worcester. A beautiful ground in a perfect setting! But a strange lack of atmosphere. When they came off the field, having bundled Worcestershire out for 131 on a good wicket, a brief ripple of clapping went round the ground, nothing more. Then the Australians batted; Woodfull and Bradman took complete charge of the county attack, but there was still remarkably little enthusiasm. It wasn't just British reticence. Very few of the players, only Woodfull, Grimmett and Oldfield in the present match, were known to the spectators. The others were not thought to be of much account. Most people had heard of Bradman, but it was difficult to distinguish one Australian from another under their green caps. After he had reached his 100, and was on his way to 150, they were more certain however. He finally made 236 in 270 minutes, and the tourists went on to win the match early on the third morning by an innings and 165 runs.

How did he do it? When the 1926 Australians played at Worcester, they had been all tied up by Fred Root and out in their first innings for 197. Without Bradman the 1930 Australians may well have been in the same boat. Freezing in their two sweaters, the other youngsters, Jackson, McCabe, Fairfax and a'Beckett looked stiff and out of touch; while Bradman on dancing feet skipped yards down the wicket to the medium-fast Root, driving him repeatedly in front of the wicket in a fashion that caused even the hardiest of old country professionals to shake their heads in amazement. Bowling on his own favourite piece of turf, on the same ground where he had perfected his famous leg-theory with the aid of that convenient breeze blowing off the Severn from the direction of third man, Root could manage only 2 – 112 this time. It was almost unfair. H. A. Gilbert, the old Oxford blue, refused to bowl any more after conceding 30 runs in 4 overs and never played for Worcestershire again.

Youthful prodigies before and after Bradman have been as brilliant, but none as consistently so. Creatures of impulse rather than reason, they go for their shots at every promising opportunity and sooner or later get themselves out, hitting too hard, cutting at balls too far up the cut, or by sundry other indiscretions. A spectacular initial burst of success and then the brilliant ones tend to fade from the scene, perhaps to re-emerge a year or two later, changed out of all recognition. In the meantime the bowlers have been thriving on the several little weaknesses they have detected. Bradman was different because from a very youthful age he was able to give total concentration to what he was doing on the field as much as off it. In the public writing-room of his Worcester hotel the *Times* cricket correspondent remembered him sitting there writing; but not only writing, preoccupied as though deep in thought.

It had been the same on the ship coming over. Though first to take part in all the deck games, forever the centre of the lively crowd on deck, he would steal away at other times and perhaps be found tinkering away at the piano in the music lounge, oblivious of the other occupants "By the way", he suddenly asked Root between overs at Worcester, "what does George Geary do with the ball in England? Does he make it turn much?" The Worcestershire match was not yet over, and already he was preparing himself mentally for the next encounter at Leicester.

Meanwhile the English critics were not particularly impressed. "Against that Worcestershire attack, mechanically wheeling up the stuff of benumbed mediocrity", wrote Neville Cardus in the *Manchester Guardian*, "almost any decent batsman would get runs." Bradman, he described in the following terms. "His batsmanship . . . is thick-set; virile, not supple; agile rather than flexible. Good, honest muscle provides the motive power. Bradman has not the volatility of mind, the sheer sensibility of Jackson. He is for his age a batsman of extraordinary scope and finish, but his style is democratic . . . Jackson and Kippax are the pedigree batsmen of the Australian Eleven." But no Englishman was much worried by any of the Australians at this stage. "It was not expected at the start," wrote Percy Fender, "that they were likely to constitute any very serious menace to England in the contest for the Ashes."

So the little-regarded Australians moved on to Leicester and this time they encountered more of a challenge. Bowling his leg-cutters at about medium-pace, turning them considerably more than he had ever managed to in Australia, George Geary on a helpful wicket was a much more dangerous proposition than Fred Root at Worcester. His very first ball removed Jackson and Bradman had to come in to play out the last 40 minutes of the day. The ball didn't come through as it did in Australia or even at Worcester. Instead it had to be watched carefully right on to the bat. At stumps he was only 9 and having soon lost Ponsford on the following Monday he continued on with great restraint until sometime after lunch, when he suddenly decided he had the measure of the bowling and began to open out. When rain finally brought the match to a premature conclusion he was 185 not out, and neither Geary nor any power in the world, it seemed, could have prevented his scoring two double-centuries in his first two innings in England." "He's not human," some of the Australians would joke with their English opponents. "You wait till he gets to 300 against you. He'll take fresh guard and go after his next 300."

But sometimes one has to take what his team-mates had to say about him with a grain of salt. Except occasionally, when he had a special object in mind, his big scores were made for good cricket reasons. Australia would have been in the soup at Leicester without him. There was nothing mechanical about his hundreds. After Leicester, particularly after Hornibrook's success at Leyton against Essex and Grimmett's 10 – 37 against Yorkshire, a good deal of the pressure was off him and he became almost light-hearted in his approach. Against Lancashire for instance, he came in to face Ted McDonald bowling at a great pace on a drying Liverpool wicket. McDonald, when his blood was up, was still one of the fastest, most dangerous bowlers in England, and Bradman tried to cut his first ball somewhere between point and the four slips. He missed, then hit a couple of boundaries and was soon out, says Cardus, to a stroke of "incredible cheekiness". He actually moved right outside his off-stump and tried to smack a straight one from McDonald past square-leg. He was bowled leg-stump.However it was a different story in the second innings when Australia was in some danger of defeat. He was most circumspect, most correct, until the danger passed.

For the Australians versus Surrey, however, he had one of those special personal reasons for making a big score. "He does not correct mistakes, nor look as if he were trying to," the Surrey captain had written about his batting in Australia. And throughout the 1929 English season, as busy with the pen as he was on the cricket field, Fender had gone on casting doubts on the ability of so many of these young Australians, implying that Chapman's task in 1928–29 had been a relatively simple one.

It was not actually a very auspicious occasion on which to put Mr. P. G. H. Fender to rights. Dark clouds, promising yet another of those cold, cheerless May days, hung low over Kennington from horizon to horizon; the gasometer in the background seemed to loom larger than ever when Woodfull and Jackson went out to open for Australia a quarter of an hour late (the wrong-sized stumps had been set). The pitch was not specially difficult, yet not specially in favour of the batsmen either, and the two of them pottered around until Jackson snicked one to the 'keeper, 1 – 11 after half an hour. "At 12.45 exactly," said the newspaper report, "a fair-haired, uncapped boy emerged from the pavilion to hearty applause."

Bradman was already a favourite in England. He couldn't be murdering the bowling all the time, but always he was busy, ever on the look-out for a cheeky single, and always it had a tonic effect upon Woodfull at the other end. Woodfull in 1930 was by no means as strokeless as his reputation suggested. Skilful as he was in shielding a younger batsman from Tate or Larwood in full cry, he certainly didn't hog the strike with Bradman as a partner. In this case he kept the runs coming with ones and twos and they added 116 together in almost even time. Not until Woodfull was out for 50 however did Bradman really go to town. The cut had been his favourite scoring shot earlier in the innings. Now he began to unleash that terrible weapon of destruction, the pull-shot. Fender was bowling with a packed off-side field and only a deep mid-on on the other side of the wicket. But Bradman would get right outside his off-stump and pivoting on his right foot smash the ball forward of square-leg. Twice he played this same shot. Fender pulled a man out of the covers to block it. Bradman stroked the third ball back along the pitch, leapt at the next and drove it through the vacant spot in the covers. The cross-bat may have offended against all the canons of classical batsmanship, but Fender was perhaps too occupied with field settings and bowling changes to spare the matter a critical thought.

At 5 – 250 Fairfax came in, 52 runs were added of which Fairfax contributed only one, and there was great interest with rain threatening to see if Bradman would reach his own personal 250 before play was stopped for the day. When he was 240 Gregory began what would obviously have to be the last over. His first five balls yielded Bradman eight runs, then to the last he was yards down the pitch off-driving it to the fence and the crowd swarmed onto the ground as the two batsmen sprinted for the pavilion. "Nobody say anything," called one of the team as they stood watching from the balcony, "Not a word."

Bradman strode into the dressing-room, threw down his gloves, and remarked, "I wonder what Fender will have to say in the morning paper this time."

Another well-known critic who watched every ball of his innings was E. H. D. Sewell. He agreed with Fender that Bradman was inclined to play this ugly, half-cock shot when he appeared to check his stroke in mid-swing, but hardly thought that this should have affected anybody's assessment of the man as a great batsman. Instead he was a little resentful that Fender had had the chance to study Bradman in great detail in 1928–29, and yet had come back and failed to warn England of what was in store.

Exactly one week later, against Hampshire at Southampton, Bradman completed 1000 runs before the end of May, the youngest player and the first Australian ever to do so. A great piece of bowling by Clarrie Grimmett, and a generous action by Lionel Tennyson assisted him to accomplish this extraordinary feat, but he was very lucky because the rain was pelting down as the last ball of the month sped towards the boundary.

Altogether, the climate apart, it had been a marvellous May for the Australians, putting them in such great heart that Press discussion of their dubious prospects in the coming series seemed so much tripe. It was true they had not yet encountered Tate or Larwood, Hammond or Hobbs, but they had an answer for them all, they believed. Grimmett was no longer just the honest toiler he sometimes looked in Australia. In the damper air, on the softer wickets, he was a match-winner. Hornibrook, left-hand, able to spin them or cut them as the occasion demanded, was the perfect foil. As for the batting, well, Australians usually take an optimistic view about their batting. Besides Bradman and Woodfull, Kippax and Richardson too were obviously at home on English wickets and in the last game before the Test at Trent Bridge young McCabe made 96 run out. Except against Tasmania, he had not at this stage made a century in first-class cricket, but there were some who believed he might yet turn out the greatest of the lot of them.

In fact the first Test proved a bit of a disappointment, though the signs were propitious at first. England dropped Duleepsinhji, the only batsman in England after Chapman likely to collar Grimmett, and as hoped the little wizard was too good for Hammond, Hendren and Woolley. But then the weather turned against Australia. Larwood was ineffective in the damp conditions, but they suited Tate and the new googly bowler, Walter Robins, and the position on the last morning was that Australia, 60 for the loss of Woodfull, needed another 369 to win and all day to get them. Bradman thought it could be done. So did Cardus and Fender; particularly when they learned that Larwood had gastritis and wouldn't play. By now the pitch should have been just to his liking.

After his 1000 runs in May, there had been a perceptible falling away in Bradman's concentration. Nature's way of conserving his energies for the all-important occasion, no doubt. Now he was geared up to the highest pitch of alertness, narrowly watching every ball, watching the bowler, watching every minute adjustment in the field. He also had to keep an eye on the clock, the score-board and make sure that McCabe when he came in at 3 – 152 was similarly alert. Patsy Hendren for instance was a great bluffer in the field. Racing after the ball, he would suddenly go through the motions of picking it up, making as though a lightning return to the stumps while the ball was still in fact 20 yards beyond him. Until one became aware of the trick, it often caused one of the batsmen to shout a premature "No".

An Australian victory was not to be however. At 229 McCabe, having made 49 out of their fourth-wicket partnership of 77, was lured into lofting a ball from Tate which Copley running hard from mid-on made into a fantastic catch, one of the most famous in Test history. That was the first hammer blow. The second occurred at 267 when Bradman, with his own score 131, played no shot to a ball from Robins that spun back sharply and took the off-stump. Bradman came to think that in going across to play the ball his left boot had become entangled in his other pad cramping his movements, but the Englishmen were certain that he had simply failed to spot the googly. Australia lost in the end by 93 runs.

A century in his first Test match in England was another landmark, but Cardus still refused to be convinced. "Neither Bradman nor Ponsford exactly looked great batsmen, yet both of them are beaters of MacLaren's highest score. From this morning I concluded their superiority over MacLaren was strictly statistical." The tourists had come to regard the Englishman's attachment to the great players of yesteryear with some amusement. They themselves were far from dismayed by one defeat, but were enjoying their cricket as much as ever, playing golf on Sundays, seeing all the sights in the odd intervals between. There was even time to take in a day or two at Wimbledon before the second Test began at Lord's on 27 June.

A good piece of news on the morning of the match was that Larwood had been dropped from the England 13. Though this was counterbalanced to some extent by the inclusion of Duleepsinhji and their old enemy, "Farmer" White. The brilliant young Indian was everything the Australians feared he might be when England batted first; a free-scoring batsman who would not be deterred by the occasion; who would quickly show the others that the best way of playing Grimmett on such a perfect wicket was to go down the track and hit him. Fortunately however he tired near the end of the day and seemed to give his hand away when he lifted Grimmett to Bradman at deep mid-off. "There you are," his uncle, Ranji, remarked to a friend in his private box, "I always told you, he's careless." So the England innings finished at 425 on the second morning, and Woodfull and Ponsford were very soon showing, in the ample time they seemed to have for every shot, that this would not be enough. Bang! Ponsford stepped out and drove Allen past mid-off, a shot he had possibly never attempted in his life off Larwood. The very energetic Gubby Allen had a fine record at Lord's, but he probably needed a little more help than he was able to get from the wicket this beautiful day. He was not quite fast enough to beat the bat by pace alone. Woodfull and Ponsford went on together till 3.30 when the King came on to the ground to shake hands with all the players, and almost immediately after that White had Ponsford caught at slip, 1 – 162.

Bradman made his way to the wicket. Slowly, as was his custom. Not with such pronounced deliberation as people would remember him going to the wicket in later years, but sufficiently to give the impression that he was trying to accustom his eyes to the light. Actually, the men from Bradman's part of the world always walk slowly when they have a heavy task ahead. They like to think it out calmly and unhurriedly before they start. Similarly he took plenty of time to gaze round the field and make last-second adjustments to his cap, gloves and so on; but then he was ready and White came in to bowl. The ball was well pitched up and Bradman met it two yards down the wicket. The crack of bat on ball echoed round the cround, the pigeons at the Nursery end took off in all directions and the ball bounced into the crowd in the region of long-off. What followed was the best innings of his life, Bradman always believed; the best, that is, in terms of technical efficiency, of maximum results attained for the minimum of effort; the best also, perhaps, for its psychological effect upon the opposition.

This was the Australians' first encounter with White since 1928–29, but Bradman knew that the left-hander would have to pitch them up more in England and was simply taking this opportunity, at the earliest possible moment, to announce that he would no longer be dictated to. Before Bradman English cricket had been full of leg-traps and silly mid-offs, inner and outer rings and all sorts of theoretical clap-trap for containing the batsman, and the young Australian despatched the lot of them straight back to the pavilion where they belonged.

After that opening shot, if White strayed in length at all, it was invariably on the short side, when Bradman would position himself like lightning and lash the ball to the leg-boundary. With his unusual grip, the top hand much further round the handle than is normal, it was almost impossible for him to hit the ball in the air unless deliberately. At the same time he belted it so hard that a fieldsman on the fence square of the wicket had small chance of cutting it off unless it went almost directly to him. By tea he had reached 50 in 45 minutes; by 6.30 he was 155 not out in 160 minutes. Cardus was quite dazed by this tremendous onslaught. He had a premonition of what was to happen from the first boundary, and now here it was stumps, and Bradman's innings could be compared only with Macartney's 100 before lunch at Leeds, with some of Trumper's greatest efforts in England in 1902; and, moreover, was still unfinished. While still searching for the right words to sum up the man, he was prepared to concede for the moment, "This Bradman is a great player fit to be mentioned with the best of them."

With Australia 2 – 404, only 21 runs behind, the tourists could feel safe from defeat; would be thinking more in terms of forcing a win. Yet Bradman, the following Monday, partnered now by Kippax, was comparatively sedate. Why was he taking it easy then, people would ask, when everybody knew he could annihilate the bowling any time he wanted. But it wasn't as simple as that. While Woodfull was with him, taking Tate or whoever was currently the more difficult, it was easier for Bradman. But Woodfull, the sheet-anchor, had gone just before stumps on Saturday and it then became Bradman's task to stop Tate. Later, when the big fellow tired, they would all be able to reap the benefit. That was the plan and it worked, except that Bradman at 254 was out to an amazing catch by Chapman at extra cover. It was a loose ball from White and Bradman lofted it slightly, almost the first ball he had hit in the air during his entire innings, though well clear of Chapman, he thought. "To this day, I cannot think how he got his hand to that ball" he remembered ruefully in his autobiography. No matter, though. The batting by this time was in charge and Woodfull could declare at tea at the record Test match total of 6 – 729.

It had been thus far one of the most thrilling and absorbing of all Test matches, at the most ancient and illustrious of all cricket grounds, and it continued in much the same vein to the very end. England, at one stage in its second innings, looked likely to be dismissed quite cheaply. Then Chapman, missed before he had scored, hit a memorable 121; Allen gave him wonderful support and the Australians were left 72 in 90 minutes to win. It seemed simple, but Ponsford was soon out bowled Robins; Bradman chopped one hard into the gully and was caught another blinder by Chapman, and all at once the game grew desperately tense. Kippax was next to go, snapped up behind off Robins, and with Australia 3 – 22, anything could happen. Woodfull was still there though. McCabe didn't appear to have a nerve in his body and the two of them pulled it round, giving Australia the victory by seven wickets.

England's defeat, by such a margin, against an Australian side so little thought of when it first arrived, plunged the country into a state of furious self-criticism. The doubts about the modern English game, the nagging dissatisfaction with it, all stilled for the time being by the great victory at The Oval in 1926, rose to the surface once again.

Where were all the great amateur batsmen of the Golden Age, the Frys, MacLarens, Spooners, Jacksons and so on? Your latter-day professional seemed either too old and a little bit past it like Hobbs and Woolley; or else, old before his time, too cautious in his methods, too anxious about his professional prospects to attempt anything that might displease Lord Harris, Lord Hawke, or the other bigwigs in the M.C.C. committee-room. Hammond, especially, had been disappointing; had seemed, away from Gloucestershire, to possess none of the dash and sparkle of Duleepsinhji; none of the vitality and audacity of the young Australians, Bradman and McCabe. English cricket was never better, it was said, than in the days when Somerset went north and beat Yorkshire and Lancashire in a single week.

That was the view of the south, of course. The north of England looked at the matter more directly. Management by Lord's was the trouble. Too many amateur nobodies in charge; too many favourite sons like Allen and Robins getting into Test matches "at expense of ow-er laads." What England most needed, the north declared, was "a virile and representative body to govern the whole game and supersede the M.C.C." Ever anxious to oblige; to demonstrate they were not insensitive of the criticisms being levelled, the three selectors, Leveson Gower (Surrey), Mann (Middlesex) and Jack White (Somerset) dropped five southerners, Woolley, Hendren, Allen, Robins and White himself, and replaced them with Sutcliffe and Larwood, restored after injury, Leyland, Dick Tyldesley and Geary of Leicestershire. The Third Test was at Leeds, one of the strongholds of the prevailing discontent, so that was a team that should please them.

Meanwhile, with the Test still some days away, the tourists were engaged against Nottinghamshire, a county match they were taking more seriously than usual. They had heard much about Bill Voce, the young left-hander; were in fact more concerned about him for the moment than they were about Larwood. Voce had begun his first-class career in 1927 as a spinner able to make the ball nip sharply away towards the slips to the discomfort of the right-hand batsman. With the encouragement of his skipper, Arthur Carr, however, he turned more and more to speed, sometimes opening with the new ball and bowling round the wicket to a cluster of leg-slips in the manner of Frank Foster and George Hirst. But his most effective attacking weapon, Carr discovered, was the short ball pitched on the line of the body. Bowled over the stumps, after the shine had left the ball, he could make it kick quite sharply on a suitable wicket, too sharply sometimes to be combated by the conventional "dead bat". He seemed to come straight at them, batsmen said; there was no obvious means of avoiding this particular delivery. Voce had his days of devastating success in the English seasons of 1928, 1929; was even more formidable when he visited West Indies with an M.C.C. side in the winter of 1929–30. On a fast wicket with a reasonable amount of bounce, such as Trent Bridge when the Australians played Nottinghamshire in July 1930, his field tended to be something like this – four men in a close-in leg-trap, two behind them of the leg-boundary, a mid-off, cover-point and third man. It was reminiscent of one of Jack Scott's unusual field-settings in Australia, placed for much the same reason.

Voce's mode of attack resembled Scott's in other ways as well. It was physically dangerous. Only two weeks before, when Nottinghamshire had been opposed to Somerset at Taunton, a ball from Voce struck the amateur, C. C. Case, causing him to stagger backwards, and half-fall, straddled over the stumps for several seconds. Dazedly he struggled upright again, picked up one of the stumps instead of his bat and was on his way off the field in the wrong direction when he bumped into Arthur Carr at mid-off. Carr gently returned him his bat in exchange for the stump and pointed him towards the pavilion.

Altogether the prospect of facing Voce on a fast wicket was sufficiently disturbing, according to the Australians' vice-captain, Vic Richardson as to leave out of the side at Nottingham four key men, Woodfull, Bradman, Grimmett and Oldfield. Whether or not he realised he was being deliberately preserved for the third Test, Bradman jumped at the idea of a few days off, his chance to see the last day of Wimbledon and Jack Crawford playing in the final of the doubles. Then, he writes, "having taken a trip up the Thames as far as Richmond, and had a look round London, I set out for Leeds . . . by car, a baby Singer. Which was something of an adventure, though a pleasant one."

Meanwhile the menace of Bill Voce had considerably abated. The left-hander soon had Jackson taken in his leg-trap, but then ran into Stan McCabe. Wisely sent in by Richardson ahead of Kippax, McCabe swung the bat at anything and everything the least bit short and although much hit about the ribs and thigh, connected often enough to cause Voce to be taken off. But the battle wasn't over yet. Larwood eventually caught-and-bowled McCabe, 58, and after lunch Voce came back looking as dangerous as ever. Jackson and McCabe were in the pavilion bruised all over; Kippax wrapped up in towels and padding and looking like the Michelin man, said Richardson, was still out there, though most uncomfortable; and Richardson told the dressing-room as he went out to bat, "Somebody's got to crack this fellow."

The South Australian was lucky perhaps, but even more successful than McCabe. Seven times he struck him to the leg-boundary, three times in one over, and reached 50 in 35 minutes. In the second innings, the wicket being considerably slower, Jackson, McCabe, Kippax and Richardson all laid about them with vigour and any hopes that Voce may have had of winning selection in the last couple of Tests gradually melted away. The Australians were immensely relieved. Despite the hammering they had meted out, they considered him a fine bowler, well worth a place.

Evidently Bradman had benefited from his little holiday from the game. Because when he came to the wicket in Australia's first innings at Leeds, everything felt just right. The wicket was easy; the outfield looked exceptionally fast; the weather was balmy. Very early on a ball from Tate got past his bat, narrowly beat the stumps, beat Duckworth, and went for four byes. It was obviously his lucky day. Even Woodfull was able to force Larwood back past the bowler. Two from Woodfull's bat was inevitably four from Bradman's, and the score mounted fast without a risk taken, without a moment's uncertainty, at least on Bradman's part, though at the other end Woodfull was just fallible enough to suggest that the bowling needed very careful watching. Bradman in fact was no less respectful of the good ball than Woodfull. The great difference between the two was that when anything a fraction loose came along, Bradman seemed able to size it up in a flash; was instantly in position to exact the maximum penalty with his customary infallible timing. Naturally the skipper saw to it that his partner received most of the strike, but even so when Bradman reached his hundred before lunch, equalling the feat of Trumper and Macartney, Woodfull was still only in his 20s.

Possibly those other great ones had displayed a wider range of shots or at any rate were less predictable in their stroke-play. They also left more to chance. Bradman just went on and on, remorselessly. There seemed no reason why he should ever get out; no means of containing him at all. Geary at one stage, and later Tyldesley, bowled with a man on the boundary behind him together with a long-off and a long-on. Such was the severity of his driving. Never before had these bowlers been so treated, and when Larwood came on with the third new ball his field also was unprecedented – one slip and a gully, with an extra man in the covers and an extra, deeper square-leg. And yet! It may have been an illusion, but Chapman's outfielders never appeared to be exactly where a critical spectator may have wished them. Time after time the ball was played just clear of Richard Tyldesley, who would be obliged to turn and chase it without ever appearing to gain upon it as it raced away to the boundary ahead of him. Perspiring furiously, the heavily-built Tyldesley finished up in the front row of the spectators, inspiring one of them to call out, "Never tha' mind, Dick la-ad. If tha' had handicap, tha'd beat ball."

At tea Bradman's score was 220 and once again R. E. Foster's Test record 287 seemed to be within his reach. Perhaps his rate of scoring fell off marginally after tea. He actually offered a sharp chance when he was 273, but at 6 o'clock he broke the record after 314 minutes' batting (one and three-quarter hours faster than Foster), and the Yorkshire crowd couldn't have given him a greater ovation if it had been Herbert Sutcliffe. When Kippax left at 423, Bradman threw himself prostrate and lay motionless, his nose buried in the grass, until McCabe arrived. He said afterwards that his wind was alright; that he felt quite fresh, but that his feet were awfully tired. All the same he seemed to carry on very nimbly, off-driving the last ball of the day for four runs to make him 309 not out and the total 3 – 458.

The next day, inevitably, was anti-climax. As so often happens with batsmen after a long innings the previous day, he was out quite soon in the morning, caught behind off Tate for 334, and the Australian innings quickly crumbled. Rain eventually caused the match to be drawn and yet the Leeds Test will always stand out in Test match history because of Bradman's great score. His 254 at Lord's may have been his best innings. The 334 at Leeds brought him the most fame. "See the actual bat with which Don Bradman made his record-breaking score, on view in Finnegan's sports-window." The world read how an unknown admirer had sent him a telegram, handed to him by Woodfull on the field of play, asking him to accept the gift of £1000. All sorts of tales circulated. He nearly didn't play at Lord's, it was said. He overslept on the first morning of the match. Jackson, the twelfth man, was all ready to take the field when with five minutes to go, Bradman rushed into the dressing-room, and was dressed and in his flannels in a twinkling.

How did some people manage to be so knowledgeable when the door to the Australian dressing-room was kept locked and all access to it carefully guarded? And the secret of his success? A potion of Carlsburga, hinted the *Star*. Frequently before an innings he was to be seen with a small glass of milky fluid in one hand and a pint glass of warm water in the other. He drained the small glass first, then immediately the other without pause for breath. It had been invented by a London chemist and removed impurities in the blood. The stories about him were legion; were told and re-told so many times that not even the original actors in them could always be sure, so long after the surrounding circumstances had been forgotten whether it had been exactly like that; whether those had been the actual words. "Not a bad bit of practice," Bradman is supposed to have remarked when he returned to the dressing-room, 309 not out, though Bradman could never remember having said it. Hordes of people swarmed round the players at the ground, at their hotel. They all had some remark or other to pass on. A week after Leeds the Australians were playing at Glasgow before a crowd absolutely unbelievable by Scottish standards. Bradman came into bat, was almost immediately struck on the pads, and given not out. He went on to make 140. The appeal caused only a momentary stir, was then instantly forgotten, but what a meal the Scots made of it afterwards. "How is he?" Preston, the unfortunate bowler, was reported to have leapt two feet in the air in ecstacy. "Not out," said the umpire, "and shut up. What do you think all these people are here for? To see

Bradman bat or you bowl?"

The story properly belonged to W. G. Grace, but by now all keen followers of the game had their own Bradman stories. At Cambridge the Australians were being shown over the university and introduced to another kind of don. ". . . and this is Mr. Bradman." "Who? Ah, yes. To be sure. And tell me, Mr. Bradman, do you bat or bowl?" Not a word of truth in any of them, but what was indisputably true was that Bradman had emerged as the cricket phenomenon of his age, a run-getter of monumental proportions, a new threat to English cricket that by one means or another would just have to be overcome. After giving the matter much thought, Neville Cardus believed that he had finally identified the reasons for his amazing success. "The secret of his stroke-power lies in his ability to move quickly, either back or forward to each ball, making its length short or over-pitched. The area of wicket wherein a ball can be pitched is considerably narrower for Bradman than for other batsmen. He either goes right back or else the whole way of the forcing stroke on punitive feet. When as a last resort he is compelled to play forward, he actually goes back on his wicket to do so, and his legs are behind the bat and his eyes on the ball."

"It isn't true," Cardus went on, "that Bradman has inaugurated a new era in batsmanship; he is substantially orthodox in technique. Nearly all his strokes at Leeds would be usable as illustrations to Fry's thoroughly scientific and pragmatic book on batsmanship. But Bradman shows us excellencies which in the past we have had to seek in different batsmen; nobody else has achieved Bradman's synthesis." Finally, what most particularly marked him off from the masters of the past, said Cardus, "is his temperament . . . who has ever heard of a young man gifted with quick eyes and feet, with mercurial spirits; who has heard of one so gifted and yet who never indulged an extravagant hit high into the air?"

That was a bit different from Cardus' earlier assessment. And indeed, it had been apparent for some time that the policy of waiting for Bradman to get himself out through his supposed lack of technique on English wickets would have to be discarded. What positive measures should be adopted then? There was an abundance of theories for getting rid of him. MacLaren for instance didn't think Bradman liked the fast ball moving from middle to off, because it prevented him using his strong card, back-play. He thought he detected a weakness against spin bowling also. "His left shoulder is never in line with the ball, so a ball spinning away to his off-stump must be ever a danger." In pursuance of this particular line of reasoning therefore, the England eleven for the fourth Test at Manchester originally included two leg-break and googly bowlers, Robins and Peebles, though Robins was replaced by Goddard of Gloucestershire when it appeared that the wicket would be a wet one. Peebles, as it turned out, did better against Bradman in this match than possibly any other bowler on the tour, though not for the reasons hoped for. As the Englishmen suspected, after his experience against Robins in the first Test, he couldn't pick the "bosie". Bradman himself didn't agree with this, though fully prepared to admit he couldn't pick Peebles' "bosie". "I watched Peebles as closely as I knew how, but it was no use. Neither by watching his hand nor the ball could I detect it and definitely, this day, his bowling was too good for me." He made only 14 before being caught.

The fourth Test proved to be another wash-out, the score in the series was still one Test-all, and yet on every side it was felt that the advantage now lay with the tourists. The Australian side as it shaped up for the deciding Test match at the Oval was undoubtedly their strongest of the summer. One by one, the out-of-form batsmen, McCabe, Ponsford, and latterly Jackson had managed to recover their form. The bowling, with Fairfax and Hornibrook back after illness and injury, with Wall improving in every match, was beginning to look really formidable. For England, on the other hand, the outlook was less promising. The batting had answered well enough, without equalling the huge totals amassed by the Australians. The bowling had been less satisfactory. Just as Hammond had failed to come anywhere near his Australian performances, so Larwood had been a big disappointment with the ball. Against the countries he was faster and more dangerous than ever. Against the Australians he seemed to have lost all confidence. Bradman was the trouble. "To bowl short of a length on those (over-prepared) wickets was simply to make the ball stand up and ask to be hit," wrote Larwood. ". . . that's why Bradman . . . was able to stand back to good-length balls, having been accustomed to the faster and concrete-like wickets in Australia and hit them at will."

Larwood had been dropped from the fourth Test, following his pounding by Bradman at Leeds; then reinstated for the final Test after it had become glaringly obvious that he was still far and away the best fast bowler in England. By then, the selectors were more concerned about Chapman. As batsman and fieldsman the big fellow continued to be an inspiration to his side, capable of turning the grimmest Test match by a dynamic innings or an "impossible" catch. As a captain, he appeared to be losing his grip. At Lord's and again at Old Trafford he was criticised for putting on the wrong bowlers for a particular batsman; putting them on at the wrong end; making them field in the deep between overs instead of trying to preserve them fresh for the next over. Similarly lax was thought to be his field placings. For Peebles' "bosie", for instance, surely a man at short-leg was demanded. But Chapman had seemed to be concerned only with saving runs this time. The horrible suspicion arose that England's very fine bowling resources were being simply thrown away. Jardine had thought the same thing in Australia, though he had said nothing at the time.

Of course captaining an M.C.C. side in Australia is a much simpler task than it is in England where the captain is constantly under the eye of the "elder statesmen" of the game, under the eye of all manner of local experts better versed in theory and the history of past contests than they are in the problems of the present. The three selectors were known to be sorely divided on the question of Chapman. To drop such a highly-regarded captain, a leader whose hold on the popular imagination was perhaps greater than any England captain before him, was to court a terrific public outcry. On the other hand there was an obvious precedent for change. In remarkably similar circumstances in 1926 with the final Test about to decide the Ashes, Chapman himself had been brought in to take the place of Arthur Carr. In the end, after prolonged deliberation, Chapman was dropped, and replaced by R. E. S. (Bob) Wyatt of Warwickshire. A cricketer of greatly admired character, a very solid batsman and useful bowler, Wyatt was pre-eminently the man for a crisis.

The difference between 1926 and 1930 however lay in the quality of the opposition. These more youthful Australians had all the terrible determination of youth. England made 405, including a stout-hearted 64 by Wyatt, but then Woodfull and Ponsford went out to wear the English attack into the ground. That was undoubtedly Woodfull's intention – to pave the way for Bradman. It didn't work out quite like that, because this time Ponsford was the brilliant one, the executioner of Larwood with magnificent shots all round the wicket; Bradman, who succeeded him, the one, forced by the dismissal of Woodfull and a change in the weather, to adopt a dogged, defensive role. When Kippax's wicket fell to make the Australian score 3 – 263, the match was still very much in the balance. Through much of Tuesday and until one o'clock on Wednesday, however, Bradman and Jackson went steadily on, scoring mostly off the back foot by strokes made very late. There was little spectacular hitting. The skill lay in getting to and right over every ball, making sure the stroke was kept down.

Two periods were especially important. At 3 o'clock when play resumed on Tuesday afternoon, 3 – 371, Larwood attacked with a vigour and determination new to him in this innings. Several balls rose awkwardly, but Bradman and Jackson got resolutely behind them in the approved fashion, and Larwood was taken off again after only three overs. They were black and blue when they came in however. Then again, the next morning after overnight rain, there was great assistance for the faster bowlers from a pitch soft on top and hard underneath. When he was 175 Bradman was struck a severe blow under the heart by a ball from Larwood and after that "for an over or two seemed inclined to draw away from Larwood . . . but he recovered his confidence and made some fine strokes to leg off the rising ball on his body." The danger period soon passed. "Bradman is such a wonder," wrote "Plum" Warner in the *Morning Post*, "that if he was batting on the tram-lines in Vauxhall Bridge Road he would make 100, probably 300." With the total 506, and the wicket much easier, Jackson departed and then Bradman and McCabe went on to 570 when Bradman was caught behind off Larwood for 232 "under circumstances which caused a certain number to think that the decision had been a mistaken one."

Once again a great innings by Bradman was the margin between victory and possible defeat. Fender in the *Star* was another to notice how Bradman had tended to draw back from Larwood during those two very awkward half-hours, yet "in this nasty period when many wickets might easily have fallen the batsmen weathered the storm by really good batting," Bradman going on to make 98 before lunch.

And so it turned out in the end that the Australians won the final Test by an innings and 39 runs and thus regained the Ashes. He was very tired; they were all very tired, but there were still six more games to be played; six more sides bursting to have the honour of meeting the Australians. One of these matches was against a Club Conference side at Lord's. In a totally different atmosphere, peaceful as a summer's day and utterly relaxed, the fielding side joined in the clapping when Bradman came out to bat. He entertained them all with an innings of 70. The club cricketers played determinedly enough, made him scamper for many a quick one or two, but gave the impression that it was rather a privilege to bowl to him; a privilege to chase the ball Don Bradman had hit. One of them, the Indian Nazir Ali, his eyes shining shining with adoration, never let his gaze leave his face. Finally it fell to the lot of Nazir Ali to have him out caught in the slips. The bowler looked most dejected, as though he had inadvertently destroyed something precious.

Everywhere people wanted to shake his hand, talk to him; become associated with him in some form or other, however fleeting. Before leaving Australia he had been persuaded to write a letter to the Young Australia Temperance Society, "The man who is a total abstainer and non-smoker must necessarily have the advantage over the man who partakes of alcoholic liquor in a contest where physical endurance plus quickness of thought and movement play a part. Personally I find a cup of tea the best thirst-quencher." The society now contrived to have this letter published in newspapers throughout Australia and proclaimed a crusade to enrol one abstainer for every run scored by Bradman in England.

Not all the publicity was as favourable. On 27 August, his twenty-second birthday, the *Daily Herald* ran a story alleging that by allowing the evening *Star* to publish his life-story, day by day for three weeks, he had broken his Board of Control contract, for which breach he would be disciplined when he returned to Australia. Good or bad, whatever could be gleaned was news to feed to a public hungry to know everything about him, this cool youngster who faced up to Maurice Tate and Harold Larwood, the terror of so many county batsmen, and destroyed them, as if it was all in the day's work. At Leeds there was a story of how he had returned to the team's hotel, 309 not out, ordered a pot of tea and promptly retired to his room for the evening. Not even the gift of £1000, it seemed, had tempted him to be more sociable. Kippax and Richardson, those convivial spirits, had hoped that the £1000 would help break the ice; would earn them and the rest of the team at least a round of drinks. But human nature is more complicated than that. In Australia he had been the butt of their dislike and resentment because he would not conform exactly to their ways, and he had come to England determined to go his own way. There was no reason why he should depart from his usual habits to please one or two who made no secret of their feelings towards him.

It was said of him, and the incident of the £1000 and his failure to share his good fortune with other members of the team helped to propagate the notion, that he was mean and selfish. Well, he certainly wasn't a big spender in those days. But "mean" in its more American sense of one lacking in generosity towards his fellows, solely out for his own advantage, was the very opposite of the man. Against Somerset for instance, he made a patient 117, not for the sake of just staying there to improve his average, but in order to concentrate upon the progress of Archie Jackson at the other end. It was one of those wretched, two-paced wickets, so common that summer, and Bradman with his greater experience of the conditions was nursing him along, demonstrating how each bowler could best be played, just as he had endeavoured to take McCabe in hand at the beginning of the season. After a shaky start, Jackson went on to score his only century in England and win a place in the final Test, but Charlie Macartney was disgusted. "Cut that sort of thing out," he told Bradman pointedly at the end of his long innings. "You're in this team to score quick runs."

If the Australians so misunderstood him, it was not surprising that the English should not quite know how to take him either. Sir Home Gordon for instance wrote later, "Bradman assumed an assurance slightly exaggerated, which didn't invariably prepossess his elders," quoting as a rather amusing example of this assurance a 1934 Bradman innings against "Tich" Freeman at Folkestone. The little googly bowler had been bowling superbly well tying down even Bradman at the start of his innings and the remark was passed at tea that Australia might have had a harder job pulling off the Ashes if Freeman had played in the Test matches. What did Bradman think of him? "Put him on again after tea," said Bradman, "and we'll see." Freeman's first over after tea was sensational. Bradman drove the first ball for four, then 6, 6, 4, 6, 4. Thirty runs off a six-ball over created a new record in English cricket.

He was not really easy to get to know. Yet it seemed that underneath his confident Australian exterior, he was deeply impressed by England, by its rulers and its traditions, by the way its affairs were ordered. In the final, official function of the tour, the Australians sat down to dinner in the splendid, oak-panelled hall of the Company of Merchant Taylors. A glittering array of gold and silver plate, the accumulated wealth of centuries, surrounded them on every side. Magnificent scenes of knightly pomp and pageantry gazed down from the stained-glass windows above. Clara Butt had come specially from the Riviera to sing, while they heard also Lord Harris lamenting the decline in present-day cricketing standards; followed by Ranji, similarly recalling the Test matches of the "Golden Age", but more sympathetically, not regretting the changes that had come about. The highlight of the evening, however, was Sir James Barrie. "When the Australians get home," he told the gathering humorously, with many pauses for effect, "they will all be taken to their hotels except 'Badman'. He has carried out this plan of his, not knowing how to get out, that he cannot now get out of anything. He won't even be able to get out of the ship, when all the others, merry and bright, leave him pacing the deck, a dark and gloomy figure. . . ."

It is very exciting to be young, to be in London in August and made much of by the great and famous of the land. The itinerary was still not complete, Bradman because of the demand playing more matches than anyone else, and yet in between innings and journeyings he still had time to speak on the new radio-telephone to Australia; to deliver broadcast messages, make a film and be photographed in every imaginable batting pose, ad nauseam. Very likely he was in breach of the spirit of his contract, along with at least six other members of the touring party. The Board of Control, when it drew up that very elaborate contract, unprecedented in length and comprehensiveness, hadn't yet envisaged film-making and other lucrative side-lines; any more than it had envisaged the tremendous popular appeal, with all the associated financial benefits, that Bradman had brought to the game at the same time.

On 17 September, the main business of the tour now definitely ended, he turned up at the headquarters of the Columbia Gramophone Company to make a piano recording, an improvisation of two pop tunes, "An Old-fashioned Locket", and "Our Bungalow of Dreams". But that was not all. From one studio he was led to another where he sat down and proceeded to write out a brief talk on the game of cricket. There was just time to read this aloud and record it before he hurried off to watch Walter Lindrum in an important billiards match at Thurston's.

There was no doubt that England had tremendously broadened his horizons. Many years later Neville Cardus was to write how, "when he first came to England in 1930, a socially uninstructed youth, he asked me to make him a list of books which I thought might help him to develop his mind and enlarge his conversation. I wrote out for him a number of titles, none of them easy reading and covering a wide field of politics and letters. A year or two later he had got through them all – and he had assimilated much." While other members of the touring party went off for a second look at Europe or visited relatives in distant parts of England and Scotland, Bradman lingered on the neighbourhood of London. A last group of six, Ponsford, Fairfax, Hornibrook, Wall, Walker and Bradman assembled at St. Pancras station for the final send-off. As usual hundreds of onlookers jostled one another to catch a glimpse, cameras clicked busily, while above the din the six players waved their farewells and exchanged parting cracks with various members of the crowd. All were in high spirits except Bradman, who seemed uncharacteristically depressed. It wasn't good-bye, he assured friends anxiously. Only au revoir. He would be back in 1934. Then the train moved slowly out, Bradman leaning further and further out of the window until he was the only one to be made out, still waving frantically.

CHAPTER FIVE

The Emergence of Bodyline

England was sorry to see him go. Australia went absolutely hysterical in welcoming him home again. While the *Oronsay* was still at sea, Bradman received a cable from his employers, Mick Simmons in Sydney, requesting him to leave the ship at the earliest possible moment after arrival in Australia. Evidently arrangements had been made for him to fly from Adelaide to Goulburn via the new aerial passenger service recently inaugurated by Kingsford Smith. He immediately cabled back to Australia for permission to go on ahead of the rest of the team and having had a favourable reply from W. H. Jeanes, the Board secretary, left the boat at Fremantle.

There was no way in which he could have avoided the publicity. Vast numbers seemed to congregate wherever he was known to be. There were dinners and functions and gala occasions. Speeches innumerable. From Perth he went overland to Adelaide by express train, while the remainder of the side continued across the Bight in the *Oronsay*. In Adelaide he was officially greeted by the Lord Mayor and members of the Board of Control, made an appearance on the stage and spoke about the tour on the radio. Then on to Melbourne in the *Southern Cloud* to find 10,000 people waiting for him at Essendon airport, though no organised reception this time, no local cricket officials nor Board members, at least not in their official capacity. The Bradman stomach, which had revolted upon its first taste of the sea, objected no less strenuously to being buffeted about in the air, but there could be no turning back at this stage. The little plane struggled doggedly on across the Southern Alps (over the same rugged terrain where 'plane and pilot, Harry Shortridge, were to disappear a few months later), before finally making a welcome return to terra firma at Goulburn. There his brother Vic was waiting to drive him home to Bowral and into the arms of his family, father, mother and sisters. Bowral, needless to say, did him proud.

However he couldn't be allowed to stay there too long. His public awaited him in Sydney. Big business was waiting to make the most of the occasion also. On 6 November, just before N.S.W.'s first Shield match of the season, he rolled up to the front entrance of Mick Simmons' in a large car driven by the racing motorist, "Wizard" Smith, three other vehicles following in procession coming to a halt immediately behind. The directors of Mick Simmons were there to receive him; to make him the guest of honour at a luncheon attended by A. W. Green, president of the N.S.W.C.A., Hal Heydon, secretary, W. C. Bull and Frank Cush, representatives of the Australian Board of Control. Then more luncheons, dinners and a grand presentation to Bradman of a two-seater Chevrolet sports car by the General Motors company. On the same day Archie Jackson arrived home. For some time his parents had been trying to discover exactly when he was expected. But without success, until that morning Mrs. Jackson got back with the shopping and found Archie in the kitchen, replaying the fifth Test with his father.

Nothing like this singling out of one particular individual had ever happened before in Australian cricket, and it made the worst possible impression on Bradman's team-mates, some of whom were prejudiced enough against him already. Two days after Bradman, the main party reached Adelaide, where the manager, W. L. Kelly, told the Press that he could describe only one member of the side as having been indispensable – Clarrie Grimmett. To which Vic Richardson, broadcasting over radio station 5 CL, added, "We could have played any team without Don Bradman. We couldn't have beaten the blind school without Grimmett." "He didn't spend twopence during the tour" muttered one member of the team. "Went back to his room after getting that £1000 and played himself gramophone records," said another.

It was a great shame, because there had been little open ill-feeling on the tour. Everybody had been too busy; too bent on winning the Ashes, to have much time for harboring grudges. And always there was the presence of Woodfull, tactfully smoothing over differences, a well-loved and respected figure for whom nobody wanted to make trouble. However when the tour was over and the players had time to reflect and see how all this concentration of publicity upon Bradman was only helping to push them further into the background, their feelings changed. An illustration of their resentment was the little story that went the rounds when N.S.W. visited Adelaide in December. Bradman had done little so far that season, but against Grimmett and South Australia under Vic Richardson he was at his most determined. Very watchful at first; after lunch, irresistible. His first 100 came in 128 minutes; the next 50 in 68; the next 50 in 38. Near the end of the day, feeling that it was unfair to his bowlers, especially to Grimmett, 26 overs, 0 maidens, 126 runs, 1 wicket, Richardson took the ball himself and placed all his men bar one on the leg-side. The rate of scoring didn't noticeably slacken however, and as he prepared to bowl the second last over of the day, Bradman grinned round the field and remarked, "O.K., boys. I'll be seeing you all again in the morning." Then the first ball of Richardson's new over clean-bowled him. "Oh, bad luck," Richardson called out after him. "Then we won't be seeing you in the morning."

Again it was a case of concocting an agreeable yarn out of the flimsiest of materials, but at least it revealed the underlying attitude in certain quarters. "Don Alexander Napoleon Bradman has hit the fussy controllers to leg. Pompous rules and regulations of the Board of Control have been cut, slashed and smitten into scraps," proclaimed a Sydney newspaper. This followed the news recently released that Bradman alone among the 1930 tourists was not yet to receive the final £150 instalment of each player's £600 tour allowance; the £150 that was retained by the Board pending a good conduct report by the tour manager. Rumour had it that Kelly had been very annoyed with Bradman for leaving the ship without seeking *his* permission first; that in Melbourne the Board of Control under its new Victorian chairman, Dr. Allen Robertson was to sit in solemn judgement to decide whether he had infringed the terms of his tour contract by indulging in too much personal publicity.

It was a very worrying few weeks for the young cricketer, reflected in a number of indifferent performances with the bat – against the other States and the newly-arrived West Indians. "My mind was most disturbed (at the time)," wrote Bradman. "I know that my concentration during that season fell away because of these extraneous matters." Perhaps he could have got away with all sorts of things, but it just happened that it was his nature to be scrupulous in such matters as contracts, to be particular in his dealings with people, as he was particular with his batting, his equipment and so on. Shortly after his great innings at Leeds, he had been approached by a firm of literary agents and invited to write his life-story. Bradman agreed, stipulating only, as his contract stipulated, that absolutely nothing concerning the current tour should be published before the team's return to Australia. He then set to work, delivering the manuscript in instalments, and was surprised to learn long before he had finished that the earlier chapters were to be serialised in an evening newspaper immediately following the fourth Test. The serialisation rights, the property of the literary agents, had been quickly disposed of to the *Star* and the *Star* intended to cash in right away. It was an unforeseen development and most unfortunate, since it could not but appear that he was deliberately flouting the wishes of the Board in regard to communicating with the Press; that he was putting himself and his own profit before all else while the fifth Test and the Ashes were still at stake.

Bradman was invited to put his side of the story to a meeting of the Board on 30 December 1930, but one section of the Board, it seems, was determined that its authority should be vindicated at all costs. Now that he was on a pedestal, every move he made would be watched and debated, the necessary measures taken to protect the Board's own position and so on. As the result of all his extra-curricular activities, Bradman had done very well out of his tour of England, Board members believed, and so, after much discussion, they decided to withhold £50, with a censure, an indication that he had overstepped the mark, but had been fined only lightly on this occasion, the breach of contract being more a "technical breach" than anything else.

The really tough times in his cricket career now lay ahead. He would have to tread warily, with enemies waiting to trip him at every turn. Still he was young, physically jumping out of his skin and the West Indians, the black members of the party at any rate, were an infectiously cheerful band of young sportsmen whom Bradman and the great majority of Australians took to at once. He had failed in his first two Tests against them, but in the third at Brisbane, he came in with the score 1 – 1, Jackson 0, and was very soon missed in the slips off their fast bowler, Constantine, when only 4. After that he could do little wrong. The Board affair was now two weeks behind him and he was free to give all his mind to his batting. He scored 223 not out, the highest score of any Australian in a Test match in Australia, then 220 against Victoria.

Meanwhile the star of the 1930–31 season was not so much Bradman as the remarkable West Indian, Learie Constantine. "A long pair of legs surmounted by broad shoulders," was how the cricket writer, Ray Robinson, remembered Constantine. He just had this way of moving in the field, loping rather, head sunk on his chest, almost a slouch, so loose-jointed he was. Sometimes the unwary batsman thought he was half-asleep or had forgotten about him, when suddenly the half-chance of a catch or run-out occurred, and a brown body hurtled acrobatically through the air, a long hand shot out to seize the ball, and that batsman was lucky if he was not caught or run-out by a ball flung back at the stumps with such tremendous velocity that very often it went on for four over-throws. "Old Electric-Heels," was the Sydney Hill's name for him. He was also a batsman capable of a hurricane hundred by the most unorthodox, most improbable strokes, but his importance in international cricket was primarily as a bowler. He could bowl all sorts, but most of all being West Indian, he loved to bowl fast.

In the first Test, West Indies v. England at Lord's in 1928, his speed for a few overs was thought by umpire Frank Chester, to be the fastest experienced in England since Kortright and Ernie Jones. When the West Indians batted, Larwood, spurred on by a comment from Chester, was faster still. Both in this Test at Lord's, and again in the second at Old Trafford, batsmen of either side were in considerable danger from short-pitched deliveries flying round their heads. Hobbs and Hammond grumbled at it, Jardine added some astringent comments of his own, but fortunately nobody was seriously hurt that summer, though the duel between Larwood and Constantine undoubtedly accelerated a tendency, always latent in first-class cricket, but now more apparent than ever, for the fast men to use their speed specifically to intimidate the batsmen.

Then in the West Indies in 1930, the young Barbadian, Inniss, was knocked to the ground by a Voce bumper, provoking Constantine to retaliate in the first Test and injure M.C.C.'s opening batsman, Andy Sandham, with M.C.C. in its second innings in a good position to win the match. Constantine was bowling with six men on the leg-side, his intention being merely to keep down the runs and force a draw, he claimed. However the injury to Sandham started a row that spluttered on intermittently throughout the tour. Accusations and counter-accusations were hurled. Much past history was recalled, but the bumpers persisted whenever the opportunity offered. Yet when West Indies visited Australia the following season there was hardly a sign of one.

Constantine himself supplies two reasons for this. "In Australia," he writes in one place, "I bowled short at Ponsford, and Grant, the captain, took me off at once. I had given Ponsford about four short balls in one over . . ." but elsewhere he remarks ". . . of all batsmen in the world the last two to whom Bodyline should ever be bowled are Bradman and McCabe." Various elements, it seemed, went into the making of a bumper war. Firstly, one must have a captain willing to incur the opprobrium of initiating hostilities, which G. C. Grant, after the fuss in the West Indies at the beginning of 1930, plainly was not. Then, he must be brave enough physically to withstand the reprisals that will inevitably be directed against his own person, the type of skipper that was A. W. Carr of Nottinghamshire, for example. "You bully," he snarled at Gubby Allen, after being hit two stinging blows on the body upon one occasion against Middlesex at Lord's. Against Surrey also, he was hit and bowled over by a ball from the fast bowler, M. J. C. Allom. "Do you call that cricket, P.G.H.?" he asked the Surrey captain, after he had got his breath back again. The Surrey team burst out laughing at the unconscious humour of this remark, but the point was that Carr was able to "stand the racket", to suffer the physical retaliation provoked by the methods of Bill Voce.

Constantine was frequently asked in later years why he hadn't bowled leg-theory at Bradman, but the West Indies were simply not equipped for that kind of campaign, and in fact their most striking success came by sticking to conventional methods. On a perfect Sydney wicket, with a nice breeze behind him to give him that extra amount of zip, Constantine aimed at the stumps and took 6 – 45 against the pride of N.S.W.'s young batting strength. He also scored 41 and 93 run out and so played the major role in a very notable victory – a great encouragement for West Indian cricket generally.

Bradman's admiration for this amazing athlete knew no bounds.

They became good friends and when the West Indian returned to the Lancashire League the following English summer, he did his best to persuade Bradman to join him there as a fellow professional. Bradman, as he makes clear in his autobiography, *My Cricketing Life*, was greatly tempted by the offer which soon reached him from the Accrington club. He would be richer if he went, as well as free of all the myriad pressures and responsibilities that beset him in Australia. Moreover, thought the Sydney *Referee*, he was still rankling over "the unkind verdict of the Board in imposing the £50 fine," (9 September 1931). Some of the Board would have liked to fine him the full £150, it was believed. And yet, long as he toyed with the idea of going to England, he knew all the time that his real business lay at home.

While the West Indies were in Australia, an M.C.C. side was in South Africa. Things seemed to be going from bad to worse for England. Having lost the first Test in Johannesburg, been out-played in the second, England was very much on top at Durban, though rain never permitted the possibility of a decision. On Kingsmead's new turf wicket made from imported Australian Bulli soil, Voce made the ball rear uncomfortably and although he was loudly jeered by the members for persistently bowling short, it was the first time any of the English faster bowlers had managed to make much impression. Thwarted by the weather and some very dour South African batting, England went on to lose the series, and English cricket to sink to its lowest point since the era of Warwick Armstrong. A South African journalist even had the gall to suggest that the coming series between South Africa and Australia would be for the world championship.

Larwood hadn't been picked for South Africa. He was too injury-prone. His stamina also was suspect. Tate similarly appeared to be in decline. Where the bowling was coming from to confront Bradman in Australia in 1932–33, God only knew, though the success of Bill Voce offered a ray of hope. In the final Test, again at Durban, the South African fast-medium right-hander, A. J. Bell, placed a field similar to Vice's leg-trap, possibly deriving from it. Bowling over the wicket, right-hand, Bell didn't come from quite the same direction; didn't inspire the same sense of unease in the batsman as Voce, but he had a pronounced inswing; could extract plenty of lift from the Australian Bulli and Bob Wyatt, for one, found him distinctly a handful. During this final Test the South African team for Australia was announced over the loud-speakers, so there was great discussion between the two sets of players about its prospects. Sandy Bell was one who might worry Bradman a bit, the Englishmen reckoned.

But Bradman's first test, when the first-class season opened in 1931–32, came from a totally unexpected quarter. Eddie Gilbert was a slimly-built Queensland Aboriginal of medium height; a fast bowler who took only a few steps to the crease and rocketed them down sometimes at amazing speed. His long arms double-jointed at the elbow, with wrists so flexible that he could bend them almost all the way back before the instant of delivery, Gilbert didn't need a run, but it was a moot point under the existing laws of cricket whether he didn't sometimes throw. Not surprisingly perhaps, the Queensland C.A. believed his action was perfectly legitimate; a great number of his Sheffield Shield opponents were convinced he threw. In 1930 when N.S.W. visited Brisbane, there was an amusing incident. In N.S.W.'s first innings, Bill Hunt, the left-hander, was bowled first ball by Gilbert by means of a delivery which he believed had been deliberately thrown. Hunt, a belligerent character, returned to the dressing-room and told his team-mates, "Just watch me, boys. You saw what that b—— did to me. Watch what I do to him." As luck would have it, Hunt was bowling when Gilbert came in to bat for Queensland, and after one or two normal deliveries, with a huge wink to Hal Hooker at mid-off, the left-hander prepared to bowl his next ball. He ran in, stopped, drew back his arm and in full view of the two umpires, the Queensland officials in the pavilion and everybody else, threw down the stumps. "All right, Eddie?" he called after the departing batsman. "Orright, Bill," the Aboriginal grinned back. There were no official repercussions.

But there was nothing particularly amusing about N.S.W.'s next visit to Brisbane in 1931. This season the wicket was the much faster one at the Woolloongabba ground, and after Queensland had been shot out for 109 on the first afternoon, Wendell Bill opening for N.S.W. was immediately caught behind off Gilbert. Bradman now came in. It was perhaps the most astonishing innings he would ever play. The wicket-keeper was standing at least half-way to the fence as Gilbert shuffled in, and his first ball saw Bradman completely beaten. The second knocked the bat out of his hand. He swung at the next two and missed by a mile; the fifth struck him on the body as he endeavoured to get out of the way; the sixth he nicked to the wicket-keeper in attempting a glance. "Gilbert just pelted them down straight at the batsmen," said the *Referee*, "and it was as much as they could do to keep out of harm's way . . . it was a most amazing scene when the world's best batsman was compelled to strike an undignified attitude before the dusky youth's lightning attack." Bradman was smiling as he walked off the field, but as he confided to team-mates in the dressing-room, he was "flabbergasted by the Aboriginal's pace, yards faster than Larwood at his top." Leo O'Connor, the former Queensland captain, had been watching the play through field-glasses and his former suspicions about the fast bowler's action were now confirmed. "Whenever Gilbert tried to get extra pace he invariably bent his arm . . . this was most noticeable in his opening overs while he was fresh."

Was Bradman being made an Aunt Sally? Earlier in the season he had been hit in a match at Wagga and had to retire, but was hardly as unlucky as Alan Kippax who had had his nose broken in Parkes, and then in this game against Queensland was struck a terrific blow on the side of the head by "Pud" Thurlow, Gilbert's opening partner. Thurlow "was so slow by comparison," said Bradman, "that Kippax had completed his stroke before the ball arrived." With six stitches in the wound, Kippax missed the next big match, played in the one following, then withdrew from the one after that still complaining of dizziness. He was never the same batsman again. "They won't get me, though," Bradman used to laugh bitterly, "I'm too quick for them." In any case there was no point in complaining, especially not when Gilbert, much slower the next day, was slaughtered by Stan McCabe who went on to make 229 not out.

By this time however, the South Africans had arrived and were already looking much more formidable than anticipated. Bell and the left-hander from Griqualand, Neville Quinn, formed a hostile opening attack, but easily their most successful bowler on hard wickets during the early part of the tour was the slow googly merchant, McMillan. South Africa batted on the first day of their match against N.S.W. and on the Saturday, in the certainty of seeing Bradman come to the crease, 33,000 turned up. They were more than a little disappointed however. In 87 minutes he made only 30, being outpaced by Fingleton and completely overshadowed by McCabe, 37 in 35 minutes. The South Africans were delighted with themselves. Bowling with two slips, a silly-leg and a silly-point, McMillan kept the great man on the defensive most of the time and finally persuaded him to spoon back a simple caught-and-bowled.

Poor, unsuspecting tourists! How could they have known that in his first Sydney grade match that season, he had made only 17 in 70 minutes against Northern Districts – 17 singles. In his next innings he made 46 run out; in the next 246 in 205 minutes against Randwick on a very uneven pitch at Coogee Oval. That painstaking 17 was not in the least like the young champion who had jumped yards down the pitch to his first ball from White in the Test match at Lord's. But it was more like the essential Bradman just the same. In special cases other considerations might prevail, but by nature he was wary, predisposed to treat every strange bowler as an object of suspicion. Not at all like Stan McCabe, 37 in 35 minutes.

While the visitors were in Adelaide Sandy Bell had been interviewed by the *Referee*. A friendly, big fellow who enjoyed airing his views about the game, he was naturally invited to say how the South Africans felt about their approaching duel with Bradman. "Bradman!" said Bell, "It takes only one ball to bowl any batsman. If the West Indians could bowl Don Bradman, I think we can . . . Bradman is an attacking bat and liable to make mistakes." Perhaps it was those incautious remarks that had caused Bradman to exercise even more care than usual in N.S.W.'s first innings; to take a very good look at them all before proceeding to execution in the second innings. He made 135 in 128 minutes this time and McMillan's analysis read: 8 overs, 0 maiden, 72 runs, 0 wicket. He did little on the tour thereafter and the performance of the whole team suffered accordingly.

As it turned out, the South Africans' best chance of matching Bell's hopes occurred at the very outset of the series, in the vital first half-hour of the first Test in Brisbane. He was swinging the ball in prodigiously in the steamy atmosphere. After getting rid of Ponsford his first ball to Bradman caught the batsman fair on the hip-bone, causing him to hobble round the stumps in agony. Quinn was even more difficult. He didn't swing as much, but was deceptively fast off the pitch and able to move it both ways. For half a dozen overs the agony continued. At 3, Bradman swung at Quinn, skied the ball and Morkel just failed to reach it at square leg. At 11, he edged the left-hander to second-slip, who dropped it. Bruce Mitchell had just stopped swearing at his fellow slip when the next Bradman edge came to him and down it went just as promptly. That was Bradman's last mistake however, almost of the entire series. In a disciplined but dominating fashion he went on to make 226 in this first Test; 219 in the return match, South Africa versus N.S.W.; 112, with a strained leg muscle, in the second Test in Sydney; 2 and 167 in the third Test in Melbourne.

The South Africans' third defeat in a row meant the series was now decided and still they hadn't seen the end of Bradman. In fact their most trying ordeal against him, in the cruel heat of Adelaide, was yet to come. Replying to South Africa's first innings 308, Australia was 1 – 9 at lunch on the Saturday, Bradman 2 not out. At tea he was 84; at stumps, 170. It was certainly hard on the visitors, and there were quite a few Australians who thought Bradman might have been content with 100 on this occasion. But if the South Africans were ever to match Australia in Test cricket, the experience could only do them good in the long run. Moreover Adelaide had waited twelve months to see Bradman again. There would have been bitter disappointment if he had deliberately thrown his wicket away, though indeed he wasn't likely to do that; he had never felt in finer fettle. Even Woodfull was seen to protest at the number of sharp singles, of fast-run twos and threes. Woodfull was out however when the score was 185 and several minutes later occurred an unfortunate incident. Bradman pulled Vincent for four to go to 97, Kippax still 0. The next ball he pulled to practically the same place, but no, it wouldn't quite go. The batsmen sprinted two, went for the third and Bradman's 100, and Kippax was run out at the 'keeper's end without facing a single ball. He left the field fuming.

So Kippax went off to tell the dressing-room all about it. The South Africans were dog-tired and fed up, their returns to the wicket whizzing so unpleasantly close to the batsmen that Bradman is alleged to have warned Cameron on one occasion, "Please tell your men that I can throw straighter and harder than any of them."[1] Mutterings and ill-feeling had crept in to mar the pleasure of one of Bradman's greatest achievements. On Monday the Australians resumed at 4 – 302 and soon it became apparent that Bell was adopting different methods altogether. He had begun the season with the two or three short-legs he had employed so successfully against the M.C.C. at Durban, but they proved of so little utility on Australian wickets that by the second Test there was nobody within coo-ee of the bat on the leg-side after the first over or two. Evidently, at this rather late hour, he had hit on an alternative line of attack.

The early morning wicket seemed to have plenty of life in it and the big man quickly discovered that by bowling short and aiming at the body, he could render the batsmen most uncomfortable. Rigg was quickly out, cocking one up off a bumper, and with Bradman and Oldfield defending grimly, the bowling had never looked so much on top. Bradman was missed in the slips when 185, survived several appeals for lbw, and in the end took 80 minutes moving from 170 to 200. The fury had expended itself by lunch-time however. After lunch the tempo of the scoring increased; by mid-afternoon Bradman was hitting them all over the place, racing towards his 300 with the cheers of the crowd echoing in his ears. At 298, with Thurlow his last remaining partner, he swung one to leg, bolted for the single, started on the second, then quickly sent Thurlow back when he saw the second run was impossible. But Thurlow had gone too far, couldn't get back and the Australian innings closed for 513, Bradman 299 not out. Australia eventually won the fourth Test by ten wickets.

It seemed then that a bouncer war was in prospect for the final encounter in Melbourne. The South Africans made no secret of the tactics they intended to pursue. The Australians, for their part, included Laurie Nash, a twenty-one-year-old Tasmanian who had disturbed the tourists by bouncing one or two at them when they visited Hobart. But the confrontation, if that is what it was intended to be, never took place. Woodfull had won the toss and put the South Africans in to bat on a very soft wicket just made for Ironmonger. The Australians were making ready to leave the dressing-room, when Bradman jumped off a bench and twisted his ankle. He couldn't field or bat that day and the match finished quickly on the second day of actual play, one day being lost through rain in between. Nash, Bell and Quinn certainly did make the ball fly however.

[1] R. S. Whitington refers to this incident in his *Bradman, Benaud and Goddard's Cinderellas*, p. 24, though it is only fair to add that Bradman himself denies having made the remark.

1. Stan McCabe and Don Bradman on the quay at Dover when arriving for their first tour of the U.K., 1930.

2. Bradman photographed on the cross-channel ferry, 1930.

3. Bradman and Richardson going out to resume their partnership against Surrey, May 1930. Off the field, however, they tended to be a less united pair.

4. Bradman in action on the way to a record-breaking 334 at Leeds.

5. Relaxing between overs during the final Test at the Oval. Archie Jackson is at the other end.

6. Fred Root's leg-trap in position, Surrey versus Worcestershire at the Oval, 30th April 1932. Hobbs is facing the bowling.

7. Jardine in the gully, Fender in the slips; Surrey versus Middlesex, 9th August 1932.

8. Larwood in action against Surrey, the Oval, July 1932.

9. Voce bowling against Surrey, the Oval 1932. It was after this match that he and Larwood were invited to dinner by Jardine to discuss tactics against the Australians.

10. Cutmore and Pope were the first English batsmen to face Larwood's fast leg-theory. Here Pope is caught by Keeton off Larwood for 25 during the Essex v. Notts match at Leyton, 4th August 1932.

11. Bowes bowling in the Surrey versus Yorkshire match at the Oval, 1932. Warner's strictures on his bowling created a stir.

12. Fender sees off Jardine before the MICC tour of India, August 1933.

13. Don Bradman and his wife Jessie returning to Australia before the bodyline series, 1932.

14. Jardine on his way to Australia for the same series.

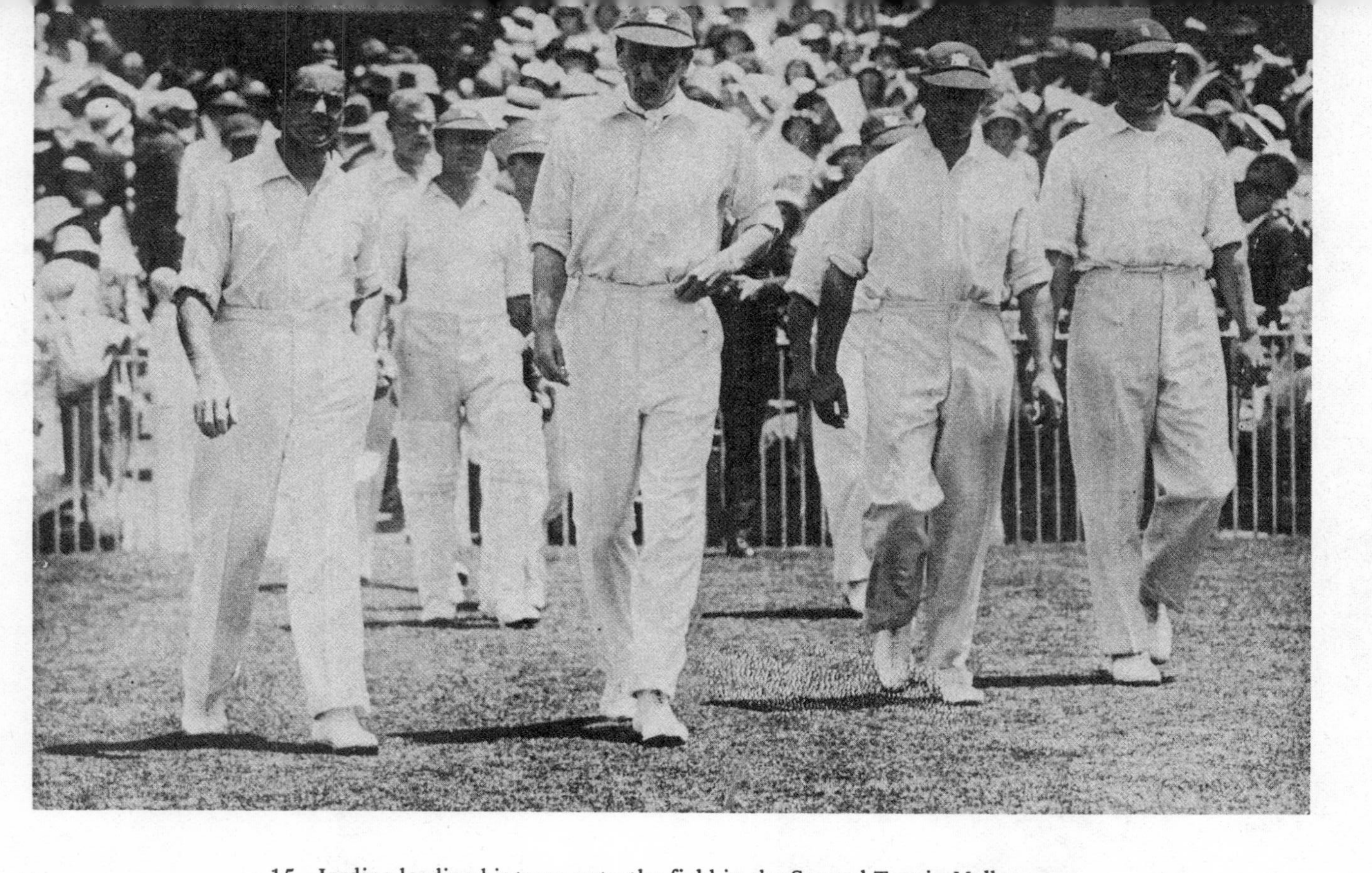

15. Jardine leading his team onto the field in the Second Test in Melbourne.

16. Fingleton ducking a ball from Larwood in the same match.

17. Third Test of the bodyline series:- Woodfull loses his bat playing Larwood.

18. In the same match Oldfield is hit by a ball from Larwood.

19. In the Fourth Test Woodfull ducks a short one from Larwood, but is hit in the ribs.

20. Larwood in action.

21. Voce *(left)* and Larwood on departure from Australia at the end of the bodyline series.

22. Woodfull designed this body protector against the merciless bowling of the English.

23. An older and strained-looking Bradman arriving at Southampton, 1934.

24. Bradman in England 1934; he is at the piano with Fleetwood-Smith and Chipperfield,

The South African tour thus rather fizzled out. The tourists went off to New Zealand and Bradman was free to take up a brand-new job. *The Sun* (21 February 1932) told the world all about it. "We kept him here for you" it proclaimed – the slogan emblazoned across a two-page spread, plastered over a montage of action shots, Bradman hooking, Bradman driving, walking out to bat, shaking hands with the great, etc., etc. "When it became known that Don was likely to become lost to cricket in Australia [reference to Accrington], F. J. Palmer took immediate action to prevent the tragedy. Radio 2 UE Ltd. and Associated Newspapers became associated with Palmers in its efforts, and negotiations were immediately entered into. . . ." "See Don at Palmers of Park Street. Hear him on 2 UE beginning 22 February at 8 p.m. Read him in *The Sun* and *Sunday Sun*."

This was Bradman in the world of big business in 1932, the biggest thing in big-name advertising since Kingsford Smith. He shrank instinctively from the notion of promoting himself in this way, but business knows no foolish scruples, imposes its own code of ethics and £1000 a year for two years and very much his own boss, was a wonderful offer – particularly when he was contemplating marriage in the near future; particularly since they both preferred to remain in Australia anyway. Mick Simmons hadn't wanted to let him go, but "There, I found that the nature of my work caused me to think and talk cricket nearly all day long. I began to ask myself how long such a state of affairs could go on."

The new job in its three parts certainly involved a lot of cricket also, but it was a much more glamorous proposition altogether and indeed he made a great success of it. "Don Bradman's Question-Box (2 UE 7.45 p.m.)" became one of the station's most popular programmes; while as a journalist he reached an audience no less wide. He enjoyed writing for the papers and took great pains over his articles. He was impartial, judicious, neither platitudinous nor too outspoken, as generous in praise of new players like Fingleton and O'Reilly as he was of old enemies like Clarrie Grimmett. "His copy was always early," wrote the *Sun* Sports Editor, A. G. Moyes, "And he wrote it himself.' There was only one possible snag. The Board had set its face against players writing for the Press, though it could hardly deny cricketers who were already journalists by occupation. But Bradman's exact status under this unusual tripartite agreement was difficult to define. He obviously didn't derive his livelihood solely from writing, in the sense that the Board understood professional journalism. Still, as he wrote to the *Sydney Morning Herald* (10 February 1932) in public explanation of his position, "I have accepted a position. I play Test cricket. If the Board of Control in its wisdom should impose such conditions as will prevent my playing, well and good. That position has not arisen yet. When it does will be time to make my decision."

All being well for the moment, then, the immediate future taken care of, a date was fixed for the wedding. Jessie Menzies was a very pretty girl, vivacious and full of fun, yet with her feet planted firmly on the ground, who came from the same steady background, the same locality in fact, as Bradman himself. Her people had been dairy farmers at Mittagong only a few miles from Bowral; they had even gone to the same school together. Don won the Gold Medal in mathematics; Jessie, in needlework. He was only eleven when he first confessed to his sister, Lily, that he intended to marry Jessie, and although the Menzies had later moved to Sydney, her youthful admirer never wavered in his resolution and on 30 April 1932, they were married in St. Paul's, Burwood. "Please keep it out of the papers," Bradman had begged his *Sun* employers, but there was no way of preventing the news from leaking out. Hundreds, perhaps thousands, of sightseers milled about the church; broke down the barriers set up to keep them at a distance, and otherwise converted a quiet suburban wedding into a gala public occasion. Eventually however they escaped unscathed and spent a few quiet weeks in East Malvern, Melbourne, before setting out on the exciting part of the honeymoon, a cricket tour of Canada and North America with a side organised and managed by Arthur Mailey.

For such international celebrities as Richardson and Kippax, Bradman and McCabe, the tour of America was little more than a cricket holiday, a very strenuous holiday, but no comparison with the grim preparations currently under way in England. It was symptomatic of the seriousness with which M.C.C. viewed its approaching tour of Australia that Jardine was now England's Test captain. He was unlikely to have been appointed in any other circumstances. Though three years in the Oxford Eleven, 1920, 1921, 1923, he had not been invited to captain Oxford in the footsteps of his father, M. R. Jardine in 1891. He was strictly an amateur, but he hardly typified the amateur approach, at least not in the sense of treating the game as a bit of fun. He had been reared more in the Victorian idea of it – the game of cricket as a character-builder; the playing fields of Eton (or Winchester, where he was educated) as a preparation for the battle of life. In the period 1920–21 when Jardine began his first-class career, England lost eight successive Test matches against Australia – she might as well have lost the War. "Oh, for the old days, the good days, the days of our strength," cried Kipling's Risaldar-major. Winning or losing was important to him, even more important than how one played the game.

He was thus very much a man of the 1920s. Arthur Gilligan, Percy Chapman were closer to the spirit of the older Edwardian England, and so their country's fortunes, with occasional interruptions, continued to drift downhill. Yorkshire, Lancashire or Nottinghamshire carried off the County Championship with monotonous regularity, not giving a fig for the glorious traditions of the game. "We don't want any bloody amateurs here," Arthur Carr was told when he was appointed skipper of Nottinghamshire just after the war, and though of course he always retained his amateur status, he became a truly professional captain whose services England was glad to employ in 1926 and again in 1929 when things were not going too well in the home series against South Africa.

Carr and Jardine were much alike in disposition. To them it was the sheerest hypocrisy to believe that a match for the County Championship, let alone a Test match, was like some gentlemanly trial-at-arms in which certain practices were frowned upon as simply not cricket. In June 1927, when Lancashire was going for its second successive County Championship, Surrey visited Old Trafford to find Ted McDonald in his most dangerous mood. McDonald was very much a bowler of moods. It greatly depended on the state of his health, or even his wife's health, claimed Peter Eckersley, one of his county captains. This day he was the very devil, with lowered arm action making the ball fly round the batsman's skull. Some of Surrey's earlier batsmen looked as if they were quite pleased to get out against him. Jardine came in after four wickets had fallen cheaply and proceeded to play a masterly innings. He was frequently hit about the upper body, but appeared to suffer no discomfort. He didn't rub the spot, nor offer any comment about the bowling to the fieldsmen; nor parade down the pitch to indicate where he thought McDonald was pitching. He made 143, driving the fast bowler mercilessly when he began to tire, and Surrey easily saved the match. This was how Jardine thought cricket should be played; that was the kind of game he really enjoyed. "After the friendly good fellowship of (ordinary) county cricket," he once wrote, "the atmosphere of a Test match comes as a nervous joy – this, one feels, is the real thing with the gloves off."

It was not surprising, then, that Jardine being an amateur and able to choose his matches, he had a decided preference for Surrey's "big" matches against the northern counties, especially when Surrey itself journeyed north and there was the likelihood of no punches pulled, plus a certain amount of hostility and aggravation from the crowds to serve as an added stimulant. Many of the amateur contingent tended to avoid these sterner contests set in the not always attractive environment of the industrial north. But then Jardine had little in common with his public school and University fellows. He wasn't particularly popular with the administrators of the game either, though he did have a good friend and consistent advocate in his Surrey captain, Percy Fender.

At one stage of 1928, hopes were being held in certain quarters that Fender might skipper M.C.C.'s side to Australia. He didn't; nor did Jardine, the outstanding amateur batsman of that summer, win the position of vice-captain, though he had been made captain of England against The Rest in a Trial match at Bristol in 1927. That job went to Jack White instead. Jardine didn't play at all in the summer of 1929; he missed most of 1930 when he would like to have played more, but was patently out of form. And then at the beginning of season 1931, there was a sudden call for Jardine. It was most extraordinary. They wanted to make him captain of England, though he was not yet even captain of Surrey. Jardine was bewildered, uncertain. "But don't worry," said M. R. Jardine, captain of Oxford in 1891. "I'll speak to the boy." And so Jardine was chosen captain for the Test match against New Zealand.

What had happened, we now know, was that England had lost to South Africa in South Africa and that Lord's was very annoyed about it and inclined to put the entire blame on A. P. F. Chapman. Though the ultimate causes of the disaster would have to be sought deeper than that. On 9 March 1931 the M.C.C.'s Board of Control of Test Matches at Home, as it was called, deferred the appointment of a Test match selection committee for several more weeks, an infallible sign that drastic measures were afoot. The hour had arrived, Fender had written in the *Star*, to "take English cricket by the scruff of the neck and shake it with such effect that some of the dead leaves will drop off, the withered branches be broken." Perhaps he didn't have the selection committee exactly in mind, but rather significantly the former 1930 selectors Leveson Gower F. T. Mann and Jack White, now disappeared at one stroke, to be replaced by "Plum" Warner, Percy Perrin, his close associate on previous England selection committees and Tommy Higson, a Manchester lawyer and businessman who would see to it that the interests of northern England were not overlooked.

The committee was appointed for a period of two years, with the express object of building up a side for Australia, and almost its first act was the appointment of Jardine as leader against New Zealand. He would not be an easy man to manage, Warner knew as an old friend of the family. He would have preferred another old Wykehamist, Hubert Ashton, but this was not a time for personal considerations, and people remembered Jardine as the greatest schoolboy captain of his generation.

New Zealand in 1931 was hardly strong enough to test his leadership qualities to the full, but by his very "presence" on the field, by the way his team jumped at the word of command, one sensed that here was a man in control of the situation. He may have had few previous opportunities of captaincy since Winchester; no very great experience of county cricket at all compared with some of his possible rivals, but he obviously knew his own mind better than anybody. No more of those eternal conferences with Hobbs between overs; no longer the feeling of some power in the pavilion pulling the strings, as there had been when Wyatt was captain of England in 1930. Discipline was that vital missing ingredient in South Africa. Discipline was what Jardine would inculcate in the body of men being assembled for the campaign in Australia. By the force of his own personal example.

How he could inspire his men was there for all to see in the final match of 1931, Yorkshire, the county champions, versus the Rest of England under Jardine at The Oval. The Rest were sent in on an awful wicket which Yorkshire, pre-eminently among the counties, was most calculated to exploit through their two outstanding young finds of the season; Bill Bowes, fast, right-hand, and Hedley Verity, a left-arm spinner. Bowes was neither specially fast nor specially accurate, but he was very tall and from this soft wicket able to impart a nasty rising angle to every delivery. Batting against him under such conditions was sheer torture. Duleep tried to hit him out of the attack and failed. Wyatt got a severe blow on the hand. Hammond batted an hour for 9, Jardine one hour and three quarters for 26. The Rest were all out 124 and even worse was to come. After Yorkshire had all the best of the wicket and led by 85 runs, Jardine's men struck another shocker at their second attempt; were at 6 – 113 at one stage, and defeat stared them in the face. Only Jardine and Wyatt were left of the recognised batsmen, Wyatt with a badly bruised hand. But they stuck it out; Wyatt for another two hours, Jardine for four hours and a half this time.

They saved the game, though one couldn't say that the Oval members were particularly impressed. They tended to be irked by Jardine and his slow batting. "Somebody once called him a stylist," Cardus wrote of this innings of his. "I would as soon call an 8-day clock a stylist. But for the purpose of keeping an end safe in Australia, Jardine is the man. He is England's reply to Woodfull. But not more than one Jardine is necessary in a cricket team, in Australia or anywhere."

"At the end of that season," Plum Warner was to recall some years later, "the committee felt some optimism for the future. The two-year period gave us a great advantage. We had another summer before us in which to build on the foundation we had created, and looking to Australia, we were of the opinion that a team abroad could be welded into a combination in a way which a team at home has not the opportunity." The success of White in Australia in 1928–29 had stimulated the search for a slow, stock bowler who might also take wickets and Verity seemed just the man. Equally important was the need to strengthen the middle-order batting and in that respect, the emergence of Leslie Ames as a possible second wicket-keeper was another notable development. Things were shaping up quite nicely. The problem of finding an opening partner for Sutcliffe was still to be solved, but all told, England looked well able to match Australia man for man, if only they could get Bradman out.

He couldn't pick the "bosie", it was said. Or didn't like the ball spinning away towards the slips. But he made 232 opposed to Peebles at The Oval. Middlesex had Robins and Surrey had a promising young leg-breaker, F. R. Brown, but it was difficult to see Brown or Robins or any other English spinner getting a ball past the Bradman bat on Australian wickets. Speed stood equally discredited by Bradman after 1930. At The Oval the shock attack, Tate and Larwood, took between them two wickets for 258. In the final Test in Melbourne in the preceding series, their combined figures were even worse, 1 – 348.

Yet it was in the faster bowlers that the selectors' best hope lay. Tate may have been slightly over the hill, but Larwood was fitter, stronger and reputedly a yard and a half faster than he had been in 1930. Against Middlesex at Lord's in June 1931, he was dynamite. Hendren and Robins were notable exceptions, but he had most of the Middlesex batsmen edging away, left-legs creeping further and further to the on-side, bats getting less and less straight. He took 6 – 64 in Middlesex's first innings, though it was very hard on his wicket-keeper. Ben Lilley retired with a badly bruised finger; Walker took his place but lasted only a short while and finally Arthur Staples, wicket-keeper number three, was ordered into line. Larwood was very fast and very dangerous and so it was a shock but no real surprise when Patsy Hendren, going for his favourite hook, was hit on the head and knocked to the ground. "He went down with a thud," Ian Peebles remembered, "his legs jerking and twitching as though he had been shot." It was a most alarming scene and he was still unconscious when taken off to St. Mary's Hospital. He proved, after all, to be not seriously hurt, but the scene was all too reminiscent of the occasion two years before at Lord's when Cameron, the South African wicket-keeper, was hit on the head, also by Larwood. A sound he would never forget, said Plum Warner.

Larwood could be terrifying; Larwood and Voce in tandem were murder. On 25 May 1932 Neville Cardus paid a special visit to Fenner's to watch the pair in action for Nottinghamshire versus Cambridge University. It wasn't a match however. A massacre is the only description. Aided by the weather, Cambridge had just defeated Middlesex by an innings. But two days later on a perfect Fenner's wicket, Larwood and Voce bowled the students out for 34 in 25 overs. In the second innings, Larwood bowled only three overs and Cambridge made 81, Voce 5 – 30. Larwood's victims looked as though they had been petrified, wrote Cardus, "petrified by the sight of his galloping run, the plunge of the left foot, the sideways fling of the body, the final hostile wheel of the arm clean over . . . Voce exploited the leg-trap and, having terrified the innocents by a hideous circle of clutching hands, often proceeded to hit the off-stump with the ball that went straight through." By a strange coincidence, Plum Warner was that day in Oxford, addressing the Oxford Luncheon Club. "In my opinion," said Warner, "Bradman is as great a batsman as any who has ever lived. The bowler who can get Bradman out for a reasonable score is going to be a tremendous fellow."

But where was he? Larwood stood at the head of the bowling averages midway through 1932. Freeman had taken the greatest number of wickets. The two were so alike, it seemed to the selection committee. They could plough through the counties at will, but when confronted by a really high-class batsman who was not afraid of them, they tended to play it safe; to concentrate on accuracy at the expense of flight or all-out speed. Chosen for North v. South in the first Test Trial at Old Trafford, Larwood bowled 31 overs and took 0 – 98. Woolley, the left-hander, drove him in front of the wicket; Hammond and Duleepsinhji played him mainly off the back foot and seemed to have ample time. Voce, under the captaincy of Bob Wyatt and employing his familiar leg-trap, looked a much better proposition for Australia.

Actually the analogy with Freeman was quite false. Larwood's was a much more complex character. Only Arthur Carr at this stage could claim to understand him thoroughly. The man was an absolute bundle of nervous energy, a marvellous natural athlete with a sensitivity about people, an intuitive understanding far greater than one may have supposed from his manner. He knew, much better than Bill Voce for example, that the knockabout methods of Nottinghamshire and Arthur Carr were looked upon askance in the summer of 1932, particularly at Lord's. For instance when Bill Bowes began bowling bumpers in the Test match against India, it was very notable that whereas on the Saturday evening he had bowled purely short stuff, he immediately began pitching them up on the following Monday morning. Again, in the Varsity match, Ken Farnes took the first Oxford wicket with a ball that was very short and reared, and Hazlerigg instantly took him off. The injuries to Cameron and Hendren were still very much in the committee's minds.

So under Chapman or White or Wyatt or any other skipper, Larwood tended to be circumspect, fearful of causing an injury that might lead to a rumpus about dangerous fast bowling. "By now I had a family and responsibilities," Larwood was to write in his autobiography. "Cricket was my livelihood, along with the chicken farm I was developing." But under Arthur Carr, reckless, commanding, hard as nails, it was different. Carr knew how to egg him on; to keep his tail up when he started to flag. He was a generous skipper also, ever ready to stand the boys a round of drinks at the right moment, to show them all a good time, and in the last resort take the rap for them, protect them from the fierce storms that were inclined to blow up in county cricket from time to time. On 23 June, in the match immediately following the Test Trial at Old Trafford, Larwood's bowling was the fastest he had ever seen in his life, Carr claimed; so fast that after hitting the stumps, the ball seemed to carry on to the boundary with practically undiminished velocity. Leicester happened to be the unfortunate visitors to Trent Bridge on this occasion, being out for 80 and 53 in a total of two hours and 40 minutes of actual cricket. Larwood and Voce each took 10 wickets, their most astonishing feat so far.

By mid-July the moment for announcing a team for Australia was fast approaching and Larwood had pretty well reasoned himself out of it. Voce, he thought, was definitely ahead of him, and Allen, and presumably Tate. How many bowlers of pace would they be taking to Australia? He had been the only really fast bowler in the party of 1928–29. Against the Gentlemen at Lord's, Larwood opened the attack on the second morning from the pavilion end – at about fast-medium; while Voce at the other end was just as ordinary, bowling over the wicket to a conventional off-side slip-field. There would be no Nottinghamshire "shock tactics" at Lord's while Jack Hobbs, most gentlemanly of Players, was skipper, and shortly after tea, the Gentlemen were 4 – 410, the two Indians, Duleepsinhji and Pataudi, having hit up the most brilliant centuries.

It was a great day for the spectators, but as an all-important try-out for Australia it was virtually useless. Possibly something was said at tea though. Because after tea Larwood took the new ball and was a different bowler. He had Jardine taken at slip, bowled Chapman, Brown and Allen in quick succession, and the Gentlemen declared at 8 – 430. However this performance had apparently come too late in the day to attract attention. His name was not in the first list of six, Jardine, Sutcliffe, Hammond, Duleepsinhji, Ames and Duckworth, announced for Australia. Even more alarming! Two sides were chosen to play a final Trial at Cardiff and Larwood found himself among The Rest. Voce and Allen were to be the opening bowlers for England.

Perhaps though the opposition to Larwood was not as great as he imagined. Or perhaps the selectors had meant him to go all the time. Jardine for instance was the last person in the world to give one a hint of reassurance, any notion of what was in his mind. The final Trial was almost entirely washed out by rain, but meantime the selectors had been busy and before its scheduled end they had issued a second list of invitees – Wyatt, Pataudi, Allen, Brown, Robins, Voce and Larwood.

He needn't really have worried. The selectors in fact had been concentrating upon the batsmen first, leaving the harder part of their task, the bowling, till later. Jardine had accepted the captaincy of the touring side, wrote P. G. H. Fender, "knowing that he was up against something bigger than normally faced by touring captains, on account of the presence in the Australian side of one player at least, who was possessed of outstanding ability. He also knew that among those from whom he had to choose his side, he had no-one who, up to that date, had shown any ability to deal even partially with the men against whom he was to play."

By the summer of 1932 Jardine had replaced Percy Fender as skipper of Surrey, but Fender continued in the team by his side, Jardine in the gully, Fender in slips, taking a common delight in treating the game of cricket not only as a test of skill, but also as an intellectual challenge, a kind of outdoor chess in which the batsman had to be thought out, the bowlers and fieldsmen to be manipulated in such a way as to bring about that result. For years Fender had been making "bricks out of straw" in the management of Surrey's rather limited bowling resources. Now in close association with Jardine, he had the opportunity of studying the problems confronting a captain of England. If the English bowling had failed before against Bradman, conceivably it was because it had not been properly handled. Take the case of Larwood for instance.

His natural ball, after the shine was gone, was a kind of in-swinger which, bowled from wide of the crease, gave the batsman the impression it was coming at his body all the time. In England, against the average county batsman, he normally pitched the ball well up on the off-stump and was usually successful enough in bowling the opposition out not to have to think about alternative methods. But in Australia, it appeared, batsmen were tending more than ever before to take guard on the off-stump, denying the bowler a sight of the stumps and ignoring every ball from the fast bowler they weren't actually forced to play. Fast bowling was the bowling the Australians liked least of all, Fender believed, but Larwood would have to attack the stumps directly, making the batsmen play every ball, the angle from which it was bowled inclining its direction towards the leg-side.

Fender had been in Australia in 1928–29 and watched Larwood giving away countless runs on the leg-side, but again he had a theory. In 1930 both he and Jardine had contributed to a book *The Game of Cricket* in which their original and distinctive approach to the game can readily be detected. In his chapter upon captaincy and field-placing, Fender had written, "The arrival of the forcing batsman at the crease is countered nowadays by a very much more clearly marked and more studied plan on the part of the fielding side . . . it is not sufficient merely to put an extra man or two in the country on such occasions. The whole side get together and working in conjunction with the bowler, a selected part of the field will be very definitely policed, while another part is equally clearly left unguarded. The bowler will then attempt not so much to avoid being hit, as to prevent the batsman from hitting the ball to any part of the field except that which is prepared for him. By so doing, the bowler will be forcing the batsman, should he attempt to score in the unguarded portion of the field, to take risks disproportionate to the gain which is likely to accrue." With a bowler of Larwood's exceptional accuracy, there was simply no limit to the number of men who might be stationed in a particular area.

Thus, or roughly thus, an idea was born. Fender and Jardine didn't always agree, nor was Jardine necessarily the junior partner in their discussions. But, "the ablest, the quickest and the most enterprising cricket brain ..." said Jardine, "is that of my old captain, Mr. P. G. H. Fender ... we occasionally differed, generally I think, because I was too conservative ... (but) ... I take this opportunity of saying he was nearly always right."

Fender had been a member of Johnny Douglas' side in Australia in 1920–21, and if he had learned anything from his first introduction to the tough school of Australian Test cricket, it was the importance of starting out with a definite plan of campaign. Recalling the first Test of the series in Sydney, he wrote, "I saw a tremendous number of things in the way of tactics which were entirely new to me. At first I found it hard to satisfy myself as to whether or not these things were actually separate schemes introduced at the moment for the undoing of a particular batsman, or really part of a general concerted plan. I made up my mind that the latter was the case ... that both bowlers and fielders were working along pre-arranged lines of attack and defence."

In those days Gregory and McDonald had been the shock troops; Kelleway and Ryder, perhaps the more conventional forces holding the line; Mailey, the sapper, undermining the enemy's defences by means of the prodigious amount of spin he imparted to the ball. In this case Larwood and Voce would be the shock troops and their first objective would be Bradman. "If he had a weakness, it lay in his ... unsound manner of playing fast bowlers."

Sometime in the middle of that English summer, the South African, Herby Taylor, arrived in England; another, it proved, who believed that England could pull off the rubber by means of "a general concerted plan" based on fast bowling. Taylor had been very impressed with the greater bounce the faster bowlers seemed to be getting from Australian wickets these days. A type of couch grass, coarser than in former years, constituted the average turf wicket and this couch had a habit of throwing out tough runners, so that while the majority of balls came through at an even height, the odd ball would strike a patch of unyielding turf and lift abruptly. Australian batsmen didn't cope with the fast, popping ball as well as their English counterparts, Taylor thought. Even Bradman hadn't looked so very impressive when Bell had bounced the ball at him in Adelaide. He had played it more safely than most of the others, but he had certainly been held in check; that terrible torrent of run-making had been dammed up for a while.

At this stage of course, the plan was pure theory. Nobody could be sure how it would work in practice. However, it chanced that Nottinghamshire were shortly due in London, so this was the opportunity to talk the matter over with Arthur Carr. "During the Surrey v. Nottinghamshire game at The Oval," wrote Carr, "he (Fender) gave me the tip that Jardine wanted to learn more about my two bowlers, Larwood and Voce, and proposed to ask the two bowlers and myself out to dinner to discuss things . . . we all went to the grill-room at the Piccadilly Hotel and although it took some time to warm up Larwood and Voce to talk in the company of their not exactly hail-fellow-well-met captain-to-be in Australia, they did eventually get going."

Larwood has also left an account of the evening. The conversation centred about Bradman evidently – particularly with reference to his possible "weakness against fast-rising balls on the leg-stump." Frank Foster and George Hirst were mentioned and "Jardine decided that Voce, being a left-handed natural inswing bowler, should concentrate on Bradman's leg-stump and bowl to his normal leg-theory field. . . . Finally Jardine asked me if I thought I could bowl on the leg-stump, making the ball come up into the body all the time, so that Bradman had to play his shots to leg. . . . I went along with the idea. I could see it was my only chance. I knew I couldn't swing the ball after two or three overs and then I could see myself pounding down on the hard Australian wickets, panting and perspiring under a blazing sun . . . he had pasted me two years ago when I could swing the ball. What would he do to me in Australia?"

Jim Cutmore was the first batsman in England to face Larwood's fast leg-theory. For eight seasons he had been opening the innings for Essex, but never in all those years of county cricket could he remember such a strange-looking field as met his eyes when he and Pope walked to the Leyton wicket on 4 August 1932, the second morning after the meeting at the Piccadilly. No fewer than six fieldsmen were stationed close to the bat on the leg-side, with two more behind them on the boundary and one solitary figure in front of the wicket on the off-side. There could be no possible doubt about Larwood's intentions. The first ball was wide on the leg-side and very short; the rest of that over and the succeeding overs were the same, except that the bowler's aim seemed to be improving all the time, more and more on the line of the batsman's body.

This was utterly unlike Essex's previous experience of Larwood. In the last couple of summers his pace had grown to a lightning speed and one or two of the county batsmen, unable any longer to pick up the flight of the ball, would play forward to every delivery, trusting to their knowledge, said Cutmore, that if the ball was short it would fly safely over their heads. Obviously some very different technique was now demanded. Cutmore found that by sliding his right foot across before the ball was delivered, being in position to swat at each rising delivery as it flashed by, he could get many of them away through the field. It was not a particularly safe method, but the first essential was to get rid of that "hideous circle of clutching hands."

Cutmore very bravely made 49, without ever feeling that he could "play himself in" against such bowling, Pope, 25 and Wilcox, 68, and at one stage Essex was 2 – 144, with Larwood resting and Voce also licking his wounds. But the "new" bowling took its toll in the end. Larwood was brought back for O'Connor and his first ball to him struck him a terrible blow in the groin, knocking his protector inside out and obliging O'Connor to be assisted from the field and later taken to hospital for treatment. After that the remaining batsmen were inclined to lash out at Sam Staples at the other end and get themselves out. He didn't expect to sight the ball, said George Reynolds Brown, Essex's No. 8, but he felt he was tall enough to hold his head well up and out of the way. For a couple of overs he was hit all over the body, and two days later the Essex side would never forget the sight of his bruises when he stripped down in the dressing-room for their next match against Somerset at Weston-super-Mare.

In the end Essex easily saved the game, severely dented Nottinghamshire's hopes of taking the Championship, and very ironically, in view of the havoc suffered by Essex, caused Carr and his men to return to Trent Bridge feeling that Larwood leg-theory was a flop. As Carr wrote, "To be effective, leg-theory demands almost perfect direction and length, and at first 'Lol' could not command these when he was bowling it. He gave a great many runs away on the leg-side. The batsmen who first played leg-theory in this country took tea with it." Nottinghamshire didn't try it again until their second-last match of the season, when theymet G lamorgan at Cardiff. On a batsman's wicket, offering absolutely nothing to the faster bowlers in the way of pace or bounce, Glamorgan were coasting easily along when Larwood switched the bulk of his field to the leg-side and directed his attack outside the leg-stump, with a view to slowing down the rate of scoring.

The move had precisely the opposite effect. Coming up to just the right height at a nice comfortable pace, the "bumpers" were an invitation to almost any batsman, let alone to one of such pugnacious temperament as Maurice Turnbull. With the enthusiastic support of Dai Davies, he smacked them to the boundary with the greatest gusto and the score mounted by leaps and bounds. Turnbull eventualy reached his first double-century in first-class cricket; Davies also hit a century and Glamorgan's 502 not only broke all sorts of club batting records, but rekindled such enthusiasm for Welsh cricket, claimed the secretary, and brought in such a rush of subscriptions as enabled the club to survive a very lean period financially, and afterwards to prosper. That evening, after getting themselves well and truly blotto, the men of Nottinghamshire are said to have strode out into the middle and urinated upon that ridiculous wicket.

Meanwhile, Larwood's new style had acquired various imitators. At Scarborough, for Essex versus Yorkshire on 11 August, Kenneth Farnes experimenting with a modified form of leg-theory was hit for 75 in four overs by Sutcliffe and Leyland. Then at The Oval on 20

August an even more notable case of fast leg-theory occurred. Bowes of Yorkshire placed five men on the leg-side for Hobbs and Sandham and proceeded to send down "very short balls which repeatedly bounced head-high and more." Fisher, a left-hander who came on after Bowes, had six men on the leg. Hobbs was extremely angry about it. He kept walking down the wicket and patting the pitch near Bowes' end, causing the crowd to boo the Yorkshireman every time he touched the ball. In a way it was reminiscent of the time when Clem Hill wandered down the wicket to tell Trumper he believed the bowler was throwing. "I know," Vic whispered back, "but don't say anything. They might take him off." Hobbs may not have approved of bumpers in theory, but nobody handled them better. He raced to 50 in 45 minutes and Bowes was taken off.

Next morning however the storm really broke. "That is not bowling," accused Plum Warner in the *Morning Post*, referring to Bowes. "Indeed, it is not cricket. If all fast bowlers were to adopt his methods, M.C.C. would be compelled to step in and penalise the bowler who bowled less than half way up the pitch . . . I appeal to Bowes and to others, if any, who may have influenced him to his present style, to get him back to orthodoxy."

Warner's strictures were later to be the subject of great discussion in Australia as well as in England, the suggestion being very plainly put that Warner was a hypocrite. But there is really no doubting his sincerity. As long ago as 1910 he had not hesitated to air his views about fast leg-theory when W. B. Burns bowled it, with six men in the short-leg area, for Worcestershire versus Middlesex at Lord's. Warner was not alone in his protests, and this form of attack, "utterly against the interest and the spirit of cricket," he wrote, was not long persisted in. Again, in his capacity as editor of *The Cricketer*, he objected no less strenuously when McDonald bowled bumpers with a strong leg-side field against Nottinghamshire in 1927. But McDonald just went on bowling bouncers when the spirit moved him and the practice spread. That was the difference between cricket before and cricket after the War.

The real question on this occasion was whether he was addressing himself primarily to Yorkshire as he appeared to be, or primarily to Jardine, captain of Surrey and captain of the touring side which Warner had helped select, and was now going to manage. Had he received some inkling of the tactics Jardine intended to pursue in Australia, and thus sought to advertise his disapproval of them? Did he know for instance, that Bowes, although not in the touring party at this stage, remained nevertheless a figure of great interest to certain of his co-selectors? These, by the way, were now five. Jardine was the fourth, automatically co-opted as appointed captain of the touring side; the fifth was Lord Hawke, who as chairman of M.C.C.'s Cricket Committee, was ultimately responsible for the tour. Once a captain has been selected,

Fender had written in *The Game of Cricket*, the authorities "should only be in an advisory position towards him so far as the actual picking of the side is concerned. They should first approve his policy and thereafter assume no more than the position of advisors to whom he turns for opinions."

In this case, it so happened, Jardine and Lord Hawke, who took the chair at the selectors' final meeting, were united in their high opinion of the Yorkshireman, while Percy Fender was another who admired him and had wanted him in the England side as early as 1931. Bowes had that invaluable quality in the fast bowler, of being able to make the ball lift; he had also developed a very useful outswinger, but more than that, he had demonstrated that he was adaptable. When there was little life or swing to be exploited from the conditions, he would station a man on the leg-boundary as a possible precaution against being swung for six in that direction, and proceed to bowl bouncers. Lord's may not have approved. The Rev. J. H. Parsons described his bowling as "disgusting," but Bowes was a disciple of Ted McDonald and never forgot the great man's advice to him at Sheffield in 1931 after Holmes and Sutcliffe had put on 323 for the first wicket against Lancashire. "You see what happens when they get things their way. They rub it in. There's no mercy. When things go your way, have no mercy. Give 'em hell and they'll think more of you for doing it." He never "hurried to offer sympathy to a victim," said Bowes. "I never said 'sorry' to a batsman whom I had hit; never went to inquire how he was. I tried to keep my face expressionless at all times." Bowes found his spells of bumpers a very paying proposition during the summer of 1932, though he didn't seem to be attracting attention at the highest level until he began bouncing them at Jack Hobbs at The Oval. He was still very much a dark horse for Australia. On 14 August three more invitations were issued – to Leyland, Verity and Tate, with a statement that Robins was unable to go for business reasons and was to be replaced by another bowler, later announced as T. B. Mitchell, the Derbyshire googly bowler.

Meanwhile Nottinghamshire still had one match to play in the County Championship, against Lancashire at Old Trafford where Ted McDonald had once been the terror of the visiting batsmen. The wicket was still damp when Larwood and Voce took up the attack before lunch. Sawdust was needed, but after lunch it began to dry out and then, reported the *Manchester Guardian*, the fun began. "Larwood came back, like a lion after meat. He had three men close in on the leg-side and two fine long-legs and he played on the leg-stump like lightning on a blasted oak."

Voce got Iddon. Larwood soon had Hopwood and in came Parkinson, "a tiny Ajax," to defy the lightning and try to shift that leg-trap. He hit one ball clean through Carr at short-leg; knocked him over backwards with another hit and made 48 before he was caught behind off a wild swing. Ernest Tyldesley was still there however, and playing one of the bravest innings of his life. Larwood took the new ball and bowled an over or two to four slips and an off-side field. Tyldesley hit him cross-bat past the bowler for four, whereupon "Larwood promptly switched his field to leg and knocked over Tyldesley's leg-stump." In Lancashire's second innings, in poor light, a leg-theory field was set at the very beginning. Paynter was bowled for 1. Tyldesley, hit in the face by his first ball, was soon bowled by another. Watson was caught behind, and Larwood had three quick wickets before rain brought play to a halt.

Fast leg-theory may have upset Lancashire, yet neither Duckworth nor Ernest Tyldesley with their previous experience of Australia could be persuaded to agree with Carr that it was likely to work out there. Still, their opinion hardly mattered for the moment. Larwood had told Jardine he thought it was worth trying. He had given him his word on that, and he intended to prove to his skipper that he was a person to be trusted. Nottinghamshire's programme was now concluded, but there remained the usual festival and end-of-season matches traditionally used by M.C.C. touring parties to bring the players together as a team, accustom them to playing with each other and so on. "For a captain to have confidence in every man on his side," Fender had laid down, "it is implied that his own knowledge of the game must include an actual, if not intimate, knowledge of the individual ability of each one. Their greatest strengths, their greatest weaknesses, their temperaments, and the way in which he can best bring out and use their powers to his own ends, must be a knowledge that he has at his finger-tips."

In this case Jardine could not be with his men in the last hectic days before the team got away, and in the three matches played under the leadership of Bob Wyatt, his trusty lieutenant, M.C.C.'s "Australian Team" met with only mixed success. An H. D. G. Leveson Gower's Eleven had the better of a rain-affected encounter at Scarborough and then at Folkestone the team suffered a real shock. Against a not over-strong Rest of England side they were all out 213, to which their opponents replied with 3 – 159 at the end of the first day. Five of M.C.C.'s front-line bowlers, Larwood and Tate, Voce, Verity and Mitchell were playing in this match; little wonder that Leveson Gower had been bold enough to criticise the composition of the touring party's attack only a few days before.

After the Rest's first wicket had fallen for 4, Woolley and Bryan Valentine, the young Kent amateur, came together and put on 108 in only 70 minutes. Woolley with his long reach was a magnificent driver, and with the ball coming nicely onto the left-hander's bat on a very fast wicket, he struck Larwood several times to the off-boundary, to which the fast bowler retaliated by dropping them shorter and shorter. Both Woolley and Valentine however were accomplished hookers of the ball, and thus partly in self-defence and partly in the hope of getting them caught hooking, Larwood switched his field to the leg-side. The two batsmen, Woolley in particular, were subjected to a barrage of short-pitched deliveries, causing Woolley at one point to walk down the pitch and ask, "Are you trying to hurt me, Harold?" Larwood looked suitably abashed, it was thought, but the bombardment continued and when Woolley was eventually dismissed by Verity for 75 he was a mass of bruises from shoulders to legs. Verity also disposed of Valentine before stumps and thenceforward M.C.C. took charge of the match.

The following morning Maurice Nichols made a few runs turning Larwood down through the leg-trap, but he was so under-confident against the fast bowler that he arranged with his batting partner, the veteran South African Herbie Taylor, that Taylor should take as much of Larwood as possible in the belief that the fast bowler would be loath to hurl his thunderbolts at him. His pace indeed was blinding. None of the players had seen faster bowling in England when the Nottinghamshire man took up the attack in the Rest's second innings. He bowled Hone for 2, Valentine for 22, Nichols for 2, in each case one of the stumps cartwheeling back as far as Duckworth standing half way to the boundary. Harry Parks on the boundary at third man had always considered himself fleet enough to cut off snicks and edges through the slips, but with Larwood's bowling he had no chance.

But cricket is the most astonishing game. In the final match of the season, Yorkshire, the county champions, versus Wyatt's Rest of England side, Larwood and Voce were quite ineffective on the comparatively lifeless surface of the Oval wicket. While Bowes for Yorkshire was in his element. With an advantage in height of 8 to 9 inches over Larwood, he found he could dig them in and get more response from a wicket like The Oval than even Larwood was able to. On the first day, reported Neville Cardus, "none of England's bowlers looked likely to get Grimmett out, let alone Bradman." But on the second day against a much superior array of batsmen than that to which the Rest bowlers had been opposed, "Bowes made his attack rear in circumstances where Larwood was unable to achieve a pennyworth of evil." Jardine and Fender, as we know, had long had Bowes in mind, though continuing to have doubts about him. He was neither quite as fast nor as accurate as their plan required. Bradman would murder anything loose. And yet against some of the most formidable players of fast bowling in England, with nothing much in the pitch to help him, the Yorkshireman took 7 – 65. The conclusion was inescapable. "Bowes will have to go to Australia," Cardus proclaimed in the *Manchester Cuardian*, "No other cricketer could have got so much life out of a sleepy wicket. To take Allen to Australia and not Bowes would be fool's folly."

Warner's opinion of his bowling methods didn't seem to matter. On the third morning of the match, while the players were waiting for the weather to allow play to resume, Bowes was plucked from the Yorkshire dressing-room and told he had been chosen for Australia. He was to take a train and go straight home, so as to be ready to join Sutcliffe and the other Yorkshire members of the touring party at Leeds Central station in three days' time.

The news, that four fast bowlers were going to Australia, certainly caused a stir in the cricket world. For several weeks now keen followers of the game had been aware of "something in the air"; of some plan for stopping Bradman evidently connected with the new form of fast leg-theory currently being tried out. But four fast bowlers! From Sussex came a report that Maurice Tate had had a nervous break-down and wouldn't be making the trip. It may have been a coincidence, but with so many other new-ball users in the side, it surely looked as if his own plans for stopping Bradman would have to be forgotten.

What then, did it all portend? In Melbourne H. Drysdale Bett, editor of the *Australian Cricketer*, had been studying the writings of the seemingly well-informed Mr. Cardus, though without being able to decide exactly what was in store. "But we have been too soft with these Antipodeans," Cardus seemed to be saying. "We want again the spirit of Grace, the Leviathan, the captain who gave nothing away. Away with mistaken notions of chivalry. Cricket is a man's game. Jardine is a man's man . . . the great crystal of Cricket is turning round . . . for us there are to be new delights . . . the poetry of Battle."

CHAPTER SIX

The Bodyline Series

On 22 September, five days after the *Orontes* left Tilbury with the M.C.C. side, the *Monowai* arrived in Sydney with the Australian cricketers who had been touring Canada and the United States. They had been away four months and in that time travelled 6000 miles across the North American continent and taken part in 51 matches. It had not all been serious cricket and mostly great fun but, as Bill Ives, Bradman's old St. George skipper, confessed to an interviewer, they had probably overdone it. Too much cricket had left some of them a bit stale. Bradman for one had suffered greatly with his teeth at various stages of the tour and was very off-colour at the end of it. Still, he had scored 3782 runs and taken more than 100 wickets. Jessie had enjoyed the trip, and after a nice rest coming back across the Pacific, he was all set for the approaching season, he told the reporters. Kippax said he wasn't going to look at a cricket bat for two weeks at least, but Bradman was playing again within a few days.

Once again, however, exactly like the aftermath of his triumphant return to Australia in 1930, trouble had been quietly brewing in the background. On the very day he arrived home the Board at its annual general meeting re-affirmed its stand against player-writers. Four years before when another M.C.C. party was on its way to Australia, various members of it had taken great exception to certain comments by Ponsford and Hendry in a Melbourne newspaper. Possibly sensing which way the wind was blowing, Ponsford now threw up his job with the *Herald* for a clerical post at the Melbourne Cricket Ground. It was a little disturbing for the Bradmans who were about to move into a new home on the north side of the Harbour on the strength of Bradman's apparently assured prospects, but not to worry too much at this stage for the Board had also announced that special cases would receive special consideration upon application for exemption from the ruling. So Bradman applied, along with young Jack Fingleton, a fellow-journalist also in the running for a Test place and was shocked to learn that his application was rejected. Fingleton's was successful. While the latter obviously belonged to the category of "one whose sole profession is journalism", Bradman could not be so considered, he was told by the chairman of the Board.

It was a bit steep. That these mainly elderly gentlemen of the Board were prepared to devote so much of their time to a disinterested running of the game was to their credit. Nobody disputed that. Nor, that in arriving at their decisions they honestly believed themselves to be acting in the best interests of all concerned. But how far were they in touch with the modern game? They were not, for instance, like the M.C.C. committee, a body composed largely of former distinguished cricketers, captains of England and the like. With one or two exceptions, the members of the Australian Board, Robertson, Oxlade, Scrymgour, Hutcheon and so on, had never been heard of as first-class cricketers. Rather they had worked their way up through the administrative ranks beginning at club level, and thus in almost every issue dividing the game, it was not surprising to find the administrators in one camp, united by the same general outlook; and such eminent former players as Alf Noble, Warwick Armstrong, Clem Hill, in an opposite camp. Only recently they had been bitterly attacked by another retired Australian Test captain, Joe Darling (*Referee*, 3 February 1932). The Board had never properly looked after the players, he alleged. In the old days it had always claimed to have no money for the purpose. Now, however it was rich and things were still the same. Poor Archie Jackson, lying seriously ill in hospital, had been granted a vote of sympathy. That was all. Possibly the modern player had more avenues for making money out of the game. In retaliation however, the Board had tightened up his contract, virtually putting a pistol to his head by making him agree to all sorts of unfair restrictions before permitting him to tour.

Not all the authorities were cast in such an unsympathetic light, of course. Canon Hughes, the clergyman who had come from Melbourne specially to marry the Bradmans and was also president of the Victorian Cricket Association, was one very good friend who would do all he could to help. There were various possible ways out of the impasse. Associated Newspapers for instance would probably release him from its share of the three-way contract, the cricket-writing part. Another large Australian corporation offered to buy up the entire contract, giving him the same money and allowing him to play as much cricket as he liked, without having to write about it at the same time. But Bradman was adamant. He would accept no release from his contract. He was determined to honour it at all costs, even if it meant having to give up Test cricket. He seemed to remember that when that contract had been signed on 30 October 1931, the Board had welcomed the agreement as a means of keeping him in Australia.

No doubt matters would sort themselves out eventually. In the meantime the Englishmen had arrived in Perth and Bradman was one of five Interstate players to represent a Combined Australian Eleven against the visitors. Frankly, the thought of 10 more days in a train, 2761 miles there, 2761 miles back, appalled him. But his responsibilities were always with him of course. Urging him to do this, do that.

The West was clamouring to see him. And it might be no bad idea to take an early look at this English team with its battery of fast bowlers.

At the same time Jardine was having an early confrontation with the Australian Press. "Could we please have the team selections in good time, Mr. Jardine? The evening papers in Sydney and Melbourne go to press at midday." The effrontery of these Australians was staggering! Was he to supply names, for the convenience of some reporter, for the sake of Sydney and Melbourne? He lost his temper with the man. "Do you think we've come all this way to provide scoops for your bloody newspaper?" There had been doubts about Jardine as an ambassador of goodwill when his appointment as leader was first announced. "He may very well win us the Ashes and lose us the Empire", exclaimed his old Winchester school-teacher, Rockley Wilson. "He is inflexible where cricket is concerned", wrote Ian Peebles in the *Daily Express*, "and has at times met with unpleasantness owing to his being outspoken. But not only has he made his authority respected among his colleagues, he has caused many a spectator to quail before his majestic presence and stinging satire."

On the ship going out Jardine had taken aside different members of the team individually, had pointed out how much was at stake, that they were engaged upon a campaign to win back the Ashes and that for the time being at least it would be necessary to regard the Australians as enemies. Allen was shocked when Jardine began his little pep-talk to him. He absolutely refused to change his attitude to the game just for the sake of winning the Ashes. "Well, don't worry." Jardine adopted that sarcastic tone of his. "You won't be playing in the Tests anyway." From time to time there would be further murmurs of dissent. But by and large, the team that arrived in Fremantle on 17 October was a team dedicated to beating the Australians at every encounter, Test or otherwise, and beating them by the widest possible margin.

There wasn't time to beat Western Australia outright because of rain but then came the match against a Combined Eleven. It seemed as though almost every inhabitant of the western half of the continent was determined to get a glimpse of Bradman. Groups of people were gathered at every wayside halt; large, noisy crowds were waiting at the bigger centres all along the line. Often he had to lock himself inside his compartment to escape their attentions. In Perth a huge mob took scarcely any notice of its other famous visitors, Richardson and McCabe, Fingleton and Lonergan. It had come to feast its eyes on Bradman alone. Police rammed a way through the mêlée so that he could reach his hotel.

The game itself however was a sad anti-climax. M.C.C. batted for most of two days, acquiring much-needed batting practice and Jardine eventually earned the resentment of the crowd for batting on and on against an attack so weak that Bradman was required to bowl 19 overs. "Take his bat and show him how, Don" they yelled. Then on the Friday night it rained and the Combined team was helpless against Verity spinning viciously. Bradman was caught in the slips for 3 and the Australians had to follow on. This time on a drier, firmer pitch, it was Allen who caused the most trouble. With a good following wind he was very fast and when he pitched several deliveries rather short, Bradman looked strangely uncomfortable as though convinced already that the Englishmen were after his skin. Watching keenly from the English dressing-room, Larwood was exultant. "If Allen can scare him, what am I going to do to him?", he told Freddie Brown. Bradman was soon snapped up at short-leg for 10 and "the ground hushed as if a national calamity had occurred."[1] He had come a long way to disappoint all those legions of admirers.

There was no hint of leg-theory in Perth however. Allen was the only fast bowler played against the Combined Eleven and he had already made it absolutely plain to Jardine that he wasn't going to bowl it. Bowes was evidently not part of the overall strategy either. Or not yet at any rate. In M.C.C.'s next match against South Australia he began bowling to the kind of field he normally used in England, off- and leg-slips distributed equally on both sides of the wicket and only one or two in front of the wicket. Vic Richardson relished Bowes' short stuff just as he had relished Voce at Nottingham. The first time Richardson hooked him to the fence at the beginning of South Australia's innings Bowes turned to Jardine and asked for another man on the leg. "No", replied Jardine, "but you can have five."

To show how unfair he was, says Bowes, "I bowled another bouncer. Vic hit this one high in the air towards the leg-boundary. Again I asked Jardine if I could have another man to leg. "I told you," came the answer, "you can have five but you cannot have one". It was an attitude I had never met before from my captain and not prepared to accept this for an answer, I continued to bowl nice, juicy long-hops down the leg-side until Jardine either gave me the extra man or took me off. He took me off". But the story had a happy ending. Jardine was an expert at dealing with injured feelings, when he chose. That evening the two men walked back to their hotel through Torrens Park and Jardine confided something of his plans concerning Bradman and the Test matches ahead. Not too much, but Bowes was content. He didn't question his skipper again.

It was indeed remarkable the way Jardine was pulling his team into shape. Sutcliffe, Leyland, Hammond, Pataudi, Wyatt, every single one

[1] It must be said that Bradman's recollection of these events does not match the recollections of three surviving members of the M.C.C. side. The above is the English version.

of his main-line batsmen was getting runs. Grimmett, of course, was their chief enemy. He was bowling immaculately against them for South Australia, not giving away any of his latest tricks but pinning the visitors down, until Larwood came in to bat. In 42 minutes, in one of the greatest displays of scientific hitting Adelaide had ever seen, he scored 81 runs and Grimmett was the principal victim. It was all over very quickly and that little burst of late hitting may not have seemed of great significance in M.C.C.'s grand total of 9 – 634 declared but Grimmett did little against Jardine's men for the rest of the tour; while Larwood developed into a Test match all-rounder, a very useful addition to M.C.C.'s store of late middle-order batsmen, Ames, Allen and Verity, which Jardine liked to refer to as his "concrete in the middle."

Freddie Brown was yet another all-rounder vaguely in the running for a Test place and none of them could be certain upon whom Jardine's choice would alight. Press reporters might complain about his giving them no prior warning of team selections, but it was worse for the players, the whole 17 of whom were more than once changed and in their flannels in the dressing-room without having been told who was going to play. There were one or two who intensely disliked being treated in this way but on the whole it would only spur them on to greater efforts still. Western Australia and the Combined Eleven were completely outplayed. South Australia and Victoria were beaten by an innings and plenty to spare, and Jardine was able to approach M.C.C.'s biggest test so far, versus an Australian Eleven in Melbourne, with a record unequalled by any former M.C.C. skipper in Australia.

The only matter of which he was not confident was his own batting and it may have been mainly for that reason that he made the surprising decision to miss the Australian Eleven match and go fishing instead. "I had one hobby which stood me in good stead throughout this tour. There is no better way of seeing a country or of forgetting the troubles of life than to pursue the gentle art of Izaak Walton". Moreover, Wyatt was an efficient and wholly reliable deputy. He knew the plans. He had led Jardine's team creditably in England before its departure for Australia and Wyatt's Test place was now assured after his recent batting success against Victoria. Jardine was not so certain about his own place.

Bradman arrived in Melbourne with Mrs. Bradman, in a much happier frame of mind than the one in which he had departed from Perth. He had never felt consistently well since returning from America; he was no longer writing regularly for the *Sun* while his dispute with the Board remained unresolved; but in Sydney on 5 November he had played an innings regarded as perhaps the most brilliant ever seen there, 238 in 200 minutes against Victoria. Woodfull just couldn't set a field to check him. 24,650 people left the ground feeling that with Bradman in this form nothing could stop Australia holding on to the Ashes, though the day had hardly improved the prospects of two young bowlers in whom the Test selectors had become interested; Fleetwood-Smith, slow left-hand, and H. H. Alexander, fast.

But alas, what a world of difference there was between the M.C.C. attack and the Victorian. Victoria had just the one fast bowler, Alexander. M.C.C. had four, Larwood, Voce, Bowes and Allen, all playing together for the first time, all obviously part of a pre-arranged plan. "We saved it up for the fifth match of the tour," said Larwood, "because we wanted to get Don in strong company before giving him the full blast of our fast leg-theory tactics." By "strong company" Larwood meant Woodfull. Bradman might be the real villain of the piece in English eyes, but Woodfull was his invaluable ally, his chief aider and abetter. Again, how purposeful was M.C.C.'s bowling, after the Victorian. Very early on, Woodfull opening for the Australian Eleven with O'Brien, the left-hander, was struck "a sickening blow" over the heart that caused play to be held up for several minutes. Fieldsmen supported Woodfull while he regained his breath and slowly recovered from the shock, and then Larwood's next ball was aimed, or so it seemed, at the very same part of the batsman's anatomy, though it didn't rise quite as high and Woodfull was able to meet it with the bat.

Bowes at the other end was nowhere near as menacing, but he kept bumping them unpleasantly on the line of the body, not allowing the two Victorians a moment's relaxation. When Larwood came off Voce took over, bowling to his now familiar leg-trap; Larwood then replaced Bowes at the far end and so it went on most of the day, the attack being shuttled between these three, and the fourth fast bowler, Allen, held in reserve, kept fresh for a renewed assault late in the afternoon, if necessary. "No one watching", said *The Australian Cricketer*, "could fail to be impressed by the effect on the batsmen's morale." In the Australian dressing-room conversation had stilled to muttered undertones, eyes never left the play, with those waiting to go in pacing up and down behind. Nobody knew what to say. They were all stunned into silence.

Somehow, with the aid of numerous snicks, no-balls and byes (the strain on Duckworth was similarly severe), the openers took the total to 51 before Woodfull was lbw, Bowes. What now would Bradman do? Bowes was the bowler and he immediately began swinging at the short ones as though determined to get rid of that close leg-field for a start. He took 13 from Bowes' second over to him and when Larwood returned in that bowler's place, he stepped back and square-cut his first ball for four. He ducked the next and hooked the third for another four. This of course was the response expected from Bradman. Accuracy was the counter prepared for it – a field accurately placed within a small compass of oval wherein the accuracy of the bowler would oblige the batsman to confine his shots. For O'Brien for instance, with his penchant for having a go outside the off-stump, Larwood had no fewer than five slips. For Bradman he had a predominantly leg-side field that included two long-legs both very fine and two slips, halfway to the fence evidently waiting for the skier from an attempted hook.

For weeks the newspapers had been full of the approaching "duel between Bradman and Larwood" as they liked to call it, and yet when this vital confrontation at last took place there was scarcely a Pressman present, expert or non-expert, who appreciated the full significance of what was going on right under their noses. Conceivably there had been faster bowling before, who knows, but certainly never before so fast and at the same time so accurate and consistently on the line of the body. Larwood claimed that his fast leg-theory was less physically dangerous to the batsman than it appeared because it was predictable. If the bagsman could feel assured of the direction of every delivery, he could take evasive action in good time. For instance in one over to Bradman five balls in succession pitched on the line of the leg-stump, five times brushing the batsman high on the hip as he moved inside them. It was true. He kept uncannily on the spot. But the incalculable factor in this situation was the pitch. On the Australian wickets of 1932–33 the ball simply didn't come through at a predictable height all the time. The batsman who remained fast at his post was bound to get hit and hit frequently, and in the end it would affect his batting whoever he was.

In this first clash with Larwood leg-theory in Melbourne Bradman was patently far from his usual self. He played some tremendous strokes, but the sense of being in absolute command, the impression he customarily conveyed, was quite lacking . . . "once he fell backwards while getting into position to play Voce and [still managed] to play him safely to the on for a single." However his end was definitely unlucky. With his score, 36, he was judged lbw to Larwood by Umpire Richards, "after moving right across his wicket to play the ball", said the *Australian Cricketer*.

After Bradman was out at 105 the middle-order batting immediately disintegrated but the tail wagged vigorously thanks to a very brave innings and the example set by P. K. Lee, a great friend of Vic Richardson's and a fellow Australian Rules footballer. Lee was the only one besides Bradman to attack the bowlers rather than let the bowlers attack him and an Australian Eleven reached a presentable 218 in reply to M.C.C.'s 282. There then followed on the third morning a totally unexpected M.C.C. collapse that caused Jardine, just back from his week-end trout-fishing excursion to the Snowy Mountains, to hasten out to the ground for an urgent lunch-time consultation with Wyatt. M.C.C. was all out 60 (Nagel, 8–32), and after that no play was possible until Tuesday, making Jardine's rush trip completely unnecessary. But it was surely significant of his current assessment of his bowlers in this hour of peril that when the Australians began their second innings needing only 125, the attack was opened this time by Larwood and Allen instead of Larwood and Bowes. There was no leg-theory in this innings but then only six overs could be bowled before the rain set in again. They were six furious and eventful overs however. In poor light Woodfull was caught behind off Larwood for 0; then Bradman late-cut him to the fence off a ball rising well above his head and wide to the off. He took two more boundaries off Allen and was missed from him, but the light was becoming very bad, a fine mist blew across the ground and Larwood took advantage of the conditions to put in a yorker which Bradman just failed to get down on.

He had now scored only 62 in four innings against M.C.C. and he was more determined than ever, despite the feeling that there was something definitely wrong with his health, to come to grips with the new bowling and conquer it. Jardine was equally as determined that he should not. Larwood, the clear victor of this first round, was rested from the next match against N.S.W. in Sydney and Jardine opened the bowling this time with Voce and Allen. Maurice Tate was also in the side, his first game since his late arrival in Australia following his illness, but what Melbourne had proved above all else was the importance of the non-stop assault. No other bowler would ever command the same degree of physical menace as Harold Larwood, but the speed and sheer aggressiveness of Gubby Allen, the consistently short-pitched deliveries of Voce and Bowes were sufficiently intimidating to ensure no let-up. Tate, although he did very well against N.S.W., was just not part of the plan and never could be.

Fingleton and Bill opened the innings for N.S.W., and "there was nothing half-hearted" about Bill Voce, said Fingleton. He bowled with studied intent at the body, the ball pitching short of the half-way mark and sometimes shorter. A Melbourne journalist "Buns" Wilmot, who made it his business to examine the pitch at the end of the first day, claimed that many balls delivered by Voce pitched within 24 feet (8 yds) of the bowling crease. Voce took only one wicket in N.S.W.'s first innings of 273. Allen and Tate got the rest. Yet Fingleton who batted all day and carried his bat for a gallant 119 would remember scarcely anything about his great innings except the bowling of Voce and the terrible battering he received that day . . . "a blow on the ribs would of a certainty be followed the very next ball by a delivery of similar length, elevation and direction. For a time several members of the English leg-trap either offered apologies when a batsman was hit or gave a rubbing palm in solace, but a continuation of such courtesies would in the circumstances have been hypocritical."

There was nothing in the pitch to account for N.S.W.'s discomfiture. When M.C.C. batted Harry Theak for N.S.W. placed a leg-field for his fast bowling and caused Sutcliffe and Wyatt no concern whatsoever. Theak was neither fast enough nor accurate enough and he had no captain like Jardine who had come to Australia with this scheme for recovering the Ashes, had thought it out in all its technical and psychological implications and would see it through, come what may, to the bitter end. For instance, the leg-theory of Larwood and Voce demanded not only certain qualities in the bowler but also a fielding side sharp enough to pick up the edges and mishits in the close-in leg-trap positions, able at the same time to stand its ground unflinchingly when the batsmen counter-attacked. It was much easier when Larwood was bowling, but the others were always liable to pitch one too short, or it simply didn't bounce as expected, and fielding in the leg-trap was like facing a one-man firing-squad with a Stan McCabe, perhaps, for executioner.

McCabe scored 67 in the N.S.W.'s first innings, the only member of the side successfully to attack the bowling rather than just patiently endure it like Fingleton, and it seemed that for the time being at least Jardine would just have to abandon this leg-side attack. Except that to retreat now would be to give in prematurely; to admit that the theory was too frail to withstand its first really severe test. No! This was rather the moment to stand firm. Two McCabe hook-shots flashed to the fence, the leg-field dived for cover – and Jardine beckoned a fifth man across to join the cordon. As it happened McCabe was out only one or two overs later, and after the match M.C.C.'s skipper wrote sternly to Fender, assuring him that their strategy was working according to plan, though so many of the Australians' shots were tending to the on-side that he had been obliged to increase Voce's leg-trap from four to five and envisaged the situation in the Test matches ahead where it might be necessary to have seven men on the leg.

This wasn't the only occasion however when his team's loyalty would be strained to the uttermost. Not only physical courage was involved, but the ability to still one's inner doubts as well. Before the year was out the news arrived from England that the Jam Saheb was one of a small group of old cricketers who had come out vehemently in opposition to M.C.C.'s tactics. Until this point Ranji's protege, the Nawab of Pataudi, had been a willing member of the leg-trap. Now, and it may have been no more than coincidence, he declined to join it. "I see His Highness is a conscientious objector" Jardine told him mockingly. Pataudi replied in kind, but defiance like this was to prove his downfall in the end. Having played in the first couple of Tests he was dropped from the remainder, received few further opportunities and returned prematurely to India.

In the meantime N.S.W. had become the third State side to be beaten by more than an innings. M.C.C. made 530 in reply to the opposition's 273 and then in N.S.W.'s second innings the wickets began falling to Voce that had morally been his in the first innings. Kippax and McCabe were each caught on the fence hooking. Hird cocked one up to the leg-trap. Bradman was bowled offering no shot. He had played on the first day feeling far from well and been lbw Tate, 18. He fielded on the Saturday, but "with a splitting head-ache, a sore throat and a temperature", and couldn't appear on the following Monday. After 26,000 on Friday, only 2000 turned up on the final day, not expecting to see him bat, but to everyone's surprise he came in at No. 6 and began cautiously but soundly enough. Five men clustered in Voce's leg-trap, but Bradman appeared to take little notice of them, simply moved across his wicket and watched the high fliers whiz past well out of harm's way. He was subdued but looking perfectly safe when an intended bumper from Voce failed to bounce as expected and knocked back his middle stump with Bradman outside the off-stump and with his back to the ball. It was a humiliating end, even for a sick man, the memory of which would leave a scar for life. "A ball pitched on the stumps", he makes the point in his *Art of Cricket*, written 25 years afterwards, "must be watched no matter how short it may be."

He went straight back to bed and for the next couple of days nobody, not even himself probably, knew whether he would be playing in the Test match beginning that Friday or not. Finally however he realised he just couldn't play the way he was, Fingleton stood by to bat in his place at first-wicket down, and a medical examination by two specialists was arranged by the Board. He was "organically sound", the doctors reported, but "seriously run-down". He needed two weeks' complete rest. There were no other details. The Stop-Press in the Sydney afternoon papers carried the brief announcement, "Bradman not fit! Will not play to-morrow", but lots of people may not have heard the news until too late, because the crowd on the first day was an excellent one, 46,709. Bradman was one of them, a spectator.

One might reasonably suppose Jardine to have been delighted by the report of Bradman's withdrawal. His first Test as skipper of England against Australia and his number one opponent out of the way! But he appears to have been too over-wrought at the time to see it in that light. "There is no pretending that the first Test match of an Australian tour is not a nerve-racking affair", he wrote in his account of the tour, *In Quest of the Ashes*. In fact he was gambling those Ashes on the success of his leg-theory and he was too pre-occupied with this question and the idea that without Bradman he still wouldn't be sure that the theory was correct, workable until the very end, to feel anything but anxiety. He still hadn't decided the final team, or at any rate told nobody of the selection until he lost the toss and knew England would have to field.

Larwood was flat out from his very first ball of this latest England–Australia Test series, but initially the advantage seemed to go Australia's way because the wicket was less lively than hoped and the fast bowling couldn't extract the lift from it that Jardine had been counting upon. The short ones went well over the batsman's head; those pitched further up rose to no more than hip-height. But after lunch the match turned back in England's favour. Larwood resumed with only one slip and an extra man on the leg-side, and in his first over, as if expecting more of a body-attack, Ponsford walked too far across his wicket and was clean-bowled. Fingleton was soon after taken in the leg-trap. Kippax was first hit by Voce, then beaten for pace by Larwood and out lbw. Larwood had taken three quick wickets and was immediately given a rest, but it was too soon for rejoicing because McCabe and Richardson, the pair who had destroyed Voce at Nottingham, were threatening to do so again.

From 4 – 87 the total rose steadily to 4 – 216 when Richardson was out one short of his 50. By this time McCabe had begun to go for his shots, gloriously hooking them off the meat of the bat and just managing to avoid the seven fieldsmen on the leg, finally causing Voce to pitch them up and aim at the wicket. Larwood on the other hand continued to strengthen his onside field, believing that he must be encouraged to go on hooking and in this way to get himself out. When the Australian innings came to an end the following morning however McCabe was still undefeated for 187 out of 360, and Jardine would have been much happier if he had known what the batsmen afterwards confessed to friends: that he felt himself to have been very fortunate; that he greatly doubted his ability to play another such innings against such bowling.

So England went into bat, needing a very big score if it was to avoid having to chase too many runs in the fourth innings, Jardine believed, and for the rest of the day he remained on tenterhooks as first Sutcliffe and Wyatt, then Sutcliffe and Hammond, set about building the foundations of a large total. When Wyatt was out after an opening partnership of 112, he returned to the dressing-room to find Jardine sitting behind a pillar, scarcely able to watch. "There's nothing to worry about", Wyatt assured him. "Batting's dead easy on that pitch. The ball's not turning an inch." But Jardine refused to be comforted. He was almost speechless, Wyatt remembered, only looking up at him every now and then to mutter "You must be bloody well mad."

But Wyatt was right. England made 524 in this innings and in fact the batting was to remain so solid throughout almost the entire series there was really no cause for anxiety at all. The Australian batting on the other hand was enough to induce nervous hysteria in even the most stout-hearted spectator. Ponsford for instance very soon walked right across his wicket in Australia's second innings, and just like Bradman in the N.S.W. match had his unguarded wicket knocked over by a straight ball from Voce. In the first innings Woodfull had been caught off a hook-shot, a stroke totally out of character which the batsman could not conceivably have attempted had it not been for those shattering experiences against the M.C.C. in Melbourne. In the second, he defended desperately for 20 minutes and was then bowled by Larwood for 0. The two mammoth scorers of the 1920s, Woodfull the "unbowlable", Ponsford the record-breaker", were both gone with only 10 on the board. "Drop them" was the cry in Melbourne. But really it was asking a lot to expect these two opening batsmen, both past 30, suddenly to accustom themselves to such unprecedented speed. It took time. He just couldn't pick up the flight of Larwood's fastest deliveries, Ponsford admitted after the match. He often didn't see the ball until it hit his bat or his body.

Fingleton and McCabe, much younger men, were better able to cope, and yet Fingleton had been so battered and bruised in three innings already against the leg-theory, that he now wore an elaborate kind of body-armour under his flannels. He certainly needed it in Australia's second innings. Up to this point he had faced only Voce's leg-theory; up to now it was mainly Voce who had been the target of the Hill. "Come on, Voce. This is supposed to be cricket. You're not playing baseball." There was plenty of booing and hooting whenever a batsman was hit, but it was basically a good-humored crowd until the Australian batting started to fall apart in the second innings and it saw Larwood pause deliberately in the middle of his second spell, motion a number of fieldsmen across to the leg-side and set out, with malice aforethought it seemed, to bowl at the batsmen. In the first innings, with Bradman unable to play and Woodfull out early, he had concentrated almost exclusively on the stumps and bowled magnificently, making McCabe's innings all the more memorable. But Jardine had been badly rattled by that great knock. Larwood leg-theory was the ultimate weapon, it seemed. Originally reserved for Bradman and possibly Woodfull, it was now to be brought out in any emergency. Exposed then to the full fury of a two-man leg-side attack, Fingleton and McCabe took the total to 61 when Fingleton fell to a catch in the leg-trap. McCabe was out at the same score and that was pretty much the end. If Ames hadn't missed a stumping in the last over, the players wouldn't have had to come back the next day for England to score just one run to win the match by 10 wickets. Larwood had taken 5 – 28 and not bowled as well as he had in the first innings.

Bradman was undoubtedly thankful for the opportunity of watching all this from the pavilion while he sought out ways and means of his own for dealing with the leg-theory. He didn't consider it cricket. For instance McCabe was an all-rounder, an indispensable member of Australia's not over-strong bowling attack. Would he be able to bowl effectively after being knocked black and blue while batting? However he couldn't convince various members of the Board of Control of his views. He would have to take the body-line in his stride. There had to be some solution to it. Very fortunately the blood-tests taken just before the Test match revealed that he wasn't suffering from anaemia as the doctors had feared and the Bradmans took off for a beach holiday on the south coast. "It was a lovely spot, only accessible by foot, with the beach at the end of a steep mountain path."

But not even paradise is free from all anxieties, it appeared. "It was the middle of summer and bush-fires were not uncommon. One fire threatened our tent for 24 hours, and it was only just when we thought the worst was going to happen to us that a sudden and fortunate change in the wind brought relief. Then I set fire to some bushes which I had cleared and the blaze got out of hand and seemed as if it would quickly eat up everything we possessed. So it would have too, if some hikers had not happened to come our way and helped us save our tent and belongings." Distractions like these however have a marvellous way of relieving a mind distracted in other directions. In that week or so away from it all a plan occurred to him, and when on 14 December they returned to Sydney he just couldn't wait to see his old friend Johnny Moyes, sports editor of the *Sun* and N.S.W. selector in 1926–27, to tell him of it.

He had to make runs, right? He was too fast on his feet to be hit, but he couldn't stay there all day just keeping out of the road of the ball and hope that the Englishmen would weary of their leg-theory. Too many wickets were likely to fall at the other end in the meantime. The Larwood of the present day was a much fitter and stronger individual than the Larwood of 1928–29; could keep going much longer, 11 overs at a stretch in one spell during the recent Test. With Voce and Allen to give you no rest at the other end. Well, what shots could he play? The hook-shot was no good. He wasn't tall enough to get on top of them and keep them down. The pull-shot was no good. With Larwood coming into the body most of the time he would be too cramped to play the shot; would be more likely to have his head knocked off. The plan, said Bradman, was this. "He would walk away from his wicket and try to hit the ball through the off-side field. If he succeeded, it would put the bowler off his balance and would force him to weaken the leg-field and strengthen the off-field. Then he would revert to normal batsmanship."

On 15 December the couple left Sydney to motor to Bowral and thence to Melbourne. Naturally he hadn't been available for the N.S.W. side to make the southern tour, but he was hoping that the N.S.W. Cricket Association would allow him to join the side for the State game in Melbourne. He would certainly need the match practice before the second Test beginning on 30 December. Also, the Association was trying very hard to have the words "solely employed in journalism" changed to "permanently employed in journalism", a possible modification of the Board's former ruling on the player-writer question that was now to be thrashed out for the last time at a special meeting of the Board on 29 December. Not until then, less than 24 hours before the second Test began, would Bradman know for certain whether he was to have a future in Test cricket or not.

They reached Melbourne on the evening of 20 December after 15 hours' driving, and never was the contrast between the countryside and the city; between the peaceful, unhurried character of the one, and the furious comings and goings of the other, more to be marvelled at. Bradman's first task was to obtain a medical certificate to prove that he was fit to play in the Shield match. Members of the Victorian Cricket Association grumbled that it was not their job to provide medical services for N.S.W. players, but the examination was duly completed. Bradman was passed fit and then the two days' play scheduled for before Christmas were washed out by rain. The game finally got under way on Boxing Day and, as it turned out, he was able to get all the practice he needed. Watchful at first against a varied attack which included Alexander and Nagel, Ironmonger and Fleetwood Smith, he gradually ran into his best form, reached his 100 in 157 minutes and then lashed out in every direction and added a further 57 in just over half-an-hour. Jardine in Tasmania was reported to have blanched when he heard the news of that.

He was fighting fit to face the Englishmen again and now the next stumbling-block was the Board. A two-thirds majority was necessary to rescind any previous Board ruling and less than two-thirds of its members, it appeared, were ready to make any concessions on the player-writer issue, just to accommodate Bradman. Nor was it thought that Bradman was prepared to make any concessions to the Board. But all this and much else was pure speculation. Following the fuss in Sydney sections of the Press had begun using the term "bodyline" in reference to leg-theory, and now another rumour began to gain ground, to the effect that not only was Bradman's position in doubt, but Woodfull's also. He was known to be very upset by the English tactics; to be contemplating even an imminent retirement from international cricket.

It was a very difficult situation for the Australian captain. Not all his fellow countrymen agreed with him in his conscientious objection to leg-theory; not by any means. In mid-December for instance the Queenslanders had arrived in Melbourne to play the first of the three matches of their southern tour under a new skipper, Eric Bensted. It was a terribly weak Queensland side, so weak in fact that loyal supporters of the game in Brisbane wondered whether Queensland would be able to retain its Sheffield Shield status. After being dismissed by Victoria for only 126, Gamble and Thurlow opened the attack for Queensland against Woodfull and Ponsford and seemed to make no impression against those broad bats whatsoever. After three overs then, Thurlow placed all but two of his field on the leg-side and bowled outside the leg-stump. Most of his deliveries were well pitched up, but several short ones hit Ponsford high on the body as he turned his back on them.

Nobody knew the reason for Bensted's sudden experiment. He might for instance have been doing no more than giving the two Test batsmen practice for their next encounter with Larwood and Voce. But, whatever the motive, there was no doubt that fast leg-theory, even in the hands of a much less competent practitioner than Larwood or Voce, had the power to upset more than one or two of Victoria's leading batsmen. Victoria made 339 in its reply, so there was obviously no call for Woodfull to retaliate through Alexander and McCormick, even supposing he had been willing to countenance the idea. But Victoria's next game in Melbourne was against N.S.W. when it quickly became apparent that Fingleton and Brown were not in the least bit interested in anything outside the off-stump. Alexander therefore aimed at the leg-stump instead, with the result that the two openers were compelled to play shots and the scoring-rate brightened with pushes and forcing strokes through the lightly-guarded leg-field. Arthur Mailey was one who thought that Woodfull would have done much better with a predominantly leg-side field-setting, even though the batsmen who followed, Bradman, McCabe and Kippax, were all stroke-makers who gave the fast bowler every chance outside the off-stump.

Woodfull however would not be moved. He couldn't forget how very soon after the Englishmen's first arrival in Melbourne and just before the Australian Eleven match, he had asked Jardine to speak to the boys at Melbourne High. The M.C.C. skipper had willingly agreed, he was punctilious about his duties and responsibilities off the field, and both he and Warner had spent several hours at the school; the visit, was a great success. Jardine was a much admired figure in Melbourne, the darling of the "Establishment" and the schoolboys alike, and the picture that Woodfull had of him at this time was of an upper-class Englishman, a little too reserved and supercilious for some Australian tastes, but the kind of person a schoolmaster would be proud to present to the boys as an example of one whom they might all look up to in this game of cricket. And then next day this same Jardine had disappeared on a fishing expedition, heedless of what his bowlers were doing to the sport, apparently unconcerned that Australian batsmen might be maimed or even killed by the onslaught. His beloved game of cricket had suddenly assumed the character of a war.

Finally, though, the morning of the match arrived and it turned out that both Woodfull and Bradman would be playing. In Bradman's case the facts that emerged were that the Board had re-affirmed its stand on the player-writer issue as most people had predicted it would, whereupon Bradman immediately informed Associated Newspapers that he would honour his contract to write about the Test matches for them. The latter however instructed him to take the field instead and Bradman then issued the following Press statement. "Through the generosity of Associated Newspapers, I have been enabled to play. Although the Board of Control continues to prevent me from earning an honourable and permanent living from the occupation of journalism, it allows others to broadcast freely though broadcasting is only temporary. The difference between the two is so small as to be ridiculous. . . . I must emphatically protest against the Board of Control being allowed to interfere with the permanent occupation of any player . . . it is certainly no encouragement for anyone to remain in Australia when such restrictions are brought in."

It proved to be a remarkable Test match from the beginning. The first surprise was the pitch. Instead of the lively surface expected of the Melbourne wicket on the first morning, it was quite docile. Neither were the conditions especially conducive to swing, and after only two overs to a conventional slip-field Larwood looked anxiously over at Jardine. "Just with the nod of the head Jardine signalled his men, and they came across on the leg-side like a swarm of hungry sharks", said Arthur Mailey. "Then the battle commenced in earnest." The run-rate was bound to be slow, with leg-theory operating now at both ends and the batsmen unable to think much about their strokes, pre-occupied with self-preservation. Voce on this comparatively gentle wicket had to bump the ball so short as to be easily avoidable. Bowes, an unexpected late inclusion in place of Verity, was the same. But Larwood was dangerous on any kind of a wicket. He was the constantly disturbing factor in the batsman's mind. As long as he was on the field, most of the Australians had been too unsettled so far to punish even the occasional bad ball; to concentrate properly on defence even against the lesser bowlers. The system worked like this. "During Larwood's absence (from the crease)", ran Mailey's report of the game, "Allen fired down a few overs and Hammond took Voce's place. With the appearance of these two bowlers the tension slackened somewhat. . . Allen's pace however was rather a surprise. After he had warmed up, he too made the ball fly and hit Woodfull in the chest. Woodfull seemed to walk into the ball in the next over. Allen bowled a good leg-ball which cannoned off Woodfull's pads and smashed into the wicket."

In seven innings against the Englishmen the Australian captain had scored but 65 runs. The sheet-anchor of the Australian batting in the two previous series against England, he had never had such a bad patch. However two promising newcomers that season, Jack Fingleton and the Victorian Leo O'Brien, who had replaced Ponsford and who now came in ahead of Don Bradman, looked completely steady and unafraid, as imperturbable as Woodfull himself. It was a shock when O'Brien was run out for 10 after more than an hour's batting; a shock, a disappointment and at the same time an occasion for relief, because the suspense of waiting for Bradman was well-nigh unendurable. Bill Bowes was bowling at the time and the scene which followed is best left to his own description, exaggerated as it undoubtedly was after the passage of time.

"The inimitable Don came in to bat amid cheering such as I had never heard before. Every step he took towards the wicket was cheered and Bradman, a cunning campaigner, came from the darkness of the pavilion and walked towards the wicket in a huge, semi-circular tour . . . he was cheered as he took up his guard, cheered as he looked round the field to see the disposition of the fieldsmen. The cheering continued at the same volume as I ran up to bowl. It was deafening. I had to stop in the middle of my run-up and wait for the noise to subside. To fill in time I asked my mid-on to move up to silly mid-on. Once again I began my run. Once again came the terrific roar. Once again I had to stop. This time I moved my fine-leg fieldsman on the boundary edge. I saw Don eyeing these changed positions with a look of determination." Finally, however, the ball was delivered. It was short, failed to bounce very high and Bradman, adjusting his hook-stroke to cope with the lower elevation, managed only to edge it onto his stumps. The crowd was stupefied. "Bradman walked off the field amid a silence that would have been a theatrical producer's triumph. The spell was broken by a solitary woman's clapping. The feeble sound rippled above the hushed throng and then an excited chatter broke out from all parts of the ground."

Even Jardine was moved to express his feelings, doing a little Indian war-dance of delight, but it was a remarkable match. Getting Bradman first ball was a tremendous coup though some of the ups-and-downs that followed were even more astonishing. Australia was all out 228, but next day on a wicket more suited to slow bowling than quick, big Bill O'Reilly aided by the great-hearted Tim Wall bundled England out for 169. Only 36,900 were there to watch this performance, but on Monday, first cricket day of the New Year 1933, the crowd had risen again to 68,188. England was up against it at this point, no doubt about it, and indicative of the seriousness of the situation, Jardine opened the attack with Larwood and Allen instead of Larwood and Voce. Allen quickly had Fingleton caught behind and after two balls of his second over, Larwood paused before walking back and looked towards Jardine, the infallible sign that he was about to switch over and attack the batsman on the leg-side.

Whatever one thought of it, on whichever side one happened to be, body-line certainly provided a thrilling, never-to-be-forgotten spectacle, frightening for the batsman perhaps, all-absorbing for the spectator. As the bowler measured out his run afresh, "the crowd counted out the yards like claps of thunder, and there was an extra special yell as he scratched his mark. Then complete silence again as he prepared to bowl. A tram miles away could be heard clattering over the points, and even Larwood's footsteps could be heard as he ran up. His arm flashed over. The ball thwacked into the wicket-keeper's gloves. There was a gasp from the crowd. The tension was snapped and again that unforgettable roar."

Just before lunch, the score 2 – 27, Bradman came in to the same thunderous reception that had greeted him in the first innings. It hadn't been much help to him then, perhaps, but he found it tremendously heartening just the same in this great crisis of his batting career. It was a grim moment, but he couldn't help smiling as the cheering died away and he heard a lone voice "Good onya, Don. Everybody in Australia is behind you, except me, and I'm a Pom." Larwood had immediately strengthened his leg-field. Bowes was given the ball at the other end. But there were to be no mistakes to encourage the bowler this time. For an over or two he watched every ball very carefully and then when Bowes bowled a really short one he hooked it gloriously to the fence to open his account. The pitch just failed to provide that extra little bit of bounce that made all the difference. The rather desperate plan that Bradman had discussed in Sydney with Johnny Moyes was simply not needed. To the ball pitched short on the line of the body the batsman was able to move across and deflect it safely down through the field. It was Bradman and Woodfull's first partnership against England since 1930 and for the first time that season it brought a sense of security to the Australian batting. Woodfull couldn't attempt some of Bradman's shots, but then no other batsman in the world could have stepped slightly back and away from his wicket like Bradman did and forced a bowler of Larwood's pace back past the bowler.

Nonetheless Woodfull kept the score moving and not until he was out with the score 78 was it apparent just how brittle the Australian batting had become these days. Richardson apart, the middle and lower sections of the order never gave a worse account of themselves and all attention concentrated on whether Bradman could reach his century before he ran out of partners. At tea he was 77 but seven wickets were down with only Wall, O'Reilly and Ironmonger remaining. Wall hung on magnificently, though without being able to score, and by the time he was out lbw to Hammond, Bradman was 96, having just taken 9 off an over from Larwood. O'Reilly was out almost immediately however and when Ironmonger came in he was still two short. The excitement was so intense that all round the ground, said Mailey, "barmen, gatekeepers, waitresses, groundsmen, cashiers, policemen," deserted their posts and rushed this way and that, searching for a spot from which to catch a glimpse.

Ironmonger survived the last two balls of Hammond's over. But then Bradman facing Voce simply couldn't manage to get the ball away. "One, two, three, four, five balls were bowled, yet Bradman still required two runs. He took a second look round the ground, gripped his bat tighter and waited for the last ball. Voce rushed up, . . . Bradman shut his teeth, and crash! the ball went soaring over the leg-fieldsmen. The batsmen ran three, Bradman was 101 and it hardly seemed to matter when Ironmonger was run out a few minutes later trying to give his partner the strike.

England needed only 251 to win but the effect on Australian morale of that wonderful century, which some people thought an even greater innings than any he had played in England, was incalculable. Wall made the initial breakthrough on a wicket that gave him no assistance at all, but O'Reilly and Ironmonger were the ones who finished the job. Their accuracy and persistence was beyond all praise, and when at three in the afternoon the last English wicket fell, 111 runs short, an exuberant crowd invaded the field to chair the Australians off and dig up pieces of the wicket to keep as mementoes of the joyful occasion. And not only were popular feelings carried away. That evening, in a gesture possibly without precedent, the Melbourne Cricket Club announced the inauguration of a Mrs. Don Bradman Testimonial Fund. In due course the Bradmans were presented with a piano with the inscription "To Mrs. Don Bradman, by numerous admirers of her husband, in recognition of his not-out century score".

Undoubtedly Jardine blamed chiefly himself for England's defeat, though Pataudi would never play for another English side under Jardine's captaincy. The skipper had made only 1 and 0 at Melbourne and was more than willing to stand down for the remainder of the series, only the entire team refused to permit it. So at Bendigo against a Victorian Country Thirteen he put himself in first, and again at Adelaide a few days later he was hard at work in the nets when a rude interruption occurred. It had long been the custom there for spectators to foregather when the players were at practice. Ordinarily they just stood and watched quietly, but for some reason this crowd was noisier than usual and when Jardine's stumps were skittled by a ball from Bowes there was an outburst of wild cheering with numerous shouted remarks and cat-calls. Soon afterwards Jardine was seen in angry conference with Bill Jeanes, as a result of which the English nets came to an abrupt end. Next day the gates were locked against the public and the Englishmen were able to practice undisturbed. Nothing more than a ripple on the surface it seemed at the time, but it proved to be the first tremors of the biggest upheaval in cricket history.

Meanwhile, all heedless of the storm about to burst, Albert Wright, the Adelaide curator, was quietly preparing one of the fastest wickets the Oval had ever known. An unusually cold spring had left the middle almost bare of grass for the early season matches, so that when the couch finally did come through in late December, it was of a fine and closely-woven texture, little trodden by human foot, the perfect surface for a fast bowler. Jardine who laid his plans meticulously in advance; who was alert to every possible development that might affect these plans, had kept himself well informed as to the latest state of the pitch, but nevertheless chose to bat when he won the toss for the first time in the series.

For Jardine personally it was a disastrous decision. By arrangement with Wyatt he had promoted himself to opening batsman and it was just his luck to have to face Wall bowling from the River End when the Adelaide wicket had never played faster nor given a fast bowler greater assistance. Wall bowled him for 3; Hammond, unsettled by several high-rising deliveries, flicked at a short one and was caught behind, and with Sutcliffe and Ames also failing England just before lunch was 4 – 30, the lowest point in the team's fortunes since landing in Australia and certainly a bitter disappointment after the very promising beginning to the tour. But Wyatt and Leyland began a revival after lunch; Paynter and Verity, the two new faces in the English side since Melbourne, carried it on, and the innings eventually lasted until after lunch on the second day. Not that 341 was a great score for the first innings of a Test match in Adelaide. Jardine was a keen student of Test match history. In 1929 England began with 334 at Adelaide and won by only 12 runs; in 1925 Australia scored 469 and only scrambled home in the end by 11 runs. For England to be certain of victory this time, Bradman would have to be knocked out of the firing-line at the earliest possible moment; fast leg-theory would just have to succeed. At 3.25, with Woodfull and Fingleton walking out to begin the innings for Australia, the moment of truth was very near.

This time England had a bit of early luck. Larwood opened from the same River End as Wall, but it was Allen from the Cathedral End who took a wicket in his first over, Fingleton nibbling at one outside the off-stump. "He wouldn't be playing in any of the Tests", Jardine had told the Middlesex fast bowler on the ship, and here in Adelaide he was opening the bowling with Harold Larwood; by sheer determination and enthusiasm he had made himself, bowling, batting and fielding in the leg-trap, into an indispensable member of the side. Not even Bradman had been altogether comfortable against him, but the next sensation occurred off the last delivery of Larwood's second over when the ball rose sharply and struck Woodfull on the chest. It must have been in almost the same place as the blow he suffered in Melbourne during the Australian Eleven match and once again he staggered away from his wicket clearly in severe pain, while the crowd hooted its head off. Jardine spoke briefly to Woodfull, then walked over to Larwood and handed him the ball, saying loudly enough for Bradman at the non-striker's end to hear quite plainly, "Well bowled Harold." This was psychology, Larwood believed, he was trying to put Bradman off, trying to unsettle him by letting him think the ball was being deliberately bowled to hit the man and that he might get the same."

After a few minutes Woodfull seemed to be alright again and Allen bowled to Bradman. He really had an amazing eye. Two deliveries from the fast bowler that were just barely short of a length; that no other batsman would have dreamed of playing other than defensively, were hooked for four and two. The over yielded six runs, not a very significant over it may have appeared from the other side of the fence, but Jardine couldn't fail to detect the note of desperation in the champion's strokes, a certain frenetic quality that Larwood leg-theory tended to induce in the batting, whoever happened to be at the crease. Frank Woolley, for instance, so noted for his fearless hooking, for the manner in which he had stood up to McDonald and more than once smashed that great fast bowler out of the attack, hardly gave the same impression of certainty facing Larwood at Folkestone. Nor Ernest Tyldesley. Nor Stan McCabe.

The fast bowler was just about to start his third over, some thought he had actually taken a couple of paces in, when he stopped at a signal from Jardine and the field was re-set for Woodfull. When it appeared that a full-scale bodyline attack was intended, the booing started again, louder and more vigorous than before, rapidly approaching the proportions of possibly the worst demonstration ever heard on the cricket-field. As Larwood ran in for the first ball of his new over, the noise swelled, hushed and then broke out into an almighty howl of rage as the Australian captain had the bat knocked out of his hands.

Australians are certainly a race of barrackers, but of good-humoured barrackers on the whole. They are not violently partisan in comparison with sporting crowds elsewhere; are usually generous in applause for their opponents and have this sentimental affection for the underdog of whatever nation. Four years before, on two separate occasions in Sydney and Melbourne, the Englishmen had been amazed at the fuss when Chapman had brought on Larwood to bowl at the elderly Ironmonger. They didn't appreciate how quick Australians are to react when they suspect that either side is attempting to take an unfair advantage.

But Chapman's offence was pale beside the action of Jardine in asking Larwood to bowl body-line after Woodfull had been hit. "Putting in the boot", this is called in Australia. "Had either he or I," wrote Jardine, "realised the misrepresentation to which we were to be subjected, neither of us would have set that particular field for that particular over." Quite so. They couldn't have realised, though the seeds of the present trouble had been sown long before. They were bound to reap the whirlwind sooner or later. "I believe", wrote Bruce Harris, a Fleet Street journalist reporting the series for the *Evening Standard*, that if some impetuous member of the crowd had set himself up as leader, any number would have followed him over the fence with unimaginable results."

Savage and sustained though the barracking was, it didn't seem to affect the actual play, or not the bowling at any rate. Bradman was soon out attempting a leg-glance and only putting up a dolly catch to Allen in the leg-trap; McCabe was out in similar fashion; finally Woodfull played Allen on and Australia was 4 – 51. Woodfull had been hit repeatedly about the body after that original blow, and as he lay on a massage-table having his bruises attended to he was visited by Plum Warner, the M.C.C. manager. Warner had come to offer his sympathy, but "I don't want to speak to you, Mr. Warner", Woodfull told him. "There are two teams out there, but only one is playing cricket. It is too great a game for spoiling by the tactics your team are adopting. I don't approve of them and never will. If they are persevered with it may be better if I do not play the game. The matter is in your hands. I have nothing further to say. Good afternoon."

Woodfull's remarks were not intended for publication of course, but somehow they did reach the Press and when the English players learned what the Australian captain had said, with the implication that their tactics were unsporting, they were as angry as their opponents. Another story current in Adelaide that week-end related how Jardine too had paid a visit to the Australian dressing-room. Not on any errand of sympathy however. The door was answered by Vic Richardson, with just a towel about his waist. "I would like to speak to Woodfull", Jardine demanded. "One of your men called Larwood a bastard. I want an immediate apology". But Richardson only looked at him derisively, turned and called out, "Hey, which of you bastards called Larwood a bastard instead of Jardine?"

At this stage the Australians believed Jardine to be more culpable than Larwood, though very soon it didn't matter, because with one or two exceptions, the two sets of players didn't speak to one another for the rest of the series. "Interest in the actual cricket disappeared", wrote Kippax, after Woodfull's disgusted utterance had been made public. Inevitably, in the circumstances, the players were tending to become less and less concerned with the game, more and more with each other. During the match Australian newspapers published a memorable picture of Leyland struggling to make his ground in the course of a sharp single. At full stretch his bat is safely inside the crease, but the batsman is half on his knees up the pitch, his head buried in his body, twisted away from the direction of the fieldsman as though fearful that the return is being aimed at him rather than at the stumps.

On Monday play resumed with Australia 4 – 109 and Ponsford and Richardson came out to bat to the sight of a body-line field settling into position for the first ball of the day. With the wicket now a shade easier and Voce apparently handicapped by an ankle injury, the ordeal by bodyline was perhaps not quite as severe as on the previous Saturday, yet it was to prove the most trying day of the entire series. All through the morning, during a splendid partnership between Ponsford and Oldfield, Larwood bombarded the batsmen with leg-theory to the accompaniment of a continuous ground-fire of booing and jeering from the crowd. Ponsford, developing the method he had first used against Thurlow in Melbourne, his body literally bulging with padding, turned his back on most of the short ones and looked safer against Larwood than he had ever looked. Eleven enormous bruises from shoulder to hip were the price he had to pay however.

Six were out for 194 when Ponsford was bowled behind his legs by Voce for 85, but Oldfield, joined first by Grimmett and later by Wall, was batting as well as he had ever batted in his life. Then the accident happened. Sooner or later, if this thing continues, Hobbs had predicted on the occasion when he was the target of Bowes' bumpers at The Oval, somebody will be killed. Not because any deliberate hurt to the batsman was intended. Simply because of the high element of risk involved. In this case, said Larwood, "I had stopped bowling bodyline and the field was set mainly on the off. I wouldn't have pitched one short at Bertie, only he could bat and he had settled in . . . Bert swung at it going for a hook, but it came off the wicket slower than he expected. He had spun almost right round, having just about completed the stroke when it hit him on the right side of the temple. I think the result would have been even worse if the peak of his cap had not broken the force of the ball. An X-ray revealed more than a black eye – he had suffered a linear fracture of the right frontal bone."

One can follow the line of thought. If you have a powerful weapon at your disposal, you don't use it indiscriminately, not against the lesser batsmen as a rule. But it is nice to feel that it is there in the bag, ready to be pulled out in case of emergency. Just so with the bodyline weapon generally. Fast leg-theory had come a long way since the day it had been conceived in England as a scientific means of curbing Bradman merely by restricting his strokes. In the heat of conflict it had developed into more of a pyschological instrument. The batsman's instinct normally is only to protect his wicket. But when the ball is hurtling about his ears, threatening to do him permanent injury, the normal instincts of batsmanship fly out the window. Batting is a different game altogether when you believe the bowler is bowling at you. It is different for the bowling and fielding side as well. They have to be more like the boxer for whom it is necessary to hate his opponent while he is in the ring with him. The ordinary niceties of the game can no longer be afforded Between wickets, Jardine would recline on the grass, making derisive remarks about each incoming batsman. He had come to Australia in 1928, the very image of British officer-class hauteur, and allowed himself to become obsessed by the natives. Strictly speaking, he should never have been permitted another spell of duty in the colonies.

Arthur Mailey, who understood the reason for body-line; who initially had quite enjoyed the spectacle of the bowler getting his own back on the batsman on those unsympathetic Australian wickets, was shocked by the events of Adelaide. In fact the injury to Woodfull, the near-fatal accident to Oldfield, had caused many an old international to think again. Jack Ryder for instance had been inclined at first to scoff at the Australian batsmen for their "timidity", remembering how he had dealt with Larwood in 1928–29; with Gregory before that. Gregory had sometimes tried to intimidate the batsman by bowling short, had occasionally caused injuries, but body-line, Ryder was now prepared to acknowledge, was different.

"One. Two. Three. Four. Five. Six. Seven. Eight. Nine. Out, you bastard," the members of an infuriated mob shouted at Larwood as he walked back to bowl. "Go home, you Pommy bastard", they shouted at Jardine as he came down to field on the fence. The average Test match spectator is not necessarily a cricket expert, but you didn't have to be an expert to feel it in your bones that this wasn't cricket, with a ring of fieldsmen lurking just out of sight, like vultures waiting for their prey. Finally, even the Board was convinced that something should be done about it. On 18 January, the fifth day of the match, a cable went off to Lords, "Bodyline bowling has assumed such proportions as to menace the best interests of the game . . . in our opinion it is unsportsmanlike. Unless stopped at once it is likely to upset the friendly relations existing between Australia and England."

A glance at Australia's totals in the five Test matches of the series shows the ravages body-line was causing. The home side did reasonably well in its first innings 360, 228, 222, 340, 435; the second innings by comparison were lamentable – 164, 191, 193, 175, 182. There weren't any deteriorating pitches to blame. The Englishmen tended to do as well, if not better, in their second efforts. The wear and tear on the nerves was more the cause. Similarly, the trend is reflected in the performances of the individual batsmen. After his 187 not out at Sydney in the first Test, McCabe played no innings higher than 32 until this final Test in Sydney. Fingleton scored 83 in the first innings in Melbourne; then 1, 0, 0, and was dropped. Ponsford's Test scores after his 85 in Adelaide were 3, 19 and 0, when he too was dropped. Richardson made a wonderful 83 in Brisbane, following it with 32, 0, and 0, for Australia, then 0 and 20 for South Australia v. M.C.C. in the tourists' last match in Australia.

Bradman and Woodfull were the exceptions to the general rule, but they had always been exceptional, each in his own way. In Australia's second innings in Adelaide, Bradman came in, No. 4 in the batting order, after the second wicket had fallen to Larwood with only 12 on the board. Having just secured Ponsford's scalp by tempting him to cut and having him caught in the gully, Larwood continued to attack outside the off-stump and Bradman in rare form pulled him, cut him and drove him for three boundaries. The bowler left the field for a few moments, came back and Bradman immediately cover-drove him for another boundary. One notable consequence of body-line was that Bradman, like most of the Australian batsmen, was being encouraged to exploit a greater range of shots than ever before. Larwood changed the direction of his attack to the other side of the wicket and Bradman glanced him through the tightly-guarded leg-field with the greatest facility. He couldn't be allowed to go on like this any longer. In the second over of Larwood's second spell, the body-line field was placed, whereupon, said Mailey, "Bradman swung wildly at every ball. The brilliant off-drives, back-cuts and leg-glances were killed by the introduction of the leg-field."

It was a perfect illustration of what the authors of leg-theory had set out to achieve. Bradman, even at his very best, could do little with the leg-theory. His wild swings simply failed to connect. At the other end Verity was bowling maiden after maiden to Woodfull. Some change in tactics was needed. So while Woodfull, encased in a body-protector, now took most of Larwood, Bradman tore into Verity. He had already forced Hammond out of the attack. He now hoped to get rid of Verity, a very necessary endeavour since, if successful, no obvious bowler would be left to plug up one end, Voce still being troubled by his ankle. Unfortunately for Australia his efforts were unavailing. After hitting the slow bowler over long-on for six (his first six in Australia and first in a Test match), he was caught-and-bowled next ball and Australia was 3 – 100.

Bradman had made 66 out of 88 in only 73 minutes, a magnificent display of attacking batsmanship in answer to defensive bowling of the highest order. "Defensive tactics in bowling," Fender had written in *The Game of Cricket*, "never include the type which permits the batsman to rest inactive ball after ball." (How well Jardine had been putting that particular precept into practice.) "Defensive bowling must never cease worrying the batsman . . . while always making the batsman play, must make it as difficult as possible for him to get runs unless he risks his wicket for the purpose." It was the peculiar genius of Larwood's leg-theory of course that by playing upon his opponent's nerves, he could still "make the batsman play" him even when he wasn't directly attacking the stumps. His dismissal of Ponsford in the second innings was a case in point.

Not everybody understood that however. The same evening, over Adelaide radio, Bradman was criticized by Kippax for "throwing his wicket away." As the most accomplished batsman in the side, said Kippax, his duty was rather to stay there and try to stick it out, like

Woodfull. In fact the Australian captain went on the next day to carry his bat for 73 out of a total of 193; a very gallant innings, though not enough to prevent Australia going down by 338 runs. That was the trouble. Sticking it out didn't conquer bodyline. Sticking it out was alright at one end, but it didn't achieve very much unless the runs were coming at the other end and in this case the rest of the batting, Bradman and Woodfull aside, totalled only 42. Bradman hadn't let the side down, any more than Woodfull. Australians would continue to pin their hopes on these two above all others and trust they would find some better method of overcoming bodyline next time.

No doubt about it, Bradman was in tremendous form at the moment. His next encounter with the Englishmen was for N.S.W. versus M.C.C. in Sydney the following week. It had rained on and off throughout the first two days and the wicket on the third morning with N.S.W. due to bat a second time was a "sticky". "I remember watching Hedley (Verity) stick his finger deep into the turf" wrote Hammond, "stand up in the Australian sunshine with a satisfied sigh and mutter 'Poor Don'. . . . But Don from the pavilion saw Verity test the turf and guessed what he said. I saw him give Hedley a very hard look when they faced one another along the pitch. Don played the game of his life that day and despite everything Verity could do, the young Australian got 70 of the best runs of his life before I managed to bowl him with an off-spinner. No one ever said 'Poor Don' to him without suffering for it, if flesh and blood and sheer dogged skill and courage could make them suffer. The very fact that he had been chased out of his wicket by Larwood and that now conditions were against him and in favour of Verity made him a thousand times more obstinately decisive than ever."

No Englishman with a life-time's experience of wet wickets could have played Verity and Hammond better. In forward defence he went all the way forward. When he went back, he went further than any of his colleagues, using the full depth of the crease. How he managed to play so close to his stumps without ever disturbing them with bat or feet is impossible to explain, except to say that he seemed to carry in his mind a blueprint of the exact position of his bat and himself in relation to the rest of the field, a product of the almost total concentration of which he was capable. Bradman's second-innings 71 out of 128 was not quite enough to save the game for N.S.W. but at one stage M.C.C. needing 110 were six down for 70. The tourists won the match by four wickets.

His value to N.S.W. was beyond computation. Because of illness and the visit of M.C.C., he could play in only three Shield matches that season, but with him N.S.W. was invincible. The final Shield game of the season was against South Australia in Sydney immediately following the N.S.W. v. M.C.C. match. There was still rain around, but except that the surface was a little greasy, the wicket was perfect. The challenge to the N.S.W. batting this time came more from the southerly that suddenly blew up. Fingleton and Bradman were going along very comfortably before lunch when a strong breeze, blowing over Wall's left shoulder and providing just the right assistance for his in-swing, made the fast bowler almost unplayable. He bowled Fingleton to make N.S.W. 2 – 87, took three more wickets in that over, and went on to achieve the extraordinary figures of nine wickets for five runs in one short spell before and after lunch. Bradman in fact was the only batsman dismissed by the fast bowler to be neither bowled nor caught behind. With the last man in, he miscued a hook and was caught at square-leg, having made 56 of N.S.W.'s 113. Wall's final analysis was 10 – 36.

The weather was not much better for N.S.W.'s second innings. But the southerly had dropped, reducing Wall to more normal proportions, and the South Australians were resigned to yet another Bradman century, probably a double-century against them, when he suddenly missed one from the off-spinner, P. K. Lee and was bowled for 97, the first time he could remember ever getting out in the nineties. He had long since abandoned all ideas of trying to get him out, the bowler claimed modestly. At the moment of delivery he was more concerned with calculating how much he had won on Astute, 8–1 winner of the Maiden Handicap at Rosehill that afternoon, and was as amazed as anybody when the ball broke in sharply and beat the bat. The innings made Bradman's Shield average for the season exactly 150. Next day N.S.W. won the match and the Sheffield Shield for the second year in succession.

Bradman's average in all games against the M.C.C. on the other hand was only 32 at this stage of the tour. Whether he would have the chance to improve it; whether there would be any further matches for him against the Englishmen was still undecided. Immediately following he Board's cable protesting against the M.C.C.'s "unsportsmanlike" tactics, Jardine had called a meeting of all members of the touring party, desiring to hear their general opinion of M.C.C.'s tactics. Jardine in fact was the only one of the 17 not present, so they would all be able to express themselves freely, he had explained. If they felt, in view of the hostility leg-theory had aroused, of the even greater hostility they might expect to encounter if it was continued, that this was the time to call it off, they had only to say so and he would abide by their decision. Sutcliffe was in the chair, and the mood of the meeting, said Bowes, was summed up in the words of Maurice Leyland, "What, give up leg-theory just because it's got 'em licked?" The next day the players issued a Press statement expressing unanimous loyalty to their captain.

The team was solidly behind him (there may have been one or two exceptions), he felt sure of that. Warner, on the other hand, was obviously against him. What was the attitude at Home, then, Jardine wondered. In his account of the tour, *In Quest of the Ashes*, he makes it quite clear that he wanted the tour to continue for the time being, but that there would be no fourth Test in Brisbane unless Lord's was able to extract from the Australian Board a public withdrawal of the allegation "unsporting". Thus there was a lull in hostilities for the moment. The return encounter with N.S.W. passed off peacefully enough, though another body-line crisis loomed ahead in Brisbane, where the Aboriginal, Eddie Gilbert was fully recovered from his shoulder injury and would be delighted to bowl leg-theory at the Englishmen. He had never bowled it before, he told the Press, but he felt sure that if he kept plugging away at the leg-stump with a leg-field, he would have much more success than hitherto.

Once again, as before the Melbourne Test, Woodfull was talking about retiring from Test cricket, plainly intimating that Richardson would be his successor, and that Richardson would retaliate with leg-theory using Gilbert, Thurlow, Alexander, Tobin of South Australia, whoever was able and willing. To add spice to the rumours, Tobin was reported to be a strong tip for Brisbane. He wouldn't hesitate to bowl bumpers if called upon, he claimed.

But indeed the great Australian retaliation campaign never got off the mark. None who knew the Australian skipper believed he really meant to carry out his threat to retire at that stage. Having come so far, he was much more likely to see it through. Moreover, Australia could hardly embark upon bodyline having so lately stigmatised it as unsporting. It was thought that Alexander might bowl it for a Victorian country side against the M.C.C. at Ballarat. However he didn't, after explicit instructions from the Victorian Cricket Association forbidding it, while at the same time Frank Gough, back as captain of Queensland in place of Bensted, announced that there would be no "Body-bowling" by Queensland under his captaincy. "It was detrimental to the game and would surely cause the withdrawal of the married men", he explained. The position in early February then was that much of the will to retaliate had been sapped; that Tobin, having been selected for Australia, had then completely lost all form; finally, that Gilbert, after modifying his action to satisfy the umpires, found he just couldn't recapture his former speed. Even without bodyline however he proved a great ordeal for Jardine when the M.C.C. skipper opened the innings against Queensland, taking in with him this time Hedley Verity.

It was near the end of the first day. There was time only for a couple of overs when Jardine, wearing his Harlequins cap, took strike and Gilbert urged on by the crowd "to get stuck into the Pommie bastard" ran in for his first ball. He may not have been as quick as formerly, but he was still very fast and quite obviously aiming at the batsman. Several deliveries flew just wide of the mark, but before the end of the over he scored one hit, on the point of the hip-bone. Jardine staggered and almost fell, but he waved back assistance as one or two players and the umpire approached him. He stood up, his face very white, and took fresh guard. Otherwise he showed no signs of being hurt and very soon he and Verity were on their way stiffly back to the pavilion, two tall Englishmen oblivious to the chant of "Bastard, Bastard" that came from a portion of the crowd that had surged onto the field and now attempted to block their way.

Police formed a lane for them and his back straight as a ramrod Jardine mounted the few wooden steps to the dressing-room door . . . walked to the table in the centre of the room, ignoring the odd remark of "Well played, skipper," and still looking straight ahead, asked if all but the England players would leave the room. When this was done, he collapsed on the table and speaking through teeth clenched in agony said, "This hip. It's giving me hell." There was in this short time an area about the size of a saucer all discoloured and in the centre an area of nearly raw flesh." "That was real courage", said Hammond, "when a cricketer sees that spirit in his skipper he remembers it always and tries to play on for his side as long as he can stand on his two feet."

Queensland was duly beaten by more than an innings, completing a grand slam of innings victories against the four Shield states, and the next day the news arrived that the Board had at last replied to M.C.C.'s quest for reassurance. "We do not regard the sportsmanship of your team as being in question." The fourth Test was on. Woodfull won the toss for the third time out of four and Richardson accompanied him to the wicket, the first time he had opened for Australia since failing in that role in 1928–29. Fingleton's confidence had been shot to pieces by the bodyline. Richardson, previously at No. 6, had at least been spared having to face a fresh Larwood and Voce in every innings and of course he possessed the ideal fighting temperament that revelled in combat.

Larwood switched to leg-theory in his fourth over of the morning, then back to off-theory for Richardson; tried leg-theory again after lunch, but all to no avail. The opening partnership had put on 133 when Bradman came in to bat and Larwood half-way through a muggy Brisbane summer's day was clearly tired. Though instantly brought back to attack the new batsman with leg-theory, he couldn't command quite his usual hostility. Bradman, uncertain at first, survived and the Australians finished the day 3 – 251, Bradman and Ponsford together and awakening all sorts of expectations. Throughout the series the sports-writers had been seizing on some brief moment of success to proclaim "Bodyline mastered at last," but it really did look like it this time.

Very late that evening Larwood returned home to his Brisbane hotel "feeling very rosy", he said. In the lounge a group of sports-writers were still talking cricket and the fast bowler bet them 10/- apiece that he would bowl the "Boy Wonder" within his first three overs of the morning. He was in many ways a very likeable sportsman. The Press liked him of course, because he provided such excellent copy, though not only for that reason. His fellow-cricketers nearly all liked him; even with many individual Australians on that turbulent tour he was very popular. There were occasions nevertheless when this seemingly mild and amiable cricketer would be transformed; would bowl like one possessed.

In the Queensland match for instance he appeared to have Oxenham caught at short-leg. The batsman made no attempt to go however. Larwood appealed first to the umpire at his end, who said "not out", his sight of the ball had been obscured by the bowler; then to the umpire at square-leg, who was similarly unhelpful. Until this point in the Queensland innings Jardine had been diligent to avoid any occasion that might revive controversy. But Larwood was wild. "I said to myself, 'I'll make you wish you'd left the wicket when you were out.' I dropped him several short ones at my fastest. They reared past his face. He went white." After a couple of overs of this, Oxenham succeeded in getting himself out to Allen at the other end and the effect on the rest of the batting was catastrophic. Queensland had seemed to be batting very soundly until the Oxenham incident. Now the innings collapsed precipitately. In its second attempt the side could manage only 81.

Larwood's greatest natural asset as a fast bowler", thought Hammond, "was a tremendous upsurge of real hostility, even anger against anybody who hit him hard." Or in any way got the better of him. Bradman knew him for an enemy from the moment in Melbourne in 1929 when he played a ball down the pitch, Larwood fielded it and the ball was returned into Duckworth's gloves "with a venom that was impossible to misunderstand." "When I bowled against Bradman," he was to confess to Fingleton many years later, "I always thought he was out to show me up as the worst fast bowler in the world. Well, I took the view that I should try and show him up as the worst batsman." There were must certain aspects of life that made him feel intensely resentful.

Thus, in spite of the heat, the slowing wicket, the absence of Voce at the other end, he managed to find a little extra that following morning of the Test match. To a tremendous cheer Ponsford hit his first ball of the day to the leg-boundary, but after that he had both batsmen ducking and weaving, moving in one direction or another before the ball was bowled, even letting go deliveries that passed perilously close to their stumps. Since the second innings in Adelaide, Bradman had been inclined to follow the practice he had once outlined to Johnny

Moyes in Sydney – to retreat to leg and force the bowler on the off-side. One beautiful square-cut off Allen rocketed to the fence, but then in Larwood's third over, he drew away from a ball that only just missed the wicket. The next ball was also short and on the leg-stump and in stepping away to try to slash it through the covers he had his leg-stump sent flying. He had made 76. In Larwood's next over Ponsford too was out. In his usual fashion. Moving too far across and making no attempt to cover a ball that went through to take his leg-stump. From 3 – 251 Australia had slumped to 5 – 267.

It is easy in retrospect to see that those few overs sealed the fate of the Ashes. Neither of the two young left-handers, Bromley and Darling, looked likely to stay very long. Or rather, when it appeared they might make a stand, Larwood switched back to leg-theory and their end was not long in coming after that. The Australians were all out 340. Their bowlers then fought back magnificently on an unhelpful wicket and England, six wickets for 216, was in some trouble until the arrival of Eddie Paynter at the crease. The little Lancastrian who had only got into the touring party at the last moment after Duleepsinhji had had to drop out; who had been included at Jardine's special desire on account of his gutsiness and determination, had already proved his worth in Adelaide. But now in Brisbane at the end of the first day he went down with tonsillitis and had to be taken to hospital. He didn't see how he could possibly bat, Warner told Jardine after visiting the patient on Sunday morning. But Jardine only smiled his grim smile and recalled the occasion when British troops suffering badly from fever had made that famous march to Kandahar.

Voce assisted to get him to the ground on the Monday afternoon and somehow he was made ready and went out to bat eventually making 83. The last four English wickets added 140 and Australia collapsed as usual in its second innings for 175. Larwood, Allen, Verity, and Mitchell shared the wickets. But it was pre-eminently Larwood who won the match for England by four wickets. While he was around, none of the Australians, not even Woodfull, could concentrate wholly upon their batting. For a while perhaps. But not for very long. Bodyline had won the series alright. But was it cricket? "The worst of Jardine's Realpolitik," wrote Neville Cardus in the London *Observer*, "is that it will satisfy the lust for sports and conquest, but nothing else."

CHAPTER SEVEN

The Decline of Bodyline

The series had already been decided, the M.C.C. had now been five long months in Australia, but there was still no sign, in the preparations being made for the final Test in Sydney, of any let-up in the battle between the players. Great numbers watched members of both sides hard at work in the nets; more huge gates were taken when the match began in hot weather on 23 February. Perhaps the spectators were not drawn merely in the hope of seeing blood, but one couldn't help sensing, in the very intensity of the duel, in the spectacle of the batsmen ducking and dodging to a continual roaring by the crowd, at least some of the atmosphere of the old Roman arena.

Towards the end of the second day Larwood was ordered in second-wicket down to act as night-watchman. He was furious, having to bat so soon after 32 overs of fast bowling, and fully intended to throw his wicket away the moment he reached the crease. But as luck would have it he survived a first few reckless swings of the bat and the spectators were given a rare treat. "I attacked the bowling at every opportunity," said Larwood. "I remember 'Bull' Alexander bumping them down at me in every over, doing his best to hit me. I knew he was trying. The Hill enjoyed it immensely. They roared as each bumper reared past me . . . 'Knock his bloody head off, Bull,' they yelled." They didn't particularly wish him harm. They just loved the excitement of it all. When he was eventually out for 98 made in two hours 20 minutes, the crowd gave him a tremendous ovation, not only on account of his fine and brave innings, but also in recognition of the man who had made that series the most gripping and memorable in Test history.

Australia assisted by a plethora of dropped catches made 435 in its first innings, to which England, aided by Larwood's 98, now replied with 454. But the actual score-board may not have been of great significance in this kind of gladiatorial contest. The most enduring memory of the match was of Larwood steaming in to bowl, his run-up growing progressively faster and more furious hour by hour, as though his only object was to finish his quarry off once and for all. "It seemed that Larwood was anxious to claim a hit on Bradman in this final Test," wrote Jack Fingleton, "a thing the Englishmen had not done previously." Bradman made 48 and 71 and Larwood registered one hit, a paralysing blow high-up on Bradman's left arm as he drew back to square-cut, so it was not easy in the end to decide actually who won the contest. Larwood had been limping badly long before Bradman's second innings was complete, but Jardine made him stay on the field until the enemy was finally defeated for the last time, and the pair walked off together, neither speaking a word, Larwood claimed, "probably the two greatest antagonists ever to meet on the cricket-field." (*The Larwood Story, p. 171*).

England won the match by eight wickets. That man of inflexible purpose had triumphed once again, though once again he would not escape personally unscathed. "Don't give *him* a drink," somebody shouted from the Hill when the drinks-waiters arrived on one occasion. "Let the bastard die of thirst." Or, when Jardine offered O'Brien a drink, "Don't touch it. Make him taste it first." Finally when England began its last innings he was obliged to appeal to the umpire against Alexander's habit of running onto the pitch after delivery. Alexander changed to round-the-wicket, but Jardine continued to object and the highly-annoyed bowler needed no further provocation to attack the M.C.C. skipper with a stream of bumpers. One of them caught him a frightful blow in the ribs and the crowd went wild with delight, throwing things into the air, cheering and huzzaing as though the final act in the drama had arrived and the villain of the piece was now being made to pay for his crimes.

The cricket had come to that. If the M.C.C. thought fit to introduce this new body-line element into bowling, it must expect the rest of the cricket world to follow suit and the humble followers of the game to behave accordingly. In M.C.C.'s final match of the tour against South Australia, Richardson made no bones about setting a body-line field for his opening bowlers, Tobin and Williams, and when the tourists left Sydney for New Zealand shortly afterwards there was not a single Australian Test cricketer to see them off. Behind their backs, in every class of cricket from Moore Park to the best grade standard, from Sydney to the back of Bourke, body-line boomed, batsmen brandished their bats in threatened retaliation, once players assaulted one another, and numerous games were broken up in angry recriminations. There were no repercussions in New Zealand but before Jardine's men arrived home, the English domestic season had opened with an outcrop of fast leg-theory in an Oxford Freshmen's Trial. For B. W. Hone's side, a young freshmen, R. C. H. Armitstead pounded them down on the leg-side with four men close-in and two deep. He caused more concern to the wicket-keeper than to the opposing batsmen, but it effectively slowed the game down. No doubt techniques would improve, until something was done about it.

In Australia Bradman had taken advantage of the end of the cricket season to plunge into his writing. Bodyline was merely a phase, he realised. It had evolved naturally and innocently, one of the bowler's responses to the current superiority of bat over ball. Nobody could blame the bowler for seeking to redress the balance but surely alternative methods could be found more in keeping with the spirit of the game. For instance he thought the proposed new lbw rule well worth consideration. By a small amendment to the existing law, allowing the bowler to gain a decision in the case of a ball pitched outside the off-stump, not only off-spin bowlers would be assisted, but leg-break bowlers against left-handers, as well as natural in-swingers like Larwood who would be able to bowl at the stumps with the chance of getting an lbw instead of having to resort to this latest abomination of trying to intimidate the batsman into cocking up a catch on the leg. If this reform didn't help the bowler sufficiently, well what about making the stumps two inches higher or adding a fourth stump. Any steps taken in aid of the bowler compelled the batsman to improve his technique in order to meet the challenge. The inevitable result would be increased efficiency all-round.

Released from the strain of the "bodyline" series, he was full of enthusiasm and ideas. In May of 1933 he set about studying the laws of the game, "particularly necessary" for captains, specifically in order to sit for the N.S.W. Cricket Umpires Association examination, to be held on 1 August. He had no intention of becoming an umpire, but if he hoped to become proficient in the laws of the game and their interpretation there was no better way of starting out than with a definite object in view. He passed with flying colours and immediately turned to another absorbing interest, the coaching and encouragement of schoolboys. Coaching, selecting teams, organising exhibition matches, was an obligation under the terms of his contract with F. J. Palmer's, but Bradman didn't merely coach and advise the boys. He took them away with him on extensive country tours, looked after like a "father and mother combined" in the words of one of them; it was no surprise that of these young cricketers he took so much trouble with "almost every one played first-grade cricket and many of them played for N.S.W.".

In September 1933 for example, a team of "Sun–Palmer" colts led by Don Bradman played a Mick Simmons Radio Club team under Stan McCabe more than 500 miles from Sydney in the North Coast centre of Lismore. Bradman hit up 71 in 30 minutes before a crowd of many thousands and it would be impossible to exaggerate the enthusiasm for cricket that this one occasion created in the surrounding district. Queensland and N.S.W. and N.S.W.C.A. sides had played in Lismore from time to time, but a personal visit from Don Bradman was a different matter altogether. Fathers took their sons out to play cricket in the back-yard; cricket clubs were besieged by non-cricketers wanting to play for perhaps the first time in their lives; and when nine months later the Test matches began in England, Lismore people organised late-night parties which went on until the broadcast descriptions of the Tests ended in the early hours of the morning. Cricket had suddenly become a completely new thing in their lives.

The bodyline series seemed light-years away in the Australian summer of 1933–34. A crowd of almost 15,000 people were there to watch Bradman batting against Queensland at the S.C.G. and they had a marvellous day. Two seasons before against South Africa he had been unhappy about his big hitting, and one afternoon at the S.C.G. No. 2 the *Referee* correspondent had watched him hitting balls into the air in every direction, not worrying where they landed at first, until finally he got it right and then bang, bang, bang, it didn't seem to matter where the ball pitched, Bradman stepped out to meet it and a succession of gigantic sixes went soaring over a distant fence. Now, as he journeyed out to the ground in the company of his father, the elder Bradman happened to mention that he had never seen him hit a six on the S.C.G. "Well, if I get to 200 today," replied his son, "I will hit a six or die in the attempt." He resumed batting that morning 122 not out, reached his 200 in another 80 minutes, and instantly began looking for sixes. He hit two off Levy's first over; was missed off Levy at cover; hit two more sixes off Levy's next over and went to 250 in a further 16 minutes. Levy's first four overs had cost him 60 runs when Bradman was out for 253, throwing his wicket away to Brew at the other end.

It would afterwards be alleged by Jack Fingleton and others that the bodyline series had left a permanent scar on Bradman's batting; that he was never quite the same again. True, he had been complaining about an inability to concentrate, a certain mental restlessness that season, but the effect upon his batting was certainly not apparent to the average onlooker in 1933–34. 32,587, a Shield record, turned up for the first day's play, N.S.W. versus Victoria later in the month, though to be honest, the excitement was not all about Bradman this time. Immediately following the match the Board of Control was to announce 16 names to go to England and public interest in the selections had never been higher.

For several weeks the *Sun* newspaper in Sydney, the paper for which Bradman wrote, had been conducting a "Test barometer." Readers wrote in choosing their team and each time a player was chosen he received a vote recorded by the barometer. There were a good number of certainties on current form, Woodfull and Ponsford, Bradman, Kippax and McCabe, Oldfield, O'Reilly, Grimmett and Wall; with as many more, Fingleton, Brown and Chilvers of N.S.W.; Barnett, Bromley, Darling, Ebeling, Fleetwood-Smith, O'Brien and Rigg (Victoria), all of them on the fringe of selection and engaged in this final match of the season.

N.S.W. batted first and Fingleton and Brown greatly improved their chances by putting on 148 together before Fingleton (78) had to retire with cramp. Bradman took his place, "to participate," he wrote, "in one of the most interesting phases of cricket it was my good fortune ever to be associated with. When I went in Brown needed 34 for his century and when 52 runs were added a new ball would be used." So he deliberately held his horses, making sure young Billy Brown saw most of the strike until he reached his 100 when Bradman suddenly cut loose. The cricket that followed was unforgettable. The Victorian bowlers were all in the running for touring places, but Bradman now scored 40 in 19 minutes; his next 50 after that to reach 100 in another 30 minutes. The huge crowd was already in a frenzy of delight when Fleetwood-Smith began what was to be Bradman's final glorious over. The first ball landed on the roof of the old Members' Stand, almost the biggest hit ever seen on the Sydney Cricket Ground; the second went for another six; he was missed in the deep from the third; hit the fourth for yet another towering six on the off-side; and was finally caught on the fence by Darling off the sixth ball. He ran from the field amid a great storm of cheering, N.S.W.'s first wicket having put on 340. Brown eventually scored 205 and next morning overtook Bromley on the arometer.

The public opinion poll proved remarkably accurate. Its team differed in only two major particulars from that selected by the official selection committee of Dwyer, Woodfull and Dolling. Instead of Fingleton and Oxenham, Ebeling and Chipperfield were chosen; with Bradman surprisingly vice-captain ahead of Kippax. It was most unfortunate about Fingleton. He was surely a better bat than Darling, Bromley or Chipperfield for example, as his past record suggested; as his subsequent career would undoubtedly prove. Yet he was left out and in his grief and outrage contrived to blame chiefly Bradman. All through the summer the latter had been contributing prolifically to the *Sun*, discussing all manner of topics, commenting on the form of various candidates for selection, not hesitating on occasions to pass on well-meant advice to promising young players like Fingleton and Brown, both of whom he believed to be certainties to tour. With this thought in mind then, he had hinted in the *Sun* (28 November) that Fingleton should go further across his wicket when attempting to cut, an important consideration in England. But the criticism which Fingleton felt to be most damaging to his prospects appeared in the *Sun* only three days before the final selections were made.

Describing N.S.W.'s first innings against Victoria, Bradman wrote, "Rowe drove the ball to mid-off, called and ran, only to be left stranded as Fingleton declined the run. . . . Jack can run fast and judge a run well, but must learn to respect his partner's judgement as well as his own." It is past belief that such a remark could have influenced the selectors in any way, but the case against Bradman seemed to be made worse by his having gone to such lengths, while at the crease, to get

Brown into the team.

However there was no time to worry about what apple-carts he may have upset in Sydney, for the Bradmans had already finalised their plans to leave that city for Adelaide. N.S.W. cricket supporters had suspected he was about to go for some time. Early in December rumours went the rounds that he intended to move to Melbourne to float his own sports goods company. However it was South Australia, weakest (before the admission of Queensland) of the Sheffield Shield States, traditionally the most expert in luring cricketers from outside the State, which finally got him. During the N.S.W. match in Adelaide in mid-December he had spent a good deal of time in the home of Harry Hodgetts, a member of the Australian Board of Control and a prominent Adelaide stock-broker, and it didn't take Hodgetts long to discover his bent for finance. He invited Bradman to join him. Hodgetts had long been a great patron of sportsmen and a benefactor of South Australian cricket and while Bradman was considering the offer, he was successful in making another acquisition for South Australia – a nineteen-year-old Tasmanian, C. L. Badcock, who in three innings against Victoria within one week after Christmas scored 107, 274 and 71 not out against the State. Badcock was to be employed as a salesman with Brown Bros, the furniture manufacturers of Hindley Street.

Bradman however had never been one to make decisions in a hurry. As long ago as March 1933 he had replied to an offer from Rochdale, the Lancashire League Club, "My present contract ends on 1 February 1934. . . . I do not want to leave Australia, but if the prospects are bad and incomparable with what I could expect in England I would not hesitate to go." At that particular moment the body-line issue had engendered such a state of feeling between the two countries that the whole future of England–Australia Test cricket had been in jeopardy. By the end of the year however the tour of England by Australia was now virtually a certainty and the Lancashire proposal, though very handsome, was less alluring.

Another tempting offer at this time came from the *Sun*. The newspaper was willing to take him on full-time, he learned from Johnny Moyes, so he would then be free to go on writing, and play cricket, Test cricket, at the same time. Twelve months before he would have jumped at the chance. But since then, somehow or other, he had grown heartily sick of cricket as his whole life. "The journalistic life had its attractions," he was to write about these days, "but always I came back to the absolute necessity of being able to free my mind from cricket when the day's play was over." On 14 February Hodgetts announced to the Press that Don Bradman had agreed to join his firm and would take up residence in Adelaide on 10 March, before the Australian touring side sailed for England, in order to qualify for South Australia at the beginning of the 1934–35 season.

It was a great wrench for both of them. Little wonder he had taken so long to make up his mind. There was naturally bitter regret in Sydney at his decision; intense disappointment on the part of his family, friends and all those for whom watching Don Bradman had become one of the great pleasures of life. But one State's loss is another State's gain. "Best thing that ever happened to South Australian cricket," declared Clem Hill on receipt of the news. "Bradman will one day lead Australia's Test side. What an honour for the State after all these years." At the Premier's Conference in Melbourne that February R. L. Butler of South Australia simply couldn't restrain his enthusiasm. "I have just heard," he told the other Premiers exultantly, "Sydney has arranged to let us have Don Bradman."

The Bradmans were holidaying in the outback, five miles from the nearest telephone, at the time of the announcement. But three days later they were back in Sydney where Bradman had to report for the Board's medical examination. He passed it without trouble, yet in view of his generally fluctuating health, his proneness recently to strains and ailments, he was exempted from the side's preliminary visit to Tasmania. Thus, instead of departing on 8 March with the rest of the N.S.W. players, the Bradmans had time to complete their farewell preparations and spend a last week or two with their families before setting out for Adelaide. On 13 March, under the alias of "Mr & Mrs Lindsay", they left Melbourne on the final stage of their journey, leaving the overnight express at a small station in the Mt Lofty Ranges where they were met quietly by car and taken to the Hodgetts' home in Kensington Gardens. He had only one week before joining the boat at Adelaide, but time enough for the committee of the Kensington Cricket Club to meet and elect him to the club in the hopes that he would now be recognised as a fully-fledged South Australian member of the touring party.

Unfortunately the brief visit to Adelaide was not a great success. Adelaide was suffering from a heat-wave and Bradman from really appalling headaches. He now consulted more specialists, but again they could diagnose nothing seriously amiss; could prescribe no course of treatment except plenty of rest, at least until the team actually arrived in England. And he had other causes for anxiety as well. On 4 February the London *Sunday Times* had published a rather startling and dramatic article declaring that the 'Bradman–Larwood duel' was about to be resuscitated; was due to be refought all over again that coming summer. "Many think leg-theory will be abandoned, but it will be employed if it promises success and does not savour of undue intimidation."

Following the Board's urgent representations in the matter; following the widespread condemnation that had greeted body-line on its first appearance in England, the great majority of Australians had simply taken it for granted that such tactics would never be repeated in Test cricket, as though it had all been just a terrible mistake. Such naivety, such optimism, whichever it is, is an Australian national characteristic; but Australians had been misled also by the Press reporting of cricket events in England which had naturally enough played up the side antagonistic to body-line and generally managed to conceal the fact there were two distinct schools of thought on the subject. During the English summer those who believed in stern measures against the Australians had chosen mainly to say little and stay in the background. Now that the Australians had actually selected their team and were about to depart, the "hard-liners" were beginning to re-assert themselves. From Nottingham came the news that Larwood was fast recovering from his foot injury; was just raring to get started again when the season opened in April. Though not yet attempting to train properly before the foot was fully healed, he was keeping very fit and working from dawn to dusk on his poultry farm.

Originally, before the M.C.C. party had actually returned from Australia and New Zealand in May 1933, few people in England had been sure what to make of "body-line". First reactions could only be instinctive. "Recent happenings in Australia," said Major R. C. Campbell, secretary of the Minor Counties Association, "makes one feel that a plot had been hatched in Nottingham or London, whereupon it was decided to send no more hearty fellows as captains to Australia. The idea seemed to be "we are out for business, to kill Bradman at any price." On the other hand was the austere approach of the *Manchester Guardian*, "It is unlikely that the Australians appreciate the services Larwood has rendered to their cricket but they are sure eventually to realise that the health of the game is insecure while batsmen wax fat on bowling made docile by the world's best pitches." To which the *Yorkshire Evening Post* added "The comparative failure of Bradman will be a wholesome discipline, even for him."

Plum Warner was hopeful that when Englishmen had the chance to see body-line for themselves they would instantly recognise it for the ugly monster it was and shun it accordingly. People, he said, simply wouldn't go to watch it. But wishful thinking wasn't going to solve the problem. Not all of us are capable of seeing things the way they are, specially not when national loyalties are involved. On 7 May Larwood burst into print in the *Sunday Express* with a scathing attack upon Australia, its cricketers and its crowds. Woodfull had been hit because he was "too slow"; Bradman had been such a comparative failure because he was "frightened" and wouldn't get behind the ball. The Aussies just couldn't take it, he implied. Put out by the discomfiture of their heroes, they had not merely screamed themselves hoarse at the tourists on the cricket-field; they had lain in wait to jeer them in the streets, at their hotel, the theatre; had even attempted to molest them on train journeys.

This was a new angle on the tour, a new talking-point. Even Jardine now felt compelled to speak, to give his version. He began in the *Evening Standard* (21 May) by criticizing the barracking and the Australian authorities' failure to control their crowds. Without the barracking there would never have been the fuss, he implied. As for body-line, a "meaningless term" invented by the Press, well, the Australians had bowled leg-theory with a leg-side field against the M.C.C. in Adelaide in 1928, but "there were no complaints from us or from any of the States playing South Australia."

Clearly the question had more sides to it than may have first appeared. An M.C.C. special committee was currently examining the whole body-line controversy. But neither the unofficial discussions that certain of its members had had with Jardine and Warner and some of the senior professionals; nor the recommendations of an Australian committee of enquiry forwarded to it by cable on 28 April, had gone any way towards helping it make up its collective mind. The proposal from Australia was that Law 48 of the Laws of Cricket should be amended or added to in the following way. "Any ball delivered which in the opinion of the umpire at the bowler's end is bowled at the batsman with the intent to intimidate or injure him shall be considered unfair and 'No-ball' shall be called." The proposal went on to empower the umpire to take certain actions if the offence was repeated. But how was the umpire to read the bowler's mind; to know what he intended at the moment of delivery? How was he to differentiate legitimate leg-theory as practised for nearly 30 years from the obnoxious "body-line" that the Australians clearly had in mind? How were the committeemen to know the difference for that matter?

Perhaps if they had had the chance to see Larwood and Voce in action it would have been easier. But Larwood was crippled by his foot injury and likely to be out for the season; Voce had put on so much weight since returning from Australia that for the moment he was hardly worth watching. There was Bowes, however, as well as Constantine. Both of these had often enough been accused of using methods akin to body-line, and now the two were to be on opposite sides in the first really important occasion at Lord's that season, M.C.C. against the touring West Indians. By the end of the first day, 20 May, the rumour in Fleet Street was that the M.C.C. had seen enough of the dangers inherent in short-pitched fast bowling to enable it to take a positive stand against leg-theory. "If this is true," hinted the *Daily Express* sports gossip columnist, "will Douglas Jardine accept the captaincy of England, if it is offered to him?"

But it wasn't Bill Bowes under the captaincy of Jardine who had so impressed the committee. It was Constantine. Coming on at six in the evening, after the West Indians had been dismissed for 309, he soon had Hulme and Hearne plainly in fear for their skins. Constantine, like Larwood, had always been able to get plenty of lift from the Lord's wicket. After numerous snicks and edges from batsmen failing to get behind the line, he had Hearne caught behind and then began an over to Hulme. The first ball hit the batsman a very painful blow on the thigh and ran away down to fine-leg. The next ball did exactly the same thing, and then the third and fourth also struck home, only higher, round the ribs. In evident desperation Hulme swung blindly at the last ball but one and got it away to leg somewhere. There was an easy single in it, but W. B. Franklin, Hulme's batting partner, didn't fancy having to face even one ball from the fast bowler. "No, no, no," he shouted, "I'm staying here."

Constantine had no body-line field. G. C. Grant, the West Indies captain, had made it very clear at the beginning of the tour that he would not tolerate such tactics just as he had forbidden them to Constantine in Australia in 1930–31. "Yet, if Saturday's bowling, even allowing for no leg-field," said Sydney Southerton, editor of *Wisden*, "is at all comparable to the methods exploited in Australia, one can appreciate what was thought both by the Australian players and the better-behaved spectators." Simultaneously that week-end London newspapers referred to the impending publication of *Fight for the Ashes*, Jack Hobbs' account of the recent series in Australia wherein he had described body-line as "a most venomous thing."

Thus briefly, it seemed, leg-theory and all that it implied stood condemned in the eyes of the only body of men who could effectively condemn it. If the M.C.C.'s special committee had been obliged to pass judgement upon leg-theory on the evidence of a single half-hour, the chances are that it would have quickly reached a verdict of guilty. M.C.C.'s innings continued however on the following Monday and opinions began to waver again. Jardine was out fending off a short one from Constantine, but then Valentine and Chapman came together and showed that the batsman who was prepared to get his shoulder in line and right over the ball; to hook the bouncer whenever it appeared, had nothing to fear from either Constantine, or Martindale, or any fast bowler one would think.

After five wickets had fallen to the fast bowlers for 70, the Kent pair added 84 in an hour. This was the kind of batting that was the real answer to leg-theory, people told one another. In West Indies' second innings little George Headley was quite badly hurt by a ball from Bowes. But the delivery was not a bouncer; nor was any leg-side field in position. Headley had moved across his stumps in order to force the ball to the "on" and unfortunately missed.

On top of all this Patsy Hendren came out to bat in M.C.C.'s second innings in an extraordinary-looking piece of head-gear that had apparently been fashioned by his wife using his present cap plus the peaks of two old caps made to serve as ear-flaps. The "helmet" had been constructed two years before after Patsy had been hit by Larwood, but this was the first time he had actually worn it. One could sympathise with Hendren on this occasion, but the general effect was only to make the batsman look ridiculous; his fears about bouncers alarmist. Was the M.C.C. now to step into the fray and penalise the fast bowler for being too fast?

So the Australians received a dusty answer to their cable of 28 April. "The term 'body-line' would appear to imply a direct attack by the bowler on the batsman. The committee consider that such an implication applied to any English bowling in Australia is improper and incorrect ... the practice of bowling on the leg-stump with a field placed on the leg-side necessary for such bowling is legitimate and has been in force for many years." M.C.C. now in effect shelved the matter for the time being, waiting to see what the rest of the season might bring forth while, uncondemned, fast leg-theory flourished as never before.

Clay (Glamorgan), Watson (Lancs), Keeton (Notts) were three more victims of Bill Bowes, each of them having to be carried from the field unconscious or badly shocked, to the great indignation and violen hooting of the home crowd. She would never speak to Bill Bowes again. He was a devil, Mrs. Keeton vowed. Body-line was the only reason Jardine had brought back the Ashes, declared Maurice Turnbull, Glamorgan's captain, at a dinner in London on 30 May. The following week Arthur Carr was knocked to the ground by E. W. Clark at Northampton; in the Varsity match that year, two Oxonians, P. C. Oldfield and D. C. H. Townsend, were both out after being hit in the neck by Kenneth Farnes, the bat or ball then falling on the stumps, while finally, in the second Test at Old Trafford, Constantine and Martindale bowled undisguised body-line, six or seven men on the leg, to which Clark retaliated for England in West Indies' second innings. According to Constantine, Grant had designedly renounced his pledge made at the outset of the tour, in revenge for Yorkshire having deliberately prepared a wet wicket for the West Indians at Harrogate, so Grant believed.

Altogether it had not been a happy English season. Batsmen also continued to offend, thrusting all their pads in front of the stumps when deceived in flight; shouldering the bat and making no attempt to play the faster bowlers swinging in towards the pads. On 23 November 14 of the 17 county captains met with the M.C.C. at Lord's to discuss once again the whole question of leg-theory; to review it in the light of the past season's experience. At the end M.C.C. issued a statement. No alteration in the existing laws of the game was called for. "But standards of sportsmanship have been set up from which there can be no backsliding. The captains have been put upon their honour."

How could anything concrete have emerged? Arthur Carr wasn't there for instance. He had already told the Press before the season began: "If Larwood cannot swing the ball, I shall tell him to bowl leg-theory at the batsman. I have no moral qualms. I expect the batsmen to get a few bruises . . . Larwood is the only man who can bowl leg-theory properly . . . I myself hate to bat against him when he is bowling leg-theory and I think it will slow the game down, but it should win matches for Nottinghamshire. That is why I use it when I think fit." By the end of the season it was apparent that two or three other county captains were in substantial agreement with these views.

Meanwhile the Australian Board of Control, also very much divided in mind, had been vainly seeking assurance from the M.C.C. that no bodyline would be bowled against the 1934 touring party. Both sides were agreed that "a form of bowling which is obviously a direct attack by the bowler upon the batsman would be an offence against the spirit of the game"; but continued to disagree that this had been practised in Australia in 1932–33. "Your team can certainly take the field with the knowledge and the full assurance that cricket will be played here in the same spirit as in the past," the M.C.C. cabled back to Australia on 9 October; a form of words acceptable to R. A. Oxlade, newly-restored chairman of the Board, obviously not so to some of the Victorian and Queensland members. At the same time Harold Larwood in Nottingham was more concerned with the reactions of Don Bradman. "I see," he wrote in the *Daily Express* (10 October), "that Bradman is reported to have said the notes (cables) mean he will not encounter leg-theory in the future. All I can say is if Bradman comes here in 1934 he may be surprised . . . if I am picked I shall bowl leg-theory and I don't think the M.C.C. will order me or anyone else not to bowl with a packed leg-trap."

No matter what anybody thought or said, however, Aubrey Oxlade, leader of the majority party on the Board, was determined that the tour should go ahead; while one of his opponents, W. L. Kelly, manager of the 1930 side, told the departing tourists in a farewell address, "If cricket in 1934 is played as it was in the old days, you will regain the Ashes. If cricket or alleged cricket is played under the captaincy of a man named Jardine, I will strike that out and simply say that I wish you every success."

Kelly believed that in the attitude of Jardine lay the whole key to the Australians' visit. In October he had gone off to skipper M.C.C. on an extensive tour of India and Ceylon while in the interim rumours continued to abound: that he *would* be skippering England the following summer; alternatively that he had declared a resolve never to play against the Australians again. Jardine in fact kept his intentions strictly to himself, yet it became clear as the tour unfolded; firstly that he had no thoughts of initiating bodyline methods against the Indians; secondly that in C. K. Nayudu, the Indian skipper, he had encountered an uncompromising opponent who would eventually compel the use of bouncers by the M.C.C. fast bowlers in self-defence. In the second Test at Calcutta Nissar for India began by hitting and injuring three England batsmen; and then when India batted Dilawar Hussain, the Indian wicket-keeper and opening batsman was knocked out by a ball from Clark. For a moment the Englishmen wondered whether there was going to be a repetition of the scenes in Australia twelve months before.

Nayudu was a very exceptional Indian, a man of tall and soldierly bearing who had determined that the matches against the Englishmen should be played in the spirit of ancient Hindu warfare, no quarter asked nor given. As organiser and inspirer of cricket teams on behalf of various Indian princes and rulers, he had skippered no fewer than six Indian sides in successive matches against the M.C.C., and when the tourists reached Madras, somewhat shaken by this ordeal, Jardine was moved to refer to "Nayudu's travelling circus"; to one or two of their opponents in particular as "Nayudu's hired assassins". In Madras there was a dispute about umpires; more incidents; more bumpers; more booing of the Englishmen by the crowd, and trouble just seemed to follow them from Madras to Ceylon and back to Bombay where the tour at last concluded on 6 March. Jardine had previously notified Lord's that he would not be returning to England with the rest of the side, but not until several weeks after the others had departed did it definitely become known that he would not be available to captain England against the Australians. In the meantime Frank Tarrant, the former Victorian and Middlesex all-rounder, now a cricket coach and umpire in India, had also reported to the M.C.C., severely condemning the bowling of E. W. Clark and the generally unhelpful attitude of Jardine. What will happen if Clark kills a man, Tarrant asked. "Will he be charged with manslaughter"?

Jardine's decision not to play was certainly one great weight off the tourists' minds, but these other developments were less reassuring. Rumours had reached them from time to time, but in Australia when they set out it had seemed possible to imagine body-line safely dead and buried. Had they been living in cloud-cuckoo land, then, happily cut off from reality? Now, when they landed in England and saw how coolly they were received in some quarters; heard themselves described as "squealers" in reference to their protests of 1933–34, they wondered whether body-line was not still very much alive and kicking. They would just have to wait and see.

Bradman was not at all keen to play in the opening match against Worcestershire. He hadn't really benefited from the voyage, being such a poor sailor, but "in order to scotch the rumours going round about me," he says in his autobiography, "it was decided I should play in the first match of the tour. . . . By the time I had got to 30 I felt so fatigued that I started to have a crack at the bowling, quite expecting to get out. By some queer means however I developed a sort of second wind, and a fortunate break enabled me to play the innings in two parts. But even a night's rest left me too exhausted to continue long next morning. Still I think the effort was worth-while . . . I was really not well enough to play and how I ever managed to make 206 will always be a miracle to me."

Neville Cardus, his old friend, had journeyed specially to watch the 1934 Australians make their debut and renew acquaintances, and he didn't regret the journey for a minute. The Bradman of 1930, he thought, had been almost like a machine, "an adding machine, the robot that scored 309 in a day at Leeds and never once erred or ventured into the unknown, that never looked at a soul all day, hardly spoke, but went on with his work with the impassiveness of one resigned to everlasting efficiency." Now, "a joyous daring rendered his genius lovable and approachable." He gave the bowler hope. When he occasionally missed, he laughed. He was out in the end running up the pitch to Howorth, missing the ball and running on all the way back to the pavilion, head down, while a crowd of about 8000 people applauded in wild excitement. It was a return to the palmy days. However he had changed not only in his approach to the game, but in his physical appearance as well. For instance he had lost a lot of weight, Cardus noted. The old sturdiness of shoulder was no longer there, so that when he drove the ball, he drove it as accurately as ever, though not as violently as in 1930.

Still, even allowing for the loss of health, Cardus was puzzled. Four years before he had played so close to the body all the time, upper arms pressed to his sides. He didn't seem to any longer. Cardus may have been puzzled. But Johnny Moyes reading about the 200 in Sydney wasn't surprised, even though Bradman had told him just before leaving that he wasn't going "to try for double-centuries unless the position of the game demanded that he do so." Moyes had gone to visit the Bradmans in their North Shore home and as they talked, discussing the innumerable things that had happened in the course of the young man's career, it seemed to Moyes that he retained a "longing for the old days when he could bat as he liked without having to worry about the crowd or his average."

A double-century at Worcester (shades of 1930) was a very ominous beginning from an English point of view. Still, Worcester had no really fast bowler and when Bradman, mysteriously, began to fail against rather ordinary bowling in the next few matches the menace seemed to recede again. "People who did not know how seedy I was began to say I was done," Bradman wrote. But then on 26 May the Australians met Middlesex. "Big" Jim Smith, as he was usually known, was an enthusiastic fast bowler rather than an especially fast one, but in his first over he dismissed Woodfull for 0, almost bowled Bradman and had Ponsford, the other opener, also for a duck in his second over. Only two days before against Hampshire, Bradman was yet another to have failed to get off the mark at the very beginning of the Australian innings. But this time "something just had to be done, so I took a risk and had a go. My timing happened to be right and an innings was born for which I very heartily thank Jim Smith."

Possibly also he had been impressed by the way Patsy Hendren earlier in the day had put Grimmett to rout for the first time on the tour. One great innings often begets another. Anyway he soon saw off the faster bowlers and then launched into the slow bowlers, Robins, Peebles, Enthoven, in a manner that was purely Bradmanesque; that transcended all allegiances and turned the spectators into avid fans of Bradman in England as much as in Australia. "He danced down the pitch and hit. He flung out his left leg and drove. He lay back and pulled." At exactly, 6.30, off the last ball of the evening, he reached his 100 after just an hour and a quarter. Next day he went on to 160.

So far everything had gone swimmingly for the Australians. Ponsford and McCabe were also making hundreds of runs, while Darling, Brown and Chipperfield were three newcomers to England who all promised to make runs in the Test matches. But the best news of the lot was the form of Grimmett and O'Reilly. Grimmett was almost as good as ever on English wickets. If the leading Englishmen were more familiar with him than they had been in 1930, he had a more than compensating advantage in the support of O'Reilly at the other end. The tall, young O'Reilly was not so well-known. He possessed a slow leg-break, a slightly faster leg-break, a googly or it might have been the top-spinner, and finally an off-break, an entirely different range of deliveries from Grimmett, delivered with a very different trajectory, and all assisting to maintain the pressure on the batsmen; to generate an atmosphere of unremitting hostility about the Australian attack that it had not known for years.

On the same Saturday as Bradman scored his wonderful 160 at Lord's however, the disquieting news arrived that Larwood, Voce and Farnes had all of them indulged in unashamed leg-theory in the Nottinghamshire versus Essex encounter at Trent Bridge. The point was that Larwood had no need to employ leg-theory in county cricket. He could get wickets more quickly and efficiently operating to an off-side field. The only time he had bowled it in England previously had been when he was trying it out in 1932 in preparation for the trip to Australia. The tourists naturally jumped to the conclusion that he was intending to have another fling at them with it, although Larwood interviewed at Trent Bridge merely remarked that the newly-relaid Trent Bridge wicket would be the death of fast bowlers; that he had been exasperated by Essex's failure to force the pace on a wicket just made for batting.

What was the position, then? When Sir Stanley Jackson was appointed chairman of selectors in April that year, he immediately invited Larwood to his Knightsbridge flat for a long discussion about the Australians and their methods. A very distinguished figure in the cricket world, one not particularly identified with either side in the great cleavage of opinion that had taken place, he left Larwood with no clear impression whether he was utterly opposed to leg-theory in all circumstances or not. However Larwood felt certain that higher interests than cricket were involved; that political pressures were being brought to bear to prevent any possible damage to Commonwealth relations. Thus, when tentative enquiries were being put out some time later to discover whether he would be available for the first Test, he replied diplomatically that he was not yet properly fit. He had obviously given the matter much thought and decided on the advice of his county skipper, Arthur Carr, that his best tactic would be to await the result of the first Test and then, in the very likely event of an English defeat, hope that the pressure of public opinion would force him into the side. In Larwood's own words, "Before the (first) Test, the selectors came and asked me if I was fit. I was determined not to play, but to make their position easy, I answered I was not fit . . . if I said I was fit and wanted to play, would they have played me? I have heard that I was not to be played in the first Test in any case. If England could win without me, then I would not be played at all."

Larwood was furious because there was still no official condemnation of leg-theory, despite the angry public reactions it was apt to provoke from time to time. For instance at Chesterfield on 28 May, Yorkshire and Derbyshire were engaged in a crucial struggle for first-innings points when Derbyshire's last man, T. R. Armstrong, came to the wicket. Bowes immediately began aiming bouncers at the tail-ender and there was great local indignation. "Yorkshire have a bowler infinitely more dangerous to life and limb than I am," said Larwood and so, following in Bowes' footsteps, bowling leg-theory when it suited him, he resumed his old working partnership with Bill Voce and the revitalisation it brought to Nottinghamshire was marvellous to behold. When on 8 June the selectors announced the names of England's final eleven for the Test at Trent Bridge, the country felt let down, as though it had been offered a substitute eleven, the real England side having been withdrawn for mysterious reasons. There was no Jardine. No Larwood, Voce nor Bowes. Only one fast bowler, Kenneth Farnes. On the morning of the match, said Arthur Carr, "I came across T. A. Higson, one of the selectors, on the ground. He was wearing no hat and I jokingly said to him, "For Heaven's sake, where's your hat? Only one fast bowler! You ought to hide your face. . . ."

So England was not at its best. (At the last minute Wyatt too had to pull out and Cyril Walters in his first Test against Australia acted as skipper.) But neither was Australia. Not with Bradman still far from his old self. Woodfull sent him in second wicket down after Brown, another making his Test match debut, but his brief innings though highly entertaining was hardly what one expected of a Test match No. 4. "His first two shots," wrote Jardine (*Evening Standard*) "were wild to a degree . . . quite out of place in view of the state of the game and the fact that only five minutes remained for play before lunch." He was eventually out for 29 made off only 32 balls, but "he had never given confidence to his supporters that he might stay," (Fender, *Evening News*). Jardine and Fender were no doubt prejudiced, but Jack Hobbs (*Star*) was sympathetic to him. However the only thing he could think of to say about Bradman's two short innings at Trent Bridge was that they reminded him of the Bradman of 1932–33, facing Larwood.

On the whole it was not a very distinguished Test match. The Australians were clearly superior throughout. On the second day Chipperfield stole the show by making 99 in his first Test; McCabe was in great form in the second innings and the match finished in very exciting fashion with Grimmett and O'Reilly bowling magnificently and England just failing to stave off defeat. "When the last English batsman came in," says Bradman, "there was a quarter of an hour left for play and fielding close in at silly-leg, I wondered what death I might suffer if a catch came to me and I dropped it. Once you begin to think like this in such circumstances you can get yourself into a state of agony and I can tell you it was a relief to me when the last wicket fell lbw." That was hardly the typical, super-confident Bradman of old either. Then, as the players sprinted for the dressing-room, he caught his foot in a boundary-rope, fell awkwardly with Grimmett on top of him, and strained a thigh-muscle. He played against Northamptonshire next day, batting sixth and needing a runner.

On the third day at Trent Bridge, with England already up against it, Larwood struck a purple patch against Sussex at Horsham, taking five wickets in eight overs to finish off the Sussex innings. The next day, England now staring defeat in the face, Bill Bowes took 6 – 17 in helpful conditions against Middlesex at Lord's, almost preventing the home county getting the bare 51 second-innings runs necessary for an outright victory. Several Middlesex batsmen were hit in the process. Bradman might be in temporary eclipse, but all England was crying out for some really fast bowling to shake these wretched Australians. Farnes had done well enough in his first Test match, but on the second morning when Australia's sixth wicket had fallen at 234, only a notoriously weak tail to come, the English attack had seemed simply unworthy of the name. Grimmett came in and made 39; the innings lingered on and on and the total finally reached 374. Immediately the match ended selector Peter Perrin went off to watch Larwood and Voce in action against Essex at Westcliff; Jackson, to Huddersfield, where

Bowes was engaged. All three selectors would be at Trent Bridge for Larwood's following match against Lancashire. There were still five days before England's second Test side was announced on 18 June and the rumour was that Larwood was a certainty to play. Moreover, said Warner, "I believe he was only too ready to play."

Other pressures, however, were also at work. Carr made a century on the first day of that game at Westcliff; then Larwood took three quick wickets in the last half-hour, when the news arrived that Lancashire and Middlesex would refuse to renew their fixtures with Nottinghamshire the following season unless the "system of direct attack upon the batsmen" was abandoned forthwith. Carr was already aware of the views of Middlesex's skipper, Nigel Haig; of his threat to summon his batsmen from the field in the event of body-line being bowled at them. He had heard too that Lancashire intended to lodge a protest during their coming encounter at Trent Bridge. However Larwood proved most co-operative in this crisis, said Carr. Learning what had taken place, he came to him and promised never to bowl leg-theory for Nottinghamshire again.

In fact he never did bowl leg-theory again. But in Lancashire's first innings at Trent Bridge, for the first time in England since the tour of 1932–33, the Nottinghamshire pair gave their fellow countrymen a real taste of the bowling that had caused such a commotion in Australia. The pitch, it must be admitted, had been generously watered and Voce, pitching short with his usual leg-trap in position, quickly got rid of Watson and Hopwood, leaving Lancashire 2 – 17. Larwood, after a fruitless opening spell, then switched ends to take over from Voce. He had two short-legs for the break-back ball, but it was an orthodox fast bowler's field to which Larwood bowled in orthodox fast-bowling fashion aiming at the stumps.

What completely unsettled the Lancastrians was his pace, together with the wicket, which every now and then caused his shorter ball to rear chest-high. Tyldesley was soon out and "Iddon's innings," said Neville Cardus, "was a masterpiece of unintentional comedy." He was thrice missed in two overs, disconcerted as much by the occasions when he contrived to hit the ball as when he missed, and was finally bowled back-pedalling furiously towards square-leg. Lister was hit under the heart by one that lifted sharply and soon after caught in the slips. Parkinson and Eckersley were out instantly flicking at the ball; Sibbles was clean-bowled, and in 29 deliveries Larwood had taken six wickets for one run. Duckworth stayed for a bit but Voce soon polished off the innings and Lancashire was all out, 119.

Lancashire made a terrible fuss about it. Warner has a lurid story about meeting Duckworth three weeks later, still battered and bruised, arm in a sling and so on. "Whatever have you been doing?", I asked, and he replied, "Haven't you heard about that match with Nottinghamshire at Trent Bridge? . . . they bowled body-line at us." "What, your old friends, Larwood and Voce? You used to lecture when you returned from Australia, defending bodyline bowling and saying it was alright." "Maybe. But its tough, too tough, and makes trouble. I am not for it now." Whatever Warner had to say years later, however, his memory must have been at fault. Duckworth finished the match in one piece, and continued to play regularly for his county for the next three weeks. Undoubtedly Lancashire had prejudged the case. "Must a fast bowler change his style?", asked Cardus, "to suit the needs of batsmen who are not good players of fast bowling . . . what will happen next week if it should be a typical Lord's wicket for the Test match, a wicket that might bounce Larwood's long-hops straight at the batsman's head, leg-trap or none? Woodfull will be in a quandary. You can't protest by instinct."

But there was to be no Test match at Lord's for Harold Larwood. The irresistible logic of events had caught up with him at last, just as it would shortly catch up with Voce and Arthur Carr. Tommy Higson for one, president of Lancashire and an England selector for three years past, was determined there were going to be no more incidents concerning fast bowling; angry words were exchanged at the end of Lancashire's first innings and next day Larwood gave vent to his feelings in a front-page story in the *Sunday Dispatch.* He believed he was likely to be chosen for the second Test, he began. But "it will not matter. I have definitely made up my mind not to play against the Australians in this or any of the Tests." Clearly he considered the whole hoo-haa over body-line, including this latest episode at Trent Bridge, to be an Australian "conspiracy to bury leg-theory and brand me as a dangerous and unfair bowler. The M.C.C. have given way to political or other influences determined at all costs to placate Australia." Newspaper readers were certainly being treated to some spicy items this particular Sunday morning. In the *Sunday Express* Bill Voce backed up his colleague to the hilt. "The Australians would let me bowl leg-theory," he claimed, "because I am not as fast nor as dangerous . . . is the Australian Board, influenced by the hooligan type we who have been there know so well, to be allowed to ruin English cricket? . . . Leg-theory has been bowled in England for years without complaint . . . it is a shame that some English counties following the Australian lead have complained. Through Larwood we are only giving the Australians what Gregory and McDonald gave us in 1921." That was it. Larwood, assisted by Voce, had "put himself outside the pale of playing for England," in *Wisden's* phrase.

Was leg-theory, as developed in England and Australia, and adapted and carried to its ultimate conclusion in Australia in 1932-33, really cricket? Did it conform with the traditions of the game as it had grown up in England and been transplanted and taken root in Australia, South

Africa, New Zealand, and indeed throughout the entire Commonwealth and beyond. There can be no clear, unequivocal answer. It cannot be said for instance that the authorities at Lord's, the supposed guardians of the game, had decided the answer in the negative and proceeded to ban it categorically, acting in the interests of this worldwide cricketing community. The most that can be ventured is that various responsible persons, under pressure from this direction and that, had endeavoured in various devious and sometimes underhand ways, perhaps there were no other ways, to discourage its practice in England. That their actions were for the good of the game generally is beyond doubt. But it is a mistake to regard leg-theory, or bodyline, or whatever it is called, as being the brain-child of some evil genius or associated with any particular personality or phase of the game. It was the product of Test cricket which all the world wants before any other form of cricket.

"Let us have no shilly-shallying," Cardus had once written in defence of Jardine. "A number of English captains of cricket have wasted their public-school amenities on heroes whose greatness has come out of a hearty appreciation of things as they are . . . the Australian plays cricket to win; he has usually left it to Mr. Warner to make the Empire-binding speeches . . . for my part I admire Mr. Jardine beyond words. I dislike his view of cricket. I believe the qualities of character he possesses would suit better a leader of armies. Nonetheless . . . I see in Jardine a personal force in a period which finds the game woefully short of personality. His influence on modern cricket has been sanitary. He has cleared away cant, to the Australians he has returned tit-for-tat. It is a pity his opponent is not Warwick Armstrong." In such circumstances, Cardus concluded, '*Il faut cultiver notre Jardine.*"

But now Jardine had gone. Larwood had gone. Voce clearly wasn't wanted. Bowes played in the second Test at Lord's, but with certain limitations on his freedom of action it seemed. England made 440 in its first innings and Australia in the persons of Woodfull and Brown were going along comfortably in reply, 0 – 60 just before tea, when Bowes came back for his second spell, having a considerably-strengthened leg-field, a peculiar-looking field with not a soul in front of the wicket on the off-side. Just after tea he bowled Woodfull, and Bradman came in instead of the expected McCabe. At the same time, claimed Bowes, "Wyatt came to me and said, 'Bill, I have just had a message from the pavilion. Ask Bowes not to bowl short.' 'And what do you say as captain?' 'Well, if they want it friendly, perhaps they'd better have it that way'."

This is the reason Bowes gives for pitching them up again and moving his field back to the off-side. Perhaps Larwood's fears, that he would not have been allowed to bowl as he wished had he played, were well-grounded. However not for very long would Bowes have been permitted the luxury of three men close in on the leg. After a week's enforced rest due to his thigh injury Bradman was in cracking form. Bowes was soon taken off. Farnes' first ball to him was short and he hooked it for four and helped himself in all to 14 runs off the over. Verity came on at the other end and was hit for three fours off successive deliveries, all off-drives. Neville Cardus was in raptures. "The excitement throbbed visibly. Perfect strangers spoke to one another, the Tavern emptied."

Brown was similarly inspired. With Woodfull as his partner, he had been almost as stodgy as Woodfull. Partnered by Bradman he was no less brilliant. He had actually outpaced him, going from 40 to 77, when Verity began another over to Bradman. The left-hander had always been a great bowler at Lord's where the pitch gave his well-flighted delivery just that extra amount of bounce at the end of its deceptive flight. With his third ball he almost had Bradman caught-and-bowled. The fifth ball also jumped unexpectedly. Bradman could not check his stroke and this time Verity took the catch. "Everybody was dashed to earth again."

The talk had all been of another 250-odd to Bradman; another 6 –729 for the Australians. But Bradman was out and during the week-end the weather took a hand. Verity was an even greater bowler with a damp pitch to assist him. Australia, 2 – 192 on Saturday evening, was all out 284 soon after lunch; all out again, 118, by ten to six. Larwood's had been the name on everybody's lips a week ago. Now it was Verity's. "One of London's largest-selling dailies published a front-page story of Verity's triumph," said the Australian cricket-writer, Ray Robinson, "with never a word about the state of the wicket after heavy rain in the night." If you hadn't been there, you were left to guess "how a bowler who had taken only two Australian wickets for 113 in the preceding Test had suddenly developed the knack of getting 14 for 80 in one day."

But England was desperately short of a hero just then. The country had already resigned itself to the loss of the Ashes, when, like an angel from Heaven, Verity appeared. In particular, people rejoiced in the way he had wrestled with and finally overcome the demon Bradman. The tale would be oft-told. How with great cunning and accuracy he had been chained down champing at the bit until finally, tempted by the sight of nobody in the deep, the hapless victim swiped against the break and wrought his own destruction with only 13 to his name. In 1930 Peebles with his googly was supposed to have got the better of him. Then it was Larwood in Australia. Now, Verity. Because, it was alleged, he was no good on sticky wickets. Those who hadn't seen him on a very difficult wicket against Verity in Sydney said that he lacked the technique for it; that he was much inferior to Hobbs, Trumper and other great masters of the past in this respect. True, an English Test side would have gone on struggling against the odds, backs to the wall, heads over the bat, till the last man perished. But that is not necessarily the Australian way. He was a fatalist, Bradman told Neville Cardus. Australia was obviously not intended to win that one. However he had no doubt whatsoever that conditions would be different at Old Trafford. Cardus could expect a double-century from him there.

Unfortunately at Old Trafford Bradman was ill. Possibly possessing less resistance to infection than normally, he had gone to watch Wimbledon and contracted "Wimbledon throat," so-called because it had swept through the tennis-players. Chipperfield and Kippax were also affected badly enough for all three to be suspected of suffering from diphtheria, but there were just no possible batting replacements in sight and Chipperfield and Bradman played and on an easy wicket under a blazing sun the result was a draw. Bradman scored 30 in Australia's first innings and thus by mid-July he had still not reached the 1000 runs that were his by the end of May in 1930. In the match against Yorkshire Cardus remembered him in the field at fine-leg, "the picture of decrepitude and senile decay." He seemed scarce able to move from the spot, but stood hands on hips, eyes glued to the ground. At every opportunity he sat or squatted on his haunches, remaining there even when the ball was being delivered sometimes. Whenever possible he allowed some other fieldsman to throw in for him, though if the chance of a run-out occurred, Cardus noted, he was like a man transformed. He had been like that all the year. Periods of great lassitude, followed by sudden brief bursts of energy. Thus he had made 200 at Worcester, 160 against Middlesex, only to relapse again afterwards. Now something inside him, perhaps the stimulus was the sight of Verity or Bowes or George Macaulay among the opposition, caused him to put forth a special effort.

He went in just after lunch and was out for 140 just before tea, by which time Woodfull still hadn't reached his 50. The manner in which he forced the ball a foot or more outside the off-stump to the on-boundary was reminiscent of 1930, and his team-mates watching from the balcony of their dressing-room were seen to be almost as excited as the rest of the spectators. They needed him so badly at this stage. England, without Larwood and Voce! Australia, with Bradman only half-fit! There had been nothing between the two sides up to this point and now with the Englishmen rating their chances rather higher on the faster wicket at The Oval, it was all the more vital for Australia to win at Leeds. If only he could take things easily for the next few days, perhaps he might pull off another innings like the one at Leeds in 1930. . . .

To add to the imponderables was the nature of the ground itself. Headingley had tended to favour the Australians over the years, but the wicket was always unpredictable. If the sun was shining and the pitch was perfectly dry it was ideal for batting. If there were clouds on the other hand the faster bowlers were enabled to swing it around and move it off the seam; if it was at all damp, it was a spin bowler's paradise. When the players made their preliminary inspection of the wicket, after a little rain in the preceding few days, they felt it could be any of these things, probably all on the one day.

In fact the opening day was dull, with the prospect of rain later in the match, and Wyatt made the only possible decision in choosing to bat. Only later in the innings when he realised that the pitch still had moisture in it, just enough, that is, to give a little help to Grimmett and O'Reilly, would he come to regret batting first. At exactly half-past five England was all out 200, but then Bowes took three quick wickets before stumps so that with Australia, 3 – 39, the game was still evenly balanced. All would hinge on the weather and Bradman and Ponsford on the morrow.

The second day turned out to be sunny and hot and a crowd of 38,000, come to see Bowes polish off the Australians in quick time, perhaps to repeat his performance at Melbourne and bowl Bradman first ball, broke all Headingley attendance records. However the two balls of the fast bowler's uncompleted over of the previous evening were both short and Bradman forced them back past the bowler for four. A friend had told him jestingly that if he attempted a boundary in the first 15 minutes he would put him across his knee, but these two shots were perfectly safe and proper. He took another four from an overpitched ball from Bowes, but after that he quietened down. He went on slowly and steadily. Neither he nor Ponsford looked like getting out. The great record-breakers of the pre-bodyline era had come together at last. But Bradman's innings wasn't like 1930's, a hundred before lunch and so on. The eye at 24 is not the same as the eye at 20. This innings was rather the bridge between the giddy pace of youth and the more circumspect approach of maturity. At lunch after two and a half hours he was 76 not out, just ahead of Ponsford; at tea after a further two hours and a quarter he was 169 and well ahead of his partner. After tea the pair put on another 98 in an hour and when Ponsford was unexpectedly out, stepping back too far and dislodging a bail while hitting Verity for four, Bradman had made 223 and Ponsford 159 of their 388 partnership.

Hereabouts he really ran amuck. It didn't seem to matter where the ball pitched or who was bowling. The stolid Yorkshiremen shook their heads in disbelief, or else forgetful for the moment of whom it was happening to, watched with eyes shining and a lump in the throat while this boy smashed their favourite bowlers right and left. In a way it was more inspirational, more uplifting than 1930, because this time he had had to struggle like any ordinary mortal at the outset, had only succeeded in shaking himself free from these relatively undistinguished beginnings by the application of will-power, determination, all the human qualities dear to Yorkshire hearts, before ascending the ultimate pinnacles of batsmanship, doing what he liked with the bowling. At stumps he was 271 not out. Many years later, at the end of another great Bradman innings at Headingley, an old man sat watching his triumphant return to the pavilion, his expression torn between love and hate. His lips seemed to be mouthing words, but all he could manage to bring out as Bradman passed him was "Ee-ee. Tha' bugga."

In 1934 however Bradman was a sad sight when he returned to the Australian dressing-room. He was completely exhausted; could only sit on a bench hardly able to move while his team-mates unbuckled his pads, removed his boots and very gently and tenderly undressed him. "On Sunday," says Bradman, "I became terribly stiff and I knew that I would be lucky if I made another 20 runs." In fact with a little luck he was able to go on to 304 before being bowled by Bowes. Australia was now 6 – 550 and soon after, all out 584. McCabe (27) was third top-scorer after Bradman and Ponsford so what his country would have done without this pair, God knows. And all, it appeared, for nothing. Because England, 6 – 229 in its second innings, was rescued from inevitable defeat by rain and the score in the rubber remained one Test-all.

He had taken so much out of himself in this great innings. It just didn't seem possible, force himself to keep going as he undoubtedly would have done, to recover the strength for another such effort. And yet Providence must have been on his side. Twice before on the tour injury or illness had obliged him to rest for several matches. With the most beneficial results. Now, blessing in disguise, the torn thigh muscle incurred during England's second innings proved so painful that the decision was made to send Bradman to London for treatment while the rest of the side went north to Durham and Scotland. Sir Douglas Shields, formerly a lecturer in clinical surgery at Melbourne University, now the owner of a private nursing-home in Park Lane, was the surgeon who had operated on Larwood's badly-injured foot and made it possible for him to bowl fast again. Bradman's injury was scarcely so serious but Sir Douglas was concerned enough about his general health to prescribe a good three weeks' convalescence. He didn't play again until the match against the Army at Aldershot on 15 August, only three days before the last Test at The Oval.

England included three fast bowlers in her final eleven, Bowes, Allen and Clark. Not the trio Jardine would have selected though. He would have made Voce his first choice, particularly after the left-hander's 8 – 66 for Nottinghamshire against the tourists only a week before. However Voce had put himself totally beyond the pale by bowling naked bodyline at the Australians and he was not even considered for selection though most of England was crying aloud for his inclusion. Still, on a hard and true wicket like this one, Bowes had achieved spectacular success at The Oval in recent years and there was no lack of hostility about Clark and Allen. If the Australians' weakness was against really fast bowling, as Jardine claimed, it would surely reveal itself here, even if the English attack did lack Larwood and Voce.

Australia won the toss and batted and Bradman came in at exactly mid-day after Brown had been clean-bowled, Clark, 10, the score 1 – 21. There was a vast crowd at Kennington. The reserved seats had actually been sold out eight months before, before any other Test ground, and in perfect weather tens of thousands arrived for the opening day, queues stretching all round the ground. The encounter between Bradman and Ponsford and the English fast attack on a fast wicket was of course the acid test, and for several overs there was almost total silence as Bowes and Clark pounded up to the crease and flung them down; the only sound, the click of bat meeting ball and the occasional cries of the batsmen. At last Bradman opened his account with a four through the slips off Bowes. It was an unconvincing stroke, but an over or two later he made amends with a spanking cover-drive off Bowes, followed by a pull wide of mid-on which no other batsman in the world would have attempted from a ball barely short of a length.

Ponsford was probably the one closest to him in ability in 1934. Since the body-line series he seemed to have found all his offside shots again and Bradman's presence gave him the extra confidence he urgently needed. Indeed he was playing so well that at lunch, when he was 66, Bradman was only 43. After lunch the latter re-asserted himself however. Ponsford just won the race to their respective hundreds, but Bradman reached 150 when his partner was still 127. It was glorious batting of a kind that English spectators only saw when the Australians were in England. Allen came on after tea, 1 – 311, and was hit for 11 in his first over. He didn't often get treated like that in ordinary county cricket. The rate of runs per 100 overs had declined from 276 in the "golden" days of 1904 to only 211 in English first-class cricket in 1934.

The bowlers tried very hard, not greatly helped by the fielding, and with the total in the region of 360, Clark came on again using the leg-side field he commonly used for Northamptonshire but had not hitherto used against the Australians. Evidently the situation at tea had been considered so desperate that the embargo against anything resembling fast leg-theory had been lifted for the time being. The left-hander didn't trouble Bradman however, who now proceeded to leave his partner well behind. In the pavilion there was great stretching of legs and complaints about the monotony of "timeless" Tests and lifeless wickets, but the writing was well and truly on the wall for England. Australia had conceded over 400 runs on the first day at Lord's in 1930 and won the match, but 1 – 400, 1 – 450, 1 – 472 was too much. A few minutes before stumps, Ponsford having just reached his 200, Bradman was out for 244, attempting his two-handed tennis smash to a bumper from Bowes and just snicking the ball to Ames. By then he had done enough, more than enough, to ensure that the Australians recovered the Ashes. They won in the end by 562 runs.

CHAPTER EIGHT

Postscript

What sort of a man was it then able to inspire millions to adoration of these extraordinary achievements; capable also of engendering such hostility, such unreasoning dislike in the very few? Some of the few went to the lengths of preparing body-line to destroy him; others in more humble walks of life would merely parade their feelings by turning their backs on him. There was a member of the Sydney Cricket Ground, a patriotic Australian at that, who made it his business to leave the ground every time Bradman came into bat; who would arrange to be rung as soon as Bradman got out so that he could return to enjoy the cricket. Needless to say, he had never known Bradman personally, nor even briefly met him. He was convinced however that the man was purely out for his own advantage; that he took a sadistic delight in reducing the poor bowler to drivelling incompetence, while at the same time heaping up fame and fortune for himself.

It would be impossible to persuade such a fanatic that Bradman was essentially a very modest person and enjoyed most of all giving other people pleasure. He was barely twenty-six at the end of the 1934 tour and already he towered above his contemporaries as W. G. Grace had once towered above his. But where one was physically huge, domineering, hogging the spotlight all the time; the other was small, almost inconspicuous, very often engaged in plotting some means of escaping attention. He possessed the same outstanding gifts of character as W.G. though; the same unshakeable conviction of what could be achieved; the same contempt for mere physical limitations. It was not generally known for instance, and nobody was more averse to discussing his state of health than Bradman, that during the course of his long innings at the Oval a large blood-clot had formed in the big muscle of his right thumb. It obviously made batting very painful. None of his team-mates could understand how he was able to hold the bat, let alone score runs with it. However in the second innings he came in at his usual position of No. 3 after Clark had begun with five men around the bat in a leg-trap, another man at deep long-leg. With just such a field Voce had destroyed the Australians at Trent Bridge, and now at the Oval facing Clark, Ponsford didn't look particularly happy. Bradman, however, slammed the first short ball from Clark through the cordon for four. Shortly after Ponsford fell to a catch in the leg-trap, to which

Bradman retaliated in the next over by hooking Clark over the leg-trap and over the fence for a huge six.

He should never have played with such an injury, but a few days later he was at it again, captaining the Australians against Sussex at Hove. It was holiday time and the county of Fry and Ranji had prevailed upon him to turn out. Their biggest crowd of the season would be so disappointed if he didn't play. He could score only in singles, but Kippax was in tremendous touch and the pair added 83 in only 41 minutes. The Australians made 560 in the day, causing the spectators to feel that the season had been worthwhile, even though England had lost the Ashes, though yet again it was Lancashire or Yorkshire which had carried off the county Championship.

There could be no doubt that he had overdone it however. "It was a Saturday afternoon (22 September)," said Bradman, "and I was entertaining a friend from Bowral of all places, looking forward to going to the theatre with Arthur Chipperfield, when I became violently ill." An Australian doctor, John Robert Lee arrived; but although convinced that it was a case of acute appendicitis, he was in a quandary how to proceed. An acute appendix, if not operated on immediately, would lead to peritonitis with probably fatal results. A laporotomy, the opening up of the stomach for preliminary investigation, would be the normal course of action, but in this case there was a danger that the patient might bleed to death if operated upon, with no guarantee that it was really the appendix to blame. Which was the worse risk? To operate or not to operate? Lee went for a long drive into the countryside, turning over in his mind all the possibilities, all the various alternatives. Then he made up his mind and drove urgently back to London. Sir Douglas Shields was called in and that evening, 23 September, they operated at Sir Douglas' nursing-home in Park Lane. Every blood transfusion unit in London had been placed on the alert, no fewer than five friends of the sick man had telegraphed the hospital offering their blood, but no blood transfusion was needed. Bradman survived the operation, though still critically ill with a very high temperature.

The first news of it reached Australia on 24 September and for a brief moment in history, as his condition remained unchanged, the whole nation seemed to hold its breath. Anxious callers jammed newspaper switchboards demanding news. Churches throughout the country prayed for his recovery. Now Jessie Bradman entered the scene. She had rushed straight to the *Sun* office upon hearing the news, telling Johnny Moyes she just had to be with him; she was off to London at the earliest possible minute. It was thought at one point that she might fly to England, with Kingsford-Smith. However this proved to be impracticable. What next? The P. & O. *Maloja* had left Sydney a few days before, but there was still time to catch up with her before she left the Australian coast. A kind friend, Mrs. Frank Louat, offered to drive

Mrs. Bradman to Adelaide to pick the ship up there, but then that idea was abandoned in favour of taking the train. A cable went off to London, "It's all right, Don. I'm coming", and Jessie started out. She was met at Melbourne, and instantly sensing that something was being kept from her, insisted on ringing London. Her husband was alive, she was told. Not dead, as reported. Alive, and likely to be ill for a long time, but there was "no cause for wild rumours about his condition." On then she went greatly encouraged, and the further she travelled the more reassuring were the messages handed to her at every major stop. When she finally embarked in the *Maloja* on 1 October, it was in the marvellous knowledge that Don was over the worst and on the road to recovery. Gradually he had gained strength. On 24 October, accompanied by Dr. Lee, he was allowed to leave the hospital for a car-ride and a walk. Two days later he was able to motor down to Dover in a chauffeur-driven car to meet Jessie. Hundreds gathered near the hotel where they were to stay in order to watch the reunion. But the Bradmans managed to elude them and that precious moment remained private.

He had given almost his life for his country, and yet in high cricket circles there continued to be this persistent undercurrent of ill-feeling against the man. In Easter of 1935, after several months of travel and badly-needed rest and convalescence, the Bradmans were at last able to settle themselves permanently in Adelaide. He was accused naturally of deserting his home State, but he had been getting into the frame of mind where playing cricket, writing about it, talking about it, seemed more like an enslavement to the game than anything else; and nobody in Sydney offered him the same opportunity of getting away from cricket, at the same time of indulging his natural bent for figures and finance as the stock-broking firm of H. W. Hodgetts and Co. in Adelaide. In fact Adelaide, quiet, conservative, straight-laced in comparison with Sydney, suited the Bradmans admirably, though even here he was soon involved in controversy.

It had been envisaged, when he was first invited to Adelaide by Hodgetts, that he would very soon take charge of the South Australian side, the preliminary to his appointment as captain of Australia. None could have done a better job than Vic Richardson, the State's very successful skipper for nearly 15 years, but Richardson was now in the evening of his career, his retirement a matter that could be confidently expected before very much longer. Bradman's serious illness however, and consequent inability to make the tour of South Africa in 1935–36, upset these plans and led to the recall of Richardson to the Australian side in order to skipper the tourists. And as things turned out they did so astonishingly well under their ebullient new leader that several of his team-mates thought he should continue to captain them against England in 1936–37. If not Richardson, whose batting might not earn him a place, then at least Stan McCabe or some other integral member of the side thoroughly acquainted with the Richardson style and tactics.

How Bradman was chosen instead and Australia after losing the first two Tests went on to win the series is now ancient history, but it is worth reflecting on some of the set-backs and disappointments that the new skipper had to overcome before final victory was assured. Firstly, on the very day the M.C.C. side arrived in Adelaide for the State match, the Bradmans lost their first-born child, a son only one day old. Neville Cardus was with him that evening and he never ceased to marvel at the way Bradman had calmly talked cricket with him and given no hint of his grief and anxiety. Before long however he was wholly absorbed in the task of retaining the Ashes for Australia and now two nasty jolts were the loss of the first Test in Brisbane followed by the loss of the second Test in Sydney. The weather was partly to blame, together with Hammond's masterly 231 not out in Sydney and Bradman's comparative failure with the bat. But Australia had started the series red-hot favourites, and in the public reaction which followed Bradman was accused of letting the cares of captaincy affect his batting, and sundry other members of the side of not pulling their weight. He lacked Richardson's inspiring personality, people said. It would be better to let somebody else shoulder the burdens of leadership, leaving Bradman free to get on with the run-getting.

In fact he had already proved himself an accomplished Test match tactician. In Sydney Charlie Macartney who had once looked askance at his batting became his whole-hearted advocate. In Melbourne Woodfull praised his captaincy in the very highest terms. Yet it could not be denied that there was dissention in the ranks; that his enemies were going about rubbing their hands in glee. Bradman's response was to ignore them completely, simply to carry on more certain than ever that events would prove him right in the end. He cut out the pull-shot because it contained a slight element of risk and in three great innings won the remaining Tests almost off his own bat. But it was not to be wondered at if he sometimes appeared a little too determined to go his own way in those days, a little too concerned to justify himself and be revenged upon his enemies. The man who had welcomed the Englishmen so warmly at the outset of the tour was no longer quite the same affable opponent. He could be curt on occasions, very often with the Press, even with people who perhaps only wanted to express their sympathy. Slowly the image began to take shape of an Australian captain, implacable, remorseless, who never conceded an inch, was dedicated only to vindicating Australian cricket supremacy by the widest possible margin.

It is true that he did want very badly to win, but not at the expense of all good feeling between the two sides. When he was out, he departed with cheerful alacrity. When his side was defeated, he accepted defeat with a broad grin, only warning the victors to watch out next time. It was remarked while Len Hutton was in the process of overhauling Bradman's Test record score at the Oval in 1938 that the little man seemed desperately concerned to prevent him, harrying him by posting men all round the bat and so on. Of course. It may not be the English, but it is the Australian way. When however Hutton finally reached his goal, Bradman was the first to congratulate him and there was none who wrung his hand more warmly or took more genuine pleasure in his achievement.

Unfortunately with Bradman, some people could only see only the success side of the story; see him as the cold, calculating opportunist, the relentless antagonist and uncompromising champion of Australian rights. To others however he appeared very differently. In 1935, the Australian team under Vic Richardson having departed for South Africa, he took over the captaincy of South Australia, and it was marvellous to see the effect he had upon his young team. Against Queensland in Adelaide he hit up 233 in 191 minutes snd when he came back to the dressing-room, having effectively put paid to the menace of Eddie Gilbert, they clustered reverently around, gazing at him, hanging on his every word. In South Australia's next game in Melbourne he scored 357, after one of the Victorians had made some ill-natured remarks about him, and finally in the last first-class match of the season, 369 against Tasmania. This broke Clem Hill's record for the highest score by a South Australian and it was instantly alleged that Bradman was piqued because Richardson's name was being canvassed as Australia's next captain against England; that Hill was a strong partisan of Richardson and that this was Bradman's revenge. However members of either team detected no such object. He seemed to be mainly concerned with the innings of Ron Hamence at the other end. Hamence was making his first-class debut and Bradman was demonstrating how each bowler should best be played; how each stroke should be executed. While Hamence was at the batting end, he would be watching closely, talking to him constantly between overs, advising him – "too far off the wicket for that sort of shot, Ronnie," and so on. After Hamence was out for 121 his next pupil was B. H. Leak. Leak didn't go on to win a place in an Australian Eleven like Hamence, but he was a useful performer on the fringe of the South Australian side for several years.

It is just impossible to estimate how much Bradman's coming meant to South Australian cricket. Off the field he sometimes seemed cold, reserved. On the field, when there was a job to do, a match to win, he was full of fun, cracking jokes, chatting away to the bowlers and fieldsmen, with the result that almost everybody in Adelaide cricket felt uplifted, honoured that he had chosen to come and live amongst them. Another young protégé of Bradman's in Adelaide was the all-rounder, Mervyn Waite. He hadn't been a particularly successful member of the South Australian side under Vic Richardson, but soon after Bradman's arrival, near the end of the 1935–36 season, he broke the batting record for Adelaide district cricket with an innings of 339. (Extraordinary the way Bradman's influence seemed to transform the game in his immediate vicinity. In the Bowral district, several years after he had left it, young men who had been small boys when he played there were making scores of 320, 333, 393 . . . breaking all sorts of new records.) Under Bradman's guidance then Waite improved tremendously for South Australia, particularly with the ball, and ultimately forced his way into the Australian touring side of 1938. In 1939 however, now an Australian international and the leading wicket-taker in Adelaide district cricket, he was rash enough to make a prediction: that he would keep Bradman quiet by means of a plan. Opening the bowling for Glenelg v. Kensington he began with away-swingers to a packed off-side field which Bradman countered by swinging him repeatedly to leg. Waite then switched to in-swingers to a leg-field, only to see the batsmen stepping right away from his wicket and off-driving them. Finally the disgusted bowler, 27 overs, 1 maiden, 160 runs, 2 wickets, threw the ball to the ground in a fury. "B—— you, Don," he is supposed to have said, "I'm not going to bowl any more." Bradman went on to make 303, taking care not to break Waite's district record, but usually he threw his wicket away soon after reaching 100.

Bradman was now thirty, and something of his developing attitude to the game, of the feelings that had been growing in him during the past few years, may be gleaned from a passage in his book, *My Cricketing Life*. He is referring to the series of 1936–37 and the widespread criticism that assailed him when Australia was two Tests down, and he writes, "I did not profess to be the ideal captain, but as there was no other player good enough for the Test side who had ever captained Australia, it would have been sheer cowardice for me to abandon what appeared to be a sinking ship . . . I might add that the captaincy of an Australian Eleven is a position which is not sought after. The responsibilities attached to it are heavy, the rewards few." Thus he was again captain of Australia for the tour of England in 1938 and indeed it proved in large measure a thankless task, although he was able to do so much to help Australia retain the Ashes. He had been much blamed originally as one of the three selectors responsible for leaving Grimmett out of the touring side and even in England he found himself a target for criticism. He was booed at the Oval for not declaring Australia's second innings closed against Surrey; booed again in the first Test at Trent Bridge for batting stubbornly on after defeat had been averted, and everywhere there were dropping gates as the word spread that Bradman was no longer his old brilliant self.

In between were many happy occasions and highly satisfying performances, but the impression in 1938 was less of Bradman of the broad grin and dashing blade, rather of the jutting jaw and stern, set features as Australia battled to avoid defeat. There was also a continuing dispute with the Board of Control at home over the question of players' wives being allowed to visit England, and finally the sad disappointment during the fifth Test at the Oval when he twisted his ankle in a bowler's foot-hole and had to be carried off the field. In his absence the Australians lost the match by a colossal margin and then in their final match in England went down to Leveson-Gower's Eleven at Scarborough to mar what would otherwise have been a very fine tour record. At least one former Test match captain, H. G. Deane of South Africa in 1929, had grown grey in the experience of leading a touring side through England, and Bradman as he slowly recovered from his ankle injury vowed that this would be his last tour. "There had been times when I found it difficult to keep going and although still not old in the cricket sense I did not feel capable of standing the strain on another occasion. Whilst not making any decision public, this was how I really felt and I visualized the possibility of perhaps one more Test season in Australia before retirement."

What saved him for another English tour surprisingly enough was the War. His health broke down so badly at the beginning of 1941 that even if Test cricket had been possible during those years, it is doubtful if Bradman could have played. Fibrositis of the muscles of his back left him crippled and in great pain for long periods of time, but slowly he made progress and at the end of hostilities in 1945 he wondered if he was not sufficiently recovered to contemplate a return to the game. At that point, quite suddenly in the winter of 1945, his employer, H. W. Hodgetts & Co. went bankrupt. Bradman himself lost money in the crash and for the next few months he was heavily involved in helping to clean up the mess, a process which led in due course to the formation of Don Bradman & Co., stock and share brokers carrying on business at the former address of Hodgetts & Co. It seemed inconceivable in these circumstances that he would ever have time to take up cricket again. But the Australian Services cricketers had been performing brilliantly in England and India creating a great popular demand to see them in Australia; while at the same time South Australia, engaged in its first Interstate match after the War, was hopelessly outplayed by N.S.W. Inevitably the pressures on him to resume steadily increased. He played against Queensland at Christmas 1945 and made 68; 27 very brightly, then the remaining 40-odd rather laboriously, favouring a leg. At New Year however he scored a century against the Services which Hassett and Whitington of the opposition thought was the best innings they had seen anywhere since the last time they had encountered Bradman.

They were dismayed however to see him looking so poorly and soon after indeed he was to suffer almost his worst attack of fibrositis so far.

He was obliged to forego the Australian tour of New Zealand at the end of 1945–46 and once again all hope of his resuming Test cricket seemed to have vanished when, miraculously, he came across a new treatment for his trouble. All at once, Hammond's M.C.C. team having already landed in Australia, he realised there was a chance. Watched by Jessie and his two children, John and Shirley, he turned out for Kensington v. Glenelg at Glenelg Oval and made a smart 42 not out – after which he was chosen to captain South Australia in the State's first match of the season against M.C.C. He played scoring 76 and 3, and knew, although still far from fit and patently out of form, that he probably could return if he really wanted to. He was in fact in much the same position as before the second Test in Melbourne in 1932–33. On the one hand he had a tempting offer to write for the Press, together with a watertight excuse, on the grounds of being unfit, for not playing; on the other, was his duty to Australian cricket, to a public which in this case had been waiting through six long years of War to see him in action once again. Despite the emergence of Lindwall and Miller, Barnes and Morris and so on, the world still craved the sight of Bradman, it seemed.

There had been a definite atmosphere whenever he was batting in those far-off, pre-War days. All round the rim of the field you could hear the crowd bubbling away in a constant simmer of contentment and good fellowship. At Randwick racecourse in Sydncy the secretary of the Australian Jockey Club claimed he used to pray for rain whenever Bradman was due to bat on a Saturday afternoon. In the back of his mind would ever remain the memory of several thousands of racegoers at the Summer carnival of 1932–33 gathered intently round a tiny scoring-board in the outside betting-ring while the races went on unheeded. They were waiting for Don's hundred to be posted against Larwood and Jardine. If he was batting at midday, the crowds would come streaming out to the ground, men, women and children. The women didn't always pay great attention to the cricket; were apt to shriek in delight or dismay every time a bump ball went to hand, but they added much to the glamour and excitement of the occasion.

This was what Australians had been missing and this was what they were to be granted again when Bradman decided to make himself available for the Test series of 1946–47. Aided by the richest crop of young cricketers that Australia had produced for a generation or more Bradman led his side to victory by three Tests to nil against England in 1946–47; four Tests to nil against India in 1947–48; by four Tests to nil against England in England in 1948. Though by no means his pre-War self he inspired perhaps an even greater enthusiasm in the crowds that flocked to cricket in post-War Britain than he ever had. The scene at the Oval when he came out to play his farewell innings in Test cricket was incredible. A similar reception had greeted Jack Hobbs in his last Test match there in 1930. But Hobbs was a Surrey man whose great deeds with the bat had been on behalf of Surrey and England. Bradman was the enemy and yet when he appeared at the players' door and began to thread his way down the steps, the vast crowd rose to its feet and cheered and clapped him every inch of the way until he reached the crease. Where Yardley and his men were waiting to give him three cheers. He did not ordinarily suffer from emotion but on this occasion he did. He felt distinctly shaky as he took guard and faced up to Eric Hollies. His first ball he played well enough. The second bowled him. A great roar went up, followed by a confused hubbub of sound as though Englishmens' instinctive glee at his cheap dismissal was marred, overwhelmed almost, by the thought that they would never see him again.

The actual ending was sad then, not the script as the sentimentally-inclined would have written it, but not really important compared with what he had set out to achieve in coming to England in the first place. "Whatever inspired me to go," he would write, "I felt it had been ordained for a greater purpose than the pleasure or success of individuals – it had been my destiny to do what I could for cricket and in my heart I knew I could not have done more." The Australian players had originally come together in March, remaining together until October, and in all that time there was scarcely a cross word amongst them, nothing beyond the ordinary sum of human misadventures and the natural disappointment of those who failed to get into a Test side. Pressmen and reporters clung to the fringes of the team in greater numbers than ever before, but they were given pitifully little in the way of material likely to appeal to the world at large – a few bumpers in the Test matches; a case of one of the Australians allegedly refusing to bowl on one occasion, that was about all. On the whole the Tests were played in an exemplary spirit, bringing back in some minds the early years of the century, the so-called Golden Age of cricket.

Public interest naturally centred on Bradman, the great run-getter, the marvel of his time. Bradman had necessarily to respond to this interest, to concentrate on giving people what they had come to see, but he felt a larger responsibility as well – an overriding determination that the game should be played properly, in the kind of decent atmosphere in which the great majority of cricket followers liked it to be played. He was not of course the perfect captain, ideal in every respect. He was too cautious for that; too much afraid of losing to take any real risk, but certainly he left Test cricket in a much healthier state than he found it in 1928; in an infinitely better light than the darkness into which it was plunged in 1932–33. Only in view of his later career can we understand the part he played in the bodyline crisis.

Long before Larwood, long before overarm bowling had been invented, the bowler had to contend with batsmen unusually difficult to dislodge; batsmen who threatened to put the bowling fraternity to shame by their prowess. Confronted by W. G. Grace, F. S. Jackson, Fry, Ranji and MacLaren, fast bowlers did not hesitate to pitch them short on occasions. If they were not aiming actually to hit the batsman, at least they aimed to unsettle him, undeterred by the very considerable risk of injuring him in the process. Tibby Cotter had bowled thus to George Gunn for example; McDonald to Hobbs; Constantine to Hammond. As chance would determine, Bradman, the most prolific batsman of all time, found himself opposed by Larwood, conceivably the fastest bowler; at any rate, the most accurate. He set out against his antagonist, as all these famous predecessors had set out, to deal with the bumper by hooking it; to let the bowler understand at the earliest possible moment that the batsman would not be intimidated.

Deciding which one came out on top in some of these epic confrontations is not easy, but undoubtedly bouncers were on the increase when Bradman came into the game; the climate of opinion, after the massive run-getting of the mid-1920's, had shifted in favour of the bowler being allowed to bowl as he chose. Not sufficient to be faced by a bowler confessedly out to even the score with him, Bradman very soon had to cope with a new dimension of the problem – a captain who had worked out a scheme of field-placing which made the hook-shot too dangerous to contemplate; who had adopted body-line as a deliberate and sustained act of policy. As soon as Bradman realised the full implications of what was intended he spoke his mind on the subject to the Board of Control, and when that failed to bring any result he went out into the middle and faced up to the body-line, and continued to face up to it, as long as the menace existed.

It was the only way. Let us suppose, for instance, that he hadn't played in Melbourne. None could have blamed him, after his illness, after his treatment by the Board. But Australia would assuredly have lost that second Test match and then Jardine, quite obviously, would have been only too glad to give up his detested body-line and win the series without it. Only Bradman compelled him to go on using it and by so doing concentrated the full glare of publicity upon it so that the issue could no longer be evaded; every man would have to search into his heart and come to his own decision about it.

In May of 1934 Douglas Jardine returned at last from India and informed the Surrey committee that he wished to make himself available for the Surrey versus Lancashire game, George Duckworth's Benefit later that month. It appeared that he would not be needed however. Surrey already had an eleven. Arthur Carr was given the same short thrift by the Nottinghamshire committee when he offered to carry on the captaincy at the beginning of 1935. His services were no longer required, he was given to understand. The committee had previously made the decision to replace him with two joint captains, Rhodes and

Heane. And thus these two former captains of England were allowed to fade quietly from the scene, their passing largely unlamented, unnoticed almost by the great mass of cricket supporters.

For Nottinghamshire too, most ancient and celebrated of clubs, it was the beginning of the end of 70 years and more as a force in the county championship. Larwood and Voce were still there to open the bowling, but rarely were they the same devastating combination as of old. The challenge had gone. Throughout 1935, while England was in the process of suffering its first home defeat in a series against South Africa, both men remained adamant that they would never play for their country again. However in 1936 Voce announced that he would be available once more and very soon forced his way into the side against India. The following English winter he toured Australia, having great success with a ball that cut away to the off.

Body-line was dead by then, all over the world. South Africa had denounced it. New Zealand had denounced it. In July 1934 the cricket nations assembled at Lord's to discuss a proposed amendment to the Laws of cricket by Australia that, "If an umpire considers the bowler is intending to hurt or intimidate the batsman he shall call 'no ball' and on repetition of the offence cause him to be taken off". This they thought was impracticable, but they offered a resolution instead, confirming the principle enunciated by the M.C.C. in 1933, "that any form of bowling that is obviously a 'direct attack' by the bowler upon the batsman is an offence against the spirit of the game." The various controlling bodies undertook to do all in their power to discourage such bowling.

That was clear enough, but short-pitched bowling persisted just the same, notably by Voce against the Australians at Trent Bridge, and at the end of the season the M.C.C. felt compelled to issue a further statement: ". . . from its own observations and from reports received the M.C.C. consider there is evidence that cases of the bowler making a direct attack upon the batsman have on occasions taken place during the past season. . . . In order to eliminate this type of bowling from the game and to ensure in future that there shall be no misunderstanding as to what exactly constitutes a direct attack . . . the M.C.C. Committee have ruled "that the type of bowling regarded as a direct attack by the bowler upon the batsman and therefore unfair consists in persistent and systematic bowling of fast, short-pitched balls at the batsman standing clear of his wicket."

This then had the effect of making "direct attack" very much a matter for the umpires, the "the sole judges of fair and unfair play" as they are described in the Laws, and so it came about that in January 1935, in a Test between England and West Indies in Trinidad, "boby-line" or "direct attack" flickered briefly into life and was promptly stamped out again by the umpire, Arthur Richardson, the former

Australian Test player. Both fast bowlers, Constantine for the West Indies, Smith for England, had been unofficially warned earlier in the match. On the last day however, at a critical stage in England's second innings, Constantine was tempted to let go two or three short ones which caused Richardson at the bowling end suddenly to stride across to mid-off in the middle of an over to speak to Constantine's skipper. England had discontinued intimidating tactics, he told Grant. West Indies would have to act similarly or he would use his authority under the M.C.C.'s new ruling to prevent Constantine continuing. The fast bowler completed his over with a couple of slow ones and was taken off amid a storm of booing from the crowd. Constantine had no leg-trap in position for those few deliveries, it should be noted.

Not only "bodyline" had now been condemned, "bodyline" as practised in Australia by Larwood and Voce, but anything remotely resembling it. Bowling for Queensland against South Australia in Adelaide in December 1935, Eddie Gilbert had already struck and injured two South Australians when he was spoken to by Jack Scott, of all people, the former Shield bowler now turned umpire. He would have to pitch them up, said Scott, which Gilbert did after a short consultation with his skipper, but he continued to offend in subsequent games until finally no-balled by umpire Borwick in Sydney the following January. Borwick acted under Law 48B, the latest Australian addition to the Laws of Cricket which stated: "Any ball delivered which, in the opinion of the umpire at the bowler's end is bowled at the batsman with intent to intimidate or injure him, shall be considered unfair and 'no-ball' shall be called. . . ." Effectively it was the end of Gilbert's first class career.

First Larwood, then Voce and Bowes, Constantine, now Gilbert, fine bowlers who had been virtually forced out of cricket or had their claws blunted. But something drastic needs to be done when the game threatens to go astray. Bodyline in its ultimate form was invented for Bradman, and Bradman was never the "run-scoring machine" the "unsmiling implacable opponent" he was sometimes portrayed as. He remains at heart, despite all the power and fame that has come to him, through all the controversies that have assailed him and raged about his head, a country boy, the son of the Bowral carpenter who loved to involve himself in local activities and see everybody as involved and happy as he was.

BIBLIOGRAPHY

Foremost in the list of works consulted must be Bradman's own autobiographies, *Don Bradman's Book*, 1930; *My Cricketing Life*, 1938; *Farewell to Cricket*, 1950, together with his *The Art of Cricket*, 1958. The following titles also proved most helpful. Unless otherwise indicated, all were published in London.

CHAPTER 1.

A. G. Moyes, *Bradman*, 1948. W. O'Reilly, *Cricket Conquest*, 1949. R. S. Whitington, *Time of the Tiger*, 1970.

CHAPTER 2.

P. G. H. Fender, *Turn of the Wheel*, 1929. W. R. Hammond, *Cricket's Secret History*, 1952. M. A. Noble, *Fight for the Ashes*, 1929.

CHAPTER 3.

C. V. Grimmett, *Getting Wickets*, 1930.

CHAPTER 4.

N. Cardus, *Cricket All the Year*, 1952. P. G. H. Fender, *Tests of 1930*, 1930. (Sir) H. Gordon, *Background of Cricket*, 1939. W. R. Hammond, *Cricket My Destiny*, 1946. V. Y. Richardson, *The Vic Richardson Story*, 1968. G. Tebbutt, *With the 1930 Australians*, 1930. P. F. Warner, *Fight for the Ashes in 1930*, 1930.

CHAPTER 5.

The Game of Cricket (Lonsdale Library), 1930. A. W. Carr, *Cricket with the Lid Off*, 1935. L. N. Constantine, *Cricket and I*, 1933. L. N. Constantine, *Cricket in the Sun*, 1946. F. R. Foster, *Cricketing Memories*, 1930. T. C. F. Prittie, *Mainly Middlesex*, 1946. C. F. Root, *A Cricket Pro's Lot*, 1937. M. J. Turnbull and M. J. C. Allom, *The Two Maurices Again*, 1931. R. S. Whitington, *Bradman, Benaud and Goddard's Cinderellas*, 1964. R. E. S. Wyatt, *Ins and Outs of Cricket*, 1936. R. E. S. Wyatt, *Three Straight Sticks*, 1951.

CHAPTER 6.

W. E. Bowes, *Express Deliveries*, 1949. J. H. Fingleton, *Cricket Crisis*, 1946. D. R. Jardine, *In Quest of the Ashes*, 1933. A. F. Kippax, *Anti-Bodyline*, 1933. H. Larwood, *Body-Line*, 1933. A. Mailey, *And Then Came Larwood*, 1933. K. Perkins, *The Larwood Story*, 1965. R. Robinson, *Between Wickets*, 1946. R. S. Whitington, *Body-Line Umpire*, Adelaide, 1974. R. W. E. Wilmot, *Defending the Ashes*, Melbourne, 1933.

CHAPTER 7.

N. Cardus, *Good Days*, 1934. P. G. H. Fender, *Kissing the Rod*, 1934. D. R. Jardine, *Ashes and Dust*, 1934. H. Sutcliffe, *For England and Yorkshire*, 1935. E. W. Swanton, *Cricket and the Clock*, 1952. P. F. Warner, *Cricket Between Two Wars*, 1942.

CHAPTER 8.

S. Downer, *Goodbye, Bradman*, 1944. (Typescript, Lords). J. H. Fingleton, *Brightly Fades the Don*, 1949. I. W. Johnson, *Cricket at the Crossroads*, 1957. K. R. Miller, *Cricket Caravan*, 1950. K. R. Miller and R. S. Whitington, *Bumper*, 1953. E. W. Swanton, *Sort of a Cricket Person*, 1972. E. W. Swanton, *Follow On*, 1977.

The following newspapers and periodicals were also consulted:

In Australia: Adelaide *Advertiser*, *Australian Cricketer* (1930–5), Brisbane *Courier*, Cootamundra *Herald*, Melbourne *Argus*, *Melbourne Herald*, *Southern Mail* (Boural), *The Sun*, Sydney *Referee*, *Sydney Morning Herald*, *Truth*.

In England: The Cricketer, *Daily Telegraph*, *Evening News*, *Evening Standard*, *Manchester Guardian*, *Morning Post*, *Nottingham Journal*, *The Star*, *Sunday Chronicle*, *Sunday Dispatch*, *Sunday Express*, *Yorkshire Evening Post*.

In West Indies: Barbados *Advocate*, Port of Spain *Gazette*.

INDEX